Home-Cooked Meals Are a Breeze...
Even on Busy Weeknights!

DOESN'T it seem like life just keeps getting busier? Work, school, errands...the list goes on and on. Squeezing in time for eating meals is difficult, let alone the time to cook them. Drive-thru and take-out seem like good choices because they're speedy, but in the long run, they're not satisfying.

This book will take a big load off your shoulders because it puts an end to the "What's for Dinner" dilemma—with wholesome, home-cooked dinners in a snap.

Taste of Home's Weeknight Cooking Made Easy 2007 is packed with 304 mouth-watering recipes that let you get a tasty, homemade dinner on the table in mere minutes. Here's what sets this one-of-a-kind cookbook apart from all others:

• **Ideal ingredients.** *Taste of Home's Weeknight Cooking Made Easy 2007* provides a balance of fresh and convenience foods to offer from-scratch goodness. Plus, many of the recipes use a *reasonable number* of everyday ingredients.

• **Focus on main dishes.** Entrees are the meat and potatoes to meal planning. You'll find 240 main dishes, featuring beef, ground beef, chicken, turkey, pork and seafood in addition to meatless entree ideas.

• **Speed is key.** The majority of the recipes in this collection go from start to finish in less than 30 minutes.

• **Beautiful photos.** We know you're more likely to try recipes with a picture. So we've included a gorgeous, color photo of *each and every recipe!*

• **Prep and cooking times.** The preparation and cooking times for each dish are prominently displayed, making it easy to find recipes that fit your schedule.

• **Hundreds of helpful hints.** Each recipe features a timely tip, such as tricks that reduce preparation time, facts for buying and storing foods, substitution secrets and ideas for speedy side dishes.

• **Easy on the eyes.** *Taste of Home's Weeknight Cooking Made Easy 2007* is so easy to read because there is only one recipe on a page.

• **Recipe list by chapter.** Quickly browse through the recipes in each chapter without turning a page. Just go to the beginning of each chapter for the list of recipes.

With *Taste of Home's Weeknight Cooking Made Easy 2007*, offering your family a wholesome meal night after night couldn't be easier!

Weeknight Cooking Made Easy 2007

Taste of Home Books
©2007 Reiman Media Group, Inc.
5400 S. 60th St., Greendale WI 53129
International Standard Book Number (10): 0-89821-558-7
International Standard Book Number (13): 978-0-89821-558-8
International Standard Serial Number: 1555-0400
All rights reserved.
Printed in U.S.A.

For additional copies of this book, write *Taste of Home* Books,
P.O. Box 908, Greendale WI 53129. Or to order by credit card, call
toll-free 1-800/344-2560 or visit our Web site at
www.reimanpub.com.

PICTURED ON THE COVER:
Kielbasa Biscuit Pizza (p. 163)

Editor: Jean Steiner

Art Directors: Gretchen Trautman, Kathy Crawford

Senior Editor/Books: Mark Hagen

Vice President, Executive Editor/Books: Heidi Reuter Lloyd

Proofreader: Linne Bruskewitz

Editorial Assistant: Barb Czysz

Taste of Home Test Kitchens

Food Director: Diane Werner RD

Test Kitchen Manager: Karen Scales

Recipe Editors: Sue A. Jurack (Senior), Mary King, Christine Rukavena

Recipe Asset System Manager: Coleen Martin

Test Kitchen Home Economists: Peggy Fleming RD, Tina Johnson, Ann Liebergen, Marie Parker, Annie Rose, Patricia Schmeling, Wendy Stenman, Amy Welk-Thieding RD

Test Kitchen Assistants: Rita Krajcir, Kris Lehman, Sue Megonigle, Megan Taylor

Taste of Home Photo Studio

Photographers: Rob Hagen (Senior), Dan Roberts, Jim Wieland, Lori Foy

Senior Set Stylist: Jenny Bradley Vent

Food Stylists: Sarah Thompson (Senior), Joylyn Trickel (Senior), Kate Baumann, Kaitlyn Besasie, Alynna Malson

Reiman Media Group, Inc.

President: Barbara Newton

Senior Vice President, Editor in Chief: Catherine Cassidy

Creative Director: Ardyth Cope

Founder: Roy Reiman

Easy Weekday Menus

Whether you're eating on the run or are actually able to enjoy a sit-down dinner, here are complete meal suggestions using both recipes from *Weeknight Cooking Made Easy* and purchased items.

Orient Express

Serves 4

You don't have to pick up takeout when you have a hunger for Asian cooking—make this meal at home instead.

Green Tea
Apricot Turkey Stir-Fry (p. 140)
Hot cooked rice
Cantaloupe a la Mode (p. 299)

Italian Fare

Serves 6

There's no need to go out to a restaurant when you can create this taste of Little Italy right at home in your own kitchen.

Italian Salad (p. 266)
Three-Cheese Spaghetti Bake (p. 219)
Garlic bread
Chocolate Cheesecake Pie (p. 300)

Family Fun Night

Serves 4 to 6

Friday would be a great night to gather your gang for a spread featuring family-pleasing pizza and playing board games.

Tomato Rosemary Focaccia (p. 290)
Lemony Tossed Salad (p. 273)
Mushroom Chicken Pizza (p. 108)
Banana Split Pudding (p. 315)

Down-Home Dinner

Serves 6

Comfort foods shouldn't only grace Sunday dinner tables. Treat your family to these quick-to-fix classics tonight.

Mushroom Salisbury Steak (p. 32)
Garlic Mashed Red Potatoes (p. 280)
Cooked broccoli florets
Peach Shortcake Towers (p. 302)

Slow-Cooked Supper

Serves 8

Let dinner simmer all day in the slow cooker…and come home to the mouth-watering aroma of a hot supper.

Vegetable Beef Stew (p. 74)
Pull-Apart Herb Bread (p. 268)
Mousse-Topped Pound Cake (p. 308)

A Taste of the Tropics

Serves 4

Take your family's taste buds on a trip with this lightened-up menu reminiscent of a tropical getaway.

Halibut with Kiwi Salsa (p. 240)
Orange-Glazed Asparagus (p. 291)
Paradise Parfaits (p. 313)

Cookout Cuisine

Serves 6

Escape the heat of the kitchen by cooking the main course and side dish outdoors on the grill. Round out the warm-weather meal with a refreshing fruit salad.

Lemonade Chicken (p. 107)
Summer Vegetable Medley (p. 278)
Five-Fruit Salad (p. 263)

Kid-Friendly Food

Serves 4

The next time your kids ask you "what's for supper?" serve up a plateful of smiles with this fun fare.

Soupy Joes (p. 35)
Carrot and celery sticks
Potato chips
Frosty Caterpillar Dessert (p. 326)

Special Celebration

Serves 4

Any occasion will seem extra-special when you serve this both easy-to-make and eye-appealing menu.

Breaded Pork Roll-Ups (p. 169)
Noodles with Broccoli (p. 264)
Blueberry Graham Dessert (p. 294)

Make It Mexican

Serves 6

When your family craves south-of-the-border cuisine, head to your kitchen to prepare this zippy supper.

Baked Chimichangas (p. 86)
Zesty Corn and Beans (p. 279)
Ice Cream Tortilla Cups (p. 312)

From burgers and stews to casseroles and skillet suppers, ground beef stars in a splendid assortment of enticing entrees.

Taco Skillet (p. 25)

Speedy Ground Beef

Cheeseburger Loaf (p. 29)

Sweet-and-Sour Meat Loaf

Prep/Total Time: 15 min.

✓ Uses less fat, sugar or salt. Includes Nutrition Facts and Diabetic Exchanges.

- 1 **egg, lightly beaten**
- 5 **tablespoons ketchup,** *divided*
- 2 **tablespoons prepared mustard**
- 1/2 **cup dry bread crumbs**
- 2 **tablespoons onion soup mix**
- 1/4 **teaspoon salt**
- 1/4 **teaspoon pepper**
- 1 **pound ground beef**
- 1/4 **cup sugar**
- 2 **tablespoons brown sugar**
- 2 **tablespoons cider vinegar**

In a large bowl, combine the egg, 2 tablespoons ketchup, mustard, bread crumbs, dry soup mix, salt and pepper. Crumble beef over mixture and mix well. Shape into an oval loaf. Place in a shallow 1-qt. microwave-safe dish. Cover and microwave on high for 10-12 minutes or until the meat is no longer pink and a meat thermometer reads 160°; drain.

Meanwhile, in a small bowl, combine the sugars, vinegar and remaining ketchup; drizzle over meat loaf. Cover and microwave on high 2-3 minutes longer or until heated through. Let stand for 10 minutes before slicing.

Yield: 4 servings.

Editor's Note: This recipe was tested in a 1,100-watt microwave.

Nutrition Facts: 4 ounces (prepared with lean ground beef) equals 375 calories, 13 g fat (5 g saturated fat), 94 mg cholesterol, 960 mg sodium, 38 g carbohydrate, 1 g fiber, 27 g protein. **Diabetic Exchanges:** 3 lean meat, 2-1/2 starch.

Make Meat Loaf Tonight!

Because this meat loaf is made in the microwave, it's ideal for busy nights.

When you are shaping meat loaves, handle the mixture as little as possible to keep the final product light in texture. Combine all of the ingredients except for the ground beef. Then crumble the beef over the mixture and mix well.

After baking a meat loaf, drain any fat from the pan and let stand for 5 to 10 minutes before slicing.

Meaty Mac 'n' Cheese

Prep/Total Time: 20 min.

- 1   package (7-1/4 ounces) macaroni and cheese
- 1   pound ground beef
- 1/4 cup chopped onion
- 1-1/2 cups salsa
- 1/2 cup fresh *or* frozen corn
- 1   can (2-1/4 ounces) sliced ripe olives, drained
- 3   tablespoons diced pimientos

Shredded cheddar cheese

Chopped tomato

Set aside cheese sauce mix from macaroni and cheese package; cook macaroni according to package directions.

Meanwhile, in a large saucepan, cook beef and onion over medium heat until meat is no longer pink; drain. Add the salsa, corn, olives and pimientos; cook until heated through.

Drain macaroni; add to beef mixture with contents of cheese sauce mix. Cook and stir until blended and heated through. Sprinkle with cheese and tomato.

Yield: 4-6 servings.

Editor's Note: The milk and butter listed on the macaroni and cheese package are not used in this recipe.

**Dressed Up
Mac 'n' Cheese**

Want to "beef" up a box of macaroni and cheese and turn it into a complete meal? The hearty mixture here gets extra flavor from the addition of ground beef, tomatoes, corn, ripe olives and zippy salsa.

You could also stir in a can of tuna, peas, dried onion and pepper to taste...or leftover chili...or cubed fully cooked ham and broccoli. Try any combination you and your family can come up with!

Beef-Topped Bean Enchiladas

Prep/Total Time: 30 min.

1-1/2   **pounds ground beef**
    1   **medium onion, chopped**
    1   **jar (16 ounces) salsa**
    1   **can (8 ounces) tomato sauce**
    1   **to 2 teaspoons ground cumin**
  1/8   **teaspoon garlic salt**
    1   **can (16 ounces) refried beans**
  12   **flour tortillas (8 inches), warmed**
1-1/2   **cups (6 ounces) shredded cheddar cheese,** *divided*
1-1/2   **cups (6 ounces) shredded Monterey Jack cheese,** *divided*
    2   **cans (2-1/4 ounces** *each***) sliced ripe olives, drained,** *divided*

In a large skillet, cook beef and onion over medium heat until meat is no longer pink; drain. Stir in the salsa, tomato sauce, cumin and garlic salt; cook for 3 minutes or until heated through.

Meanwhile, spread 2-3 tablespoons refried beans over each tortilla. Sprinkle each with 1 tablespoon of cheddar cheese, 1 tablespoon Monterey Jack cheese and 1 tablespoon olives. Roll up.

Place seam side down in a greased 13-in. x 9-in. x 2-in. baking dish. Top with beef mixture. Sprinkle with remaining cheeses and olives. Bake, uncovered, at 350° for 20 minutes or until heated through.

Yield: 6 servings.

Keep Staples On Hand

You can rely on kitchen mainstays to create these family-pleasing enchiladas. Simply keep the salsa, tomato sauce and refried beans on hand in your pantry and the tortillas and cheese in the fridge.

Buy fresh ground beef on the way home from work or defrost meat stored in the freezer.

For best results, defrost ground beef in the refrigerator and use within 1 to 2 days. If defrosting in the microwave, cook immediately after thawing.

Meatball Skillet Meal

Prep/Total Time: 30 min.

1/2 cup finely chopped fresh
     mushrooms
1/3 cup quick-cooking oats
  2 tablespoons finely
     chopped green pepper
  2 tablespoons finely
     chopped onion
  2 tablespoons dried parsley
     flakes
  1 teaspoon dried basil
  1 teaspoon dried oregano
1/2 teaspoon dried thyme
1/2 teaspoon salt
1/4 teaspoon pepper
  1 pound ground beef
  4 medium carrots, sliced
  1 small zucchini, sliced
  1 can (14-1/2 ounces) diced tomatoes, undrained
  4 cups hot cooked rice

In a large bowl, combine the first 10 ingredients. Crumble beef over mixture and mix well. Shape into 1-1/4-in. balls.

In a large skillet, cook meatballs over medium heat until no longer pink; drain. Add carrots and zucchini; cook, uncovered, for 5 minutes or until tender. Stir in tomatoes and heat through. Serve over rice.

Yield: 6 servings.

Meatballs of Equal Size

One way to make meatballs that are the same size is to lightly pat the mixture into a 1-inch-thick rectangle. Using a knife, cut the rectangle into the number of meatballs needed for a recipe. Gently roll each square into a ball.

Or if you have a 1-1/2- or 1-3/4-inch-diameter scoop, scoop the mixture into equal sized portions. Gently roll each into a ball.

Pasta Beef Soup

Prep/Total Time: 25 min.

✓ Uses less fat, sugar or salt. Includes Nutrition Facts and Diabetic Exchanges.

- 1 **pound ground beef**
- 2 **cans (14-1/2 ounces** *each***) beef broth**
- 1 **package (16 ounces) frozen pasta with broccoli, corn and carrots in garlic-seasoned sauce**
- 1-1/2 **cups tomato juice**
- 1 **can (14-1/2 ounces) diced tomatoes, undrained**
- 2 **teaspoons Italian seasoning**
- 1/4 **cup shredded Parmesan cheese, optional**

In a large saucepan, cook beef over medium heat until no longer pink; drain. Add the broth, pasta with vegetables, tomato juice, tomatoes and Italian seasoning; bring to a boil. Reduce heat; cover and simmer for 10 minutes or until vegetables are tender. Serve with Parmesan cheese if desired.

Yield: 6 servings.

Nutrition Facts: 1-1/2 cups (prepared with lean ground beef and reduced-sodium beef broth and tomato juice; calculated without Parmesan cheese) equals 253 calories, 9 g fat (4 g saturated fat), 46 mg cholesterol, 680 mg sodium, 21 g carbohydrate, 3 g fiber, 20 g protein. **Diabetic Exchanges:** 2-1/2 lean meat, 1 starch, 1 vegetable.

Take Stock in Soup

Because it calls for so many convenience items most people keep on hand, Pasta Beef Soup is both flavorful and easy to prepare. But it's flexible, too, because you can use other ingredients, such as a different frozen pasta-vegetable blend. Or stir in some shredded zucchini or yellow squash. If there is any soup left over, it reheats well served another day.

Beefy Barbecue Macaroni

Prep/Total Time: 15 min.

- 3/4 **pound ground beef**
- 1/2 **cup chopped onion**
- 3 **garlic cloves, minced**
- 3-1/2 **cups cooked elbow macaroni**
- 3/4 **cup barbecue sauce**
- 1/4 **teaspoon pepper**
- **Dash cayenne pepper**
- 1/4 **cup milk**
- 1 **tablespoon butter**
- 1 **cup (4 ounces) shredded sharp cheddar cheese**
- **Additional shredded sharp cheddar cheese, optional**

In a large skillet, cook the beef, onion and garlic over medium heat until meat is no longer pink; drain. Add the macaroni, barbecue sauce, pepper and cayenne pepper.

In a small saucepan, heat milk and butter over medium heat until butter is melted. Stir in cheese until melted. Pour over the macaroni mixture; gently toss to coat. Sprinkle with additional cheese if desired.

Yield: 4 servings.

"Kick Up" the Sauce

Barbecue sauce is traditionally made with tomatoes, onion, mustard, garlic, brown sugar and vinegar. If your family likes food with a little "kick," stir in some chopped fresh chile peppers, dried red pepper flakes or Tabasco sauce to taste.

This recipe calls for 3-1/2 cups cooked elbow macaroni. Make it ahead! Cooked pasta can be refrigerated for 1 to 2 days in an airtight container. Reheat by placing in a colander and rinsing with hot water.

Slow-Cooked Spaghetti Sauce

Prep: 15 min. **Cook:** 7 hours

1 **pound ground beef** *or* **bulk Italian sausage**
1 **medium onion, chopped**
2 **cans (14-1/2 ounces** *each***) diced tomatoes, undrained**
1 **can (8 ounces) tomato sauce**
1 **can (6 ounces) tomato paste**
1 **bay leaf**
1 **tablespoon brown sugar**
4 **garlic cloves, minced**
1 **to 2 teaspoons dried basil**
1 **to 2 teaspoons dried oregano**
1 **teaspoon salt**
1/2 **to 1 teaspoon dried thyme**
Hot cooked spaghetti

In a large skillet, cook beef and onion over medium heat until meat is no longer pink; drain. Transfer to a 3-qt. slow cooker. Add the next 10 ingredients. Cover and cook on low for 7-8 hours or until heated through. Discard bay leaf. Serve over spaghetti.

Yield: 6-8 servings.

Easy Italian Entree

It's wonderful to quickly assemble Slow-Cooked Spaghetti Sauce in the morning and let it simmer all day. It fills the house with a rich, savory aroma. For a spicier sauce, you could add 1-1/2 teaspoons crushed red pepper flakes.

To accompany this saucy main dish, toss together Italian Salad (p. 266), a pleasing combination of romaine, grape tomatoes, ripe olives, onion slices, pepperoncinis and Parmesan cheese topped with homemade croutons.

Pizza Meat Loaf Cups

Prep/Total Time: 30 min.

> 1   egg, beaten
> 1/2 cup pizza sauce
> 1/4 cup seasoned bread crumbs
> 1/2 teaspoon Italian seasoning
> 1-1/2 pounds ground beef
> 1-1/2 cups (6 ounces) shredded
>   part-skim mozzarella
>   cheese

Additional pizza sauce, optional

In a large bowl, combine the egg, pizza sauce, bread crumbs and Italian seasoning. Crumble beef over mixture and mix well. Divide between 12 greased muffin cups; press onto the bottom and up the sides. Fill center with cheese.

Bake at 375° for 15-18 minutes or until meat is no longer pink. Serve immediately with additional pizza sauce if desired. Or cool, place in freezer bags and freeze for up to 3 months.

Yield: 1 dozen.

Fix-and-Freeze Convenience

It's so convenient to bake and then freeze these moist little meat loaves that are packed with pizza flavor. They're great to have on hand to reheat for an after-school snack or quick dinner on extra-busy nights. Or freeze half of them and treat your gang to the rest tonight!

Pass around extra pizza sauce to drizzle on top for even more flavor. Use lean ground beef when making these meat loaf cups and you'll cut back on the number of fat grams.

Tortilla Pie

Prep/Total Time: 30 min.

✓ Uses less fat, sugar or salt. Includes Nutrition Facts and Diabetic Exchanges.

- 1/2 **pound lean ground beef**
- 1/4 **cup chopped onion**
- 1 **garlic clove, minced**
- 1 **can (14-1/2 ounces) Italian *or* Mexican diced tomatoes, drained**
- 1/2 **teaspoon chili powder**
- 1/4 **teaspoon ground cumin**
- 3/4 **cup part-skim ricotta cheese**
- 1/4 **cup shredded part-skim mozzarella cheese**
- 3 **tablespoons minced fresh cilantro, *divided***
- 4 **flour tortillas (8 inches)**
- 1/2 **cup shredded reduced-fat cheddar cheese**

In a large nonstick skillet, cook the beef, onion and garlic over medium heat until meat is no longer pink; drain. Stir in the tomatoes, chili powder and cumin. Bring to a boil; remove from the heat. In a small bowl, combine the ricotta cheese, mozzarella cheese and 2 tablespoons cilantro.

Place one tortilla in a 9-in. round baking pan coated with nonstick cooking spray. Layer with half of the meat sauce, one tortilla, all of the ricotta mixture, another tortilla and the remaining meat sauce. Top with remaining tortilla; sprinkle with cheddar cheese and remaining cilantro. Cover and bake at 400° for 15 minutes or until heated through and cheese is melted.

Yield: 6 servings.

Nutrition Facts: One piece equals 250 calories, 9 g fat (4 g saturated fat), 28 mg cholesterol, 439 mg sodium, 22 g carbohydrate, 1 g fiber, 19 g protein. **Diabetic Exchanges:** 2 lean meat, 1-1/2 starch, 1/2 fat.

Lighter Than Lasagna

This delicious layered entree is lighter-tasting than some of the traditional lasagnas made with pasta, and it has a pleasantly mild Southwestern flavor.

The main difference between corn and flour tortillas is that flour tortillas are made with fat (usually lard or shortening) and corn tortillas are not.

Sloppy Joe Wagon Wheels

Prep/Total Time: 20 min.

- 1 package (16 ounces) wagon wheel pasta
- 2 pounds ground beef
- 1 medium green pepper, chopped
- 1 medium onion, chopped
- 1 jar (28 ounces) meatless spaghetti sauce
- 1 jar (15-1/2 ounces) sloppy joe sauce

Cook pasta according to package directions. Meanwhile, in a large skillet, cook the beef, green pepper and onion over medium heat until meat is no longer pink; drain. Stir in spaghetti sauce and sloppy joe sauce; cook until heated through. Drain pasta; transfer to a large serving bowl and top with beef mixture.

Yield: 8 servings.

Get the Kids to Help

Sloppy joe sauce gives a bit of sweetness to prepared spaghetti sauce in this meaty mixture that's served over wagon wheel pasta.

Youngsters like to help prepare fun food almost as much as they like to eat it, so let them get involved. They could read you the recipe, wash the green pepper and hand you the sauce jars. Together, you'll create fast-to-fix fare—and warm memories!

Beefy Spanish Rice

Prep/Total Time: 30 min.

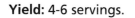

 1 pound ground beef
 1 medium onion, chopped
 1 medium green pepper, chopped
 1 garlic clove, minced
 1 can (14-1/2 ounces) stewed tomatoes
1-1/2 cups water
 1 cup uncooked long grain rice
 1 teaspoon salt
1/2 to 1 teaspoon chili powder
1/2 teaspoon dried thyme
1/4 teaspoon dried basil
1/4 teaspoon pepper
 2 tablespoons tomato paste

In a large skillet, cook the beef, onion, green pepper and garlic over medium heat until meat is no longer pink; drain. Stir in the next eight ingredients; bring to a boil. Reduce heat; cover and simmer for 20 minutes or until the rice is tender. Stir in tomato paste and cook until heated through.

Yield: 4-6 servings.

Adjust the Seasoning

This one-skillet rice dish can easily be altered to fit any taste by adjusting how spicy and saucy you make it. Simply add more or less of the chili powder and tomato paste. For a change of pace, try using ground turkey in place of the beef.

Rice is classified by its size: long, medium or short grain. Long grain rice has a length four to five times that of its width. When cooked, it produces light, dry grains that separate easily.

Pepper Patties

Prep/Total Time: 25 min.

    2 tablespoons soy sauce
  1/4 teaspoon garlic powder
  1/4 teaspoon pepper
    1 pound ground beef
    1 small onion, sliced
    1 small green pepper,
      julienned
    1 small sweet red pepper,
      julienned
    1 teaspoon vegetable oil
Hot cooked noodles, optional

In a large bowl, combine the soy sauce, garlic powder and pepper, reserving 1 tablespoon. Crumble beef over the remaining soy sauce mixture and mix well. Shape into four 1/2-in.-thick patties.

In a large skillet, saute onion and peppers in oil and reserved soy sauce mixture for 3-4 minutes or until crisp-tender. Remove and set aside.

Add patties to skillet. Cook, uncovered, for 4-5 minutes on each side or until a meat thermometer reads 160°; drain. Top patties with peppers and onion; cook until heated through. Serve over noodles if desired.

Yield: 4 servings.

Pepper Patty Particulars

When cooking beef patties, turn them with a spatula. Do not flatten them or flavorful juices will escape and the burgers will be dry. Present them on a bed of hot cooked egg noodles for a hearty dinner, alone for a lighter meal or on bread as an open-faced sandwich.

Bell peppers have a mild, sweet flavor and crisp, juicy flesh. Red bells are simply vine-ripened green bell peppers that, because they've ripened longer, are very sweet. There are also yellow, orange and purple-black bell peppers.

Spanish Noodles 'n' Ground Beef

Prep/Total Time: 30 min.

1   **pound ground beef**
1   **small green pepper, chopped**
1/3   **cup chopped onion**
3-1/4   **cups uncooked medium egg noodles**
1   **can (14-1/2 ounces) diced tomatoes, undrained**
1   **cup water**
1/4   **cup chili sauce**
1   **teaspoon salt**
1/8   **teaspoon pepper**
4   **bacon strips, cooked and crumbled**

In a large skillet, cook the beef, green pepper and onion over medium heat until meat is no longer pink; drain. Stir in the noodles, tomatoes, water, chili sauce, salt and pepper. Cover and cook over low heat for 15-20 minutes or until the noodles are tender, stirring frequently. Top with bacon.

Yield: 5 servings.

About Ground Beef

Ground beef is often labeled using the cut of meat that it is ground from, such as ground chuck or round. Ground beef can also be labeled according to the fat content of the ground mixture or the percentage of lean meat to fat, such as 85% or 90% lean. The higher the percentage, the leaner the meat.

Cutting back on beef? Trim fat and calories in this recipe by using ground turkey breast and turkey bacon instead.

Broiled Pizza Burgers

Prep/Total Time: 25 min.

          1   **pound ground beef**
          1   **tablespoon chopped onion**
          2   **teaspoons cornstarch**
          1   **can (14-1/2 ounces) diced tomatoes, undrained**
          1   **teaspoon dried oregano**
     1/4   **teaspoon salt**
     1/4   **teaspoon onion salt**
        10   **slices process American cheese,** *divided*
          4   **hamburger buns, split**

In a large skillet, cook beef and onion over medium heat until meat is no longer pink; drain. Sprinkle with cornstarch; stir until blended. Stir in the tomatoes, oregano, salt and onion salt. Cook, uncovered, for 5 minutes or until slightly thickened. Add six cheese slices; cook and stir until cheese is melted and blended.

Place hamburger buns cut side up on an ungreased baking sheet; spoon about 1/4 cup meat mixture onto each bun half. Cut remaining cheese slices in half diagonally; place over meat mixture. Broil 6-8 in. from the heat for 4 minutes or until cheese is melted.

Yield: 4 servings.

Cut Minutes from Cooking Time

These pizza-style burgers can be on the dinner table in just 25 minutes. They're even faster to fix if you use precooked ground beef you keep on hand in the freezer.

Brown several pounds of ground beef (include chopped onion and minced garlic if you like) and freeze in heavy-duty plastic bags or freezer containers for up to 3 months. One pound ground beef will yield 2-1/2 to 3 cups cooked; 4 pounds will yield 10 to 12 cups.

Taco-Stuffed Pepper Cups

Prep/Total Time: 30 min.

☑ Uses less fat, sugar or salt. Includes Nutrition Facts and Diabetic Exchanges.

- 2 medium green peppers
- 1/2 pound ground beef *or* lean ground turkey
- 2 tablespoons chopped onion
- 1 can (16 ounces) kidney beans, rinsed and drained
- 1 can (8 ounces) tomato sauce
- 3 tablespoons taco seasoning
- 1/4 cup sour cream
- 1/4 cup shredded cheddar cheese
- 1/4 cup chopped tomato

Cut tops off peppers and remove seeds. In a large kettle, cook peppers in boiling water for 3-5 minutes. Drain and rinse in cold water; set aside.

In a large skillet, cook beef and onion over medium heat until meat is no longer pink; drain. Stir in beans, tomato sauce and taco seasoning; bring to a boil. Reduce heat; simmer, uncovered, for 5-6 minutes or until heated through. Spoon into peppers.

Place in an ungreased 8-in. square baking dish. Bake, uncovered, at 350° for 10-12 minutes or until peppers are tender. Top with the sour cream, cheese and tomato.

Yield: 4 servings.

Nutrition Facts: 1 stuffed pepper half (prepared with ground turkey, fat-free sour cream and reduced-fat cheddar cheese) equals 261 calories, 6 g fat (2 g saturated fat), 52 mg cholesterol, 823 mg sodium, 31 g carbohydrate, 7 g fiber, 21 g protein. **Diabetic Exchanges:** 2 lean meat, 2 vegetable, 1-1/2 starch, 1 fat.

New Take on Tacos

When green, red or yellow bell peppers are plentiful, they create colorful containers for this spicy taco mixture that's ready in record time. Your family will surely welcome the change from ordinary hard shell tacos.

After parboiling the peppers, use tongs to easily remove them from the water. Rinsing the peppers under cold water stops them from cooking. Overcooked peppers can turn mushy and fall apart.

Cheeseburger Chowder

Prep/Total Time: 25 min.

- 1/2 **pound ground beef**
- 1 **can (10-3/4 ounces) condensed cheddar cheese soup, undiluted**
- 1-3/4 **cups milk**
- 1 **cup frozen shredded hash brown potatoes**
- 1 **can (4 ounces) chopped green chilies**
- 1 **tablespoon taco seasoning**
- 1 **tablespoon dried minced onion**
- 1/2 **teaspoon chili powder**

Coarsely crushed corn chips, shredded Monterey Jack cheese and chopped green onions, optional

In a large saucepan, cook beef over medium heat until no longer pink; drain. Stir in the soup, milk, potatoes, chilies, taco seasoning, onion and chili powder until blended. Bring to a boil.

Reduce heat; simmer, uncovered, for 5 minutes or until heated through. Garnish with corn chips, cheese and green onions if desired.

Yield: 4 servings.

Change Up The Peppers

If your family is a fan of cheeseburgers, they're going to love this chowder! The addition of chilies and Southwestern spices dress up a can of cheddar cheese soup. Use mild green chilies if they suit your tastes or try a spicier variety to give the soup even more kick.

Coarsely crush some corn chips to top off bowlfuls of the chowder, along with chopped green onions and shredded Monterey Jack cheese.

Ground Beef 'n' Biscuits

Prep: 20 min. **Bake:** 20 min.

1-1/2	pounds ground beef
1/2	cup chopped celery
1/2	cup chopped onion
2	tablespoons all-purpose flour
1	teaspoon salt
1/4	teaspoon dried oregano
1/8	teaspoon pepper
2	cans (8 ounces *each*) tomato sauce
1	package (10 ounces) frozen peas
1	tube (7-1/2 ounces) refrigerated buttermilk biscuits
1	cup (4 ounces) shredded cheddar cheese

In a large skillet, cook the beef, celery and onion over medium heat until meat is no longer pink; drain. Stir in the flour, salt, oregano and pepper until blended. Add tomato sauce and peas; simmer for 5 minutes.

Transfer to a greased 13-in. x 9-in. x 2-in. baking dish. Separate biscuits; arrange over beef mixture. Sprinkle with cheese. Bake, uncovered, at 350° for 20 minutes or until biscuits are golden brown and cheese is melted.

Yield: 6 servings.

Meaty Meal-in-One

With meat, vegetables and bread, Ground Beef 'n' Biscuits is practically a meal in itself. All you need is a tossed salad to serve alongside.

Your grocery store likely carries a delightful assortment of salad kits, which include the salad greens, dressing and other condiments all in one bag. Or turn to the Swift Sides & Salads chapter (p. 260) for a variety of garden-fresh ideas.

Taco Skillet

Prep/Total Time: 30 min.

1 pound ground beef
1 medium onion, chopped
1 can (16 ounces) refried beans
1 can (4 ounces) chopped green chilies
1/4 to 1/2 teaspoon garlic powder
3/4 cup sour cream
1/2 to 1 teaspoon ground cumin
1/2 to 1 teaspoon chili powder
1 medium tomato, seeded and chopped
1 can (2-1/4 ounces) sliced ripe olives, drained
1 small green pepper
1 cup (4 ounces) shredded Mexican cheese blend

Tortilla chips *or* taco shells
Shredded lettuce
Salsa

In a large skillet, cook beef and onion over medium heat until meat is no longer pink; drain. Stir in the beans, chilies and garlic powder; cook until heated through.

In a small bowl, combine the sour cream, cumin and chili powder; spread over beef mixture. Top with tomato, olives and green pepper. Sprinkle with cheese. Serve with tortilla chips or taco shells, lettuce and salsa.

Yield: 4-6 servings.

Freeze Taco Meat

Served with tortilla chips or taco shells, lettuce and salsa, this one-dish Mexican dinner is a fun meal for everyone!

If your family favors Mexican food, consider having taco meat ready to go in the freezer. Cook 3 pounds ground beef and 1-1/2 cups chopped onion over medium heat until meat is no longer pink; drain. Add 3 envelopes taco seasoning and prepare according to package directions. Cool and freeze in 1-pound portions.

Savory Beef and Noodles

Prep/Total Time: 20 min.

1   pound ground beef
1   can (10-1/2 ounces)
    condensed French onion
    soup, undiluted
1/2 cup beef gravy
1   can (4 ounces) mushroom
    stems and pieces, drained
1   tablespoon all-purpose
    flour
1   tablespoon water
Hot cooked noodles
Minced fresh parsley, optional

In a large skillet, cook beef over medium heat until no longer pink; drain. Stir in the soup, gravy and mushrooms. Bring to a boil. Reduce heat; cover and simmer for 5 minutes.

In a small bowl, combine flour and water until smooth; stir into beef mixture. Bring to a boil; cook and stir for 2 minutes or until thickened. Serve over hot cooked noodles. Garnish with parsley if desired.

Yield: 4 servings.

Down-Home Dinner

Are you craving country-style cooking but don't have time to spend hours in the kitchen? Savory Beef and Noodles is a speedy variation of beef stroganoff that's long on flavor. No one will be able to resist a hearty entree like this…it's true comfort food at its finest.

The recipe only calls for 1/2 cup of beef gravy. Refrigerate the remainder and serve it with mashed potatoes or leftover roast beef at another meal.

Chili Bean Nacho Skillet

Prep/Total Time: 30 min.

✓ Uses less fat, sugar or salt. Includes Nutrition Facts and Diabetic Exchanges.

1	**pound ground beef**
1/2	**cup chopped onion**
1	**can (15-1/2 ounces) chili beans, undrained**
1	**can (15 ounces) tomato sauce**
1	**can (11 ounces) Mexicorn, drained**
1	**teaspoon sugar**
1	**teaspoon chili powder**
1/2	**teaspoon dried oregano**
1/2	**to 1 cup shredded cheddar cheese**

Tortilla chips, optional

In a large skillet, cook beef and onion over medium heat until meat is no longer pink; drain. Stir in the beans, tomato sauce, corn, sugar, chili powder and oregano. Bring to a boil. Reduce heat; simmer, uncovered, for 10 minutes.

Sprinkle with cheese; remove from the heat. Cover; let stand for 5 minutes or until cheese is melted. Serve with tortilla chips if desired.

Yield: 6 servings.

Nutrition Facts: 1 cup (prepared with lean ground beef and 1/2 cup reduced-fat cheese; calculated without chips) equals 278 calories, 8 g fat (4 g saturated fat), 44 mg cholesterol, 1,040 mg sodium, 28 g carbohydrate, 6 g fiber, 23 g protein. **Diabetic Exchanges:** 2 starch, 2 lean meat.

Make It Mexican

Served with tortilla chips and a side salad, this one-skillet dish makes a wholesome Mexican meal in a matter of minutes. Toss together Fiesta Mixed Greens (p. 289) or Guacamole Tossed Salad (p. 262) to round out the Southwestern theme. Family and friends won't give you any heat!

To make homemade tortilla chips, cut flour tortillas into wedges and place on a baking sheet. Spritz with nonstick cooking spray, then sprinkle with chili powder and cayenne pepper. Bake at 375° for 7 to 10 minutes or until crisp and lightly browned.

Microwave Meatball Stew

Prep/Total Time: 25 min.

- 1 egg, lightly beaten
- 1/2 cup dry bread crumbs
- 1/2 cup finely chopped onion
- 2 tablespoons onion soup mix
- 1 pound ground beef
- 1 can (15 ounces) whole potatoes, drained and quartered
- 1-1/4 cups frozen sliced carrots
- 1-1/4 cups frozen peas
- 1 can (10-3/4 ounces) condensed cream of mushroom soup, undiluted
- 1 can (10-1/2 ounces) condensed beef broth, undiluted
- 1/2 teaspoon dried savory
- 1/4 teaspoon dried thyme
- 2 tablespoons cornstarch
- 2 tablespoons water
- 1/4 teaspoon browning sauce, optional

Microwave Cooking Clues

Most vegetables cook just beautifully in a microwave oven—they keep their color and nutrients better than with most other cooking methods. When using a microwave, stir foods such as casseroles to distribute the food for even cooking.

In a large bowl, combine the egg, dry bread crumbs, onion and soup mix. Crumble beef over mixture and mix well. Shape into 1-1/2-in. balls. Place in a microwave-safe baking dish. Cover and microwave on high for 3-4 minutes. Turn meatballs and microwave 3-4 minutes longer; drain.

In a large bowl, combine the next seven ingredients; spoon over meatballs. Combine cornstarch, water and browning sauce if desired; gradually stir into the stew. Cover and microwave on high for 1-2 minutes or until thickened and bubbly, stirring occasionally.

Yield: 4-6 servings.

Editor's Note: This recipe was tested in a 1,100-watt microwave.

Cheeseburger Loaf

Prep/Total Time: 20 min.

- 1 **pound ground beef**
- 1/4 **cup chopped onion**
- 1 **can (10-3/4 ounces) condensed tomato soup, undiluted**
- 1/2 **teaspoon garlic salt**
- 1/4 **teaspoon salt**
- 1/4 **teaspoon pepper**
- 1 **loaf (1 pound) unsliced French bread**
- 1 **tablespoon butter, softened**
- 8 **ounces process American *or* Mexican-flavored cheese, sliced**

In a large saucepan, cook beef and onion over medium heat until meat is no longer pink; drain. Add soup, garlic salt, salt and pepper; simmer, uncovered, for 5-10 minutes.

Meanwhile, slice the top third off the bread. Hollow out bottom half of loaf, leaving a 3/4-in. shell (discard removed bread or save for another use). Spread butter on cut side of bread. Place loaf on an ungreased baking sheet and broil 4-6 in. from the heat until lightly browned.

Spoon beef mixture into shell; arrange cheese slices on top. Broil 2-3 minutes longer or until the cheese is melted. Replace bread top.

Yield: 6-8 servings.

Great Sandwich Variations

Give this sandwich loaf an Italian flair by substituting spaghetti sauce for the tomato soup and mozzarella for the American cheese. Or do you prefer Southwestern flavor? Use picante sauce and Monterey Jack cheese.

To make the bread shell, use a serrated knife to cut a thin slice off the top of the loaf of bread. With a fork, pull out the bread from inside, leaving a 3/4-inch shell.

Cola Burgers

Prep/Total Time: 30 min.

    1   egg
  1/2   cup cola, *divided*
  1/2   cup crushed saltines (about 15)
    6   tablespoons French salad dressing, *divided*
    2   tablespoons grated Parmesan cheese
  1/4   teaspoon salt
1-1/2   pounds ground beef
    6   hamburger buns, split

In a large bowl, combine the egg, 1/4 cup cola, cracker crumbs, 2 tablespoons salad dressing, Parmesan cheese and salt. Crumble beef over mixture and mix well. Shape into six 3/4-in.-thick patties (the mixture will be moist). In a small bowl, combine the remaining cola and salad dressing; set aside.

Grill patties, uncovered, over medium-hot heat for 3 minutes on each side. Brush with cola mixture. Grill 8-10 minutes longer or until a meat thermometer reads 160°, basting and turning occasionally. Serve on buns.

Yield: 6 servings.

Editor's Note: Diet cola is not recommended for this recipe.

Pass Up the Ketchup

The unique combination of cola and French salad dressing added to ground beef gives these hamburgers fabulous flavor. Using the mixture as a basting sauce when grilling the moist burgers adds even more great taste, so forget the ketchup! Simply top them off with lettuce and tomato slices.

It's a snap to slice tomatoes if you use a serrated knife. Also, slices will hold their shape better if you slice from stem end to blossom end.

Santa Fe Supper

Prep/Total Time: 30 min.

1   **cup uncooked long grain rice**

1   **pound ground beef**

2   **small zucchini, cut into 1/4-inch slices**

1   **large onion, halved and sliced**

1-1/2   **cups chunky salsa,** *divided*

1/4   **teaspoon salt**

1/4   **teaspoon pepper**

1   **cup (4 ounces) shredded pepper Jack cheese**

1   **can (4 ounces) chopped green chilies, drained**

1   **cup (4 ounces) shredded cheddar cheese**

Cook rice according to package directions. Meanwhile, in a large skillet, cook beef over medium heat until no longer pink; drain. Stir in the zucchini, onion, 1 cup salsa, salt and pepper; cook until vegetables are crisp-tender.

Add pepper Jack cheese and chilies to the rice. Sprinkle cheddar cheese over beef mixture; serve with rice and remaining salsa.

Yield: 4 servings.

Add Sizzle to Supper

This zesty skillet meal is a great way to bring a little variety to your dinnertime lineup. Green chilies and pepper Jack cheese spice up the rice, while salsa, zucchini, onion and cheddar cheese dress up the ground beef mixture.

A broad selection of salsas is available in supermarkets today. They can range in spiciness from mild to mouth-searing. Be sure to pick one that your whole family will enjoy.

Mushroom Salisbury Steak

Prep/Total Time: 30 min.

1/4 cup cornstarch
2 cans (10-1/2 ounces *each*) condensed beef consomme, undiluted
1 jar (6 ounces) sliced mushrooms, drained
4 teaspoons Worcestershire sauce
1 teaspoon dried basil
1 egg, lightly beaten
1/2 cup soft bread crumbs
1 medium onion, finely chopped
1/2 to 1 teaspoon seasoned salt
1/4 teaspoon pepper, optional
1-1/2 pounds ground beef
Hot mashed potatoes *or* cooked noodles

In a large bowl, combine the cornstarch and consomme until smooth. Stir in mushrooms, Worcestershire sauce and basil; set aside.

In another large bowl, combine egg, bread crumbs, onion, seasoned salt and pepper if desired. Crumble beef over mixture and mix well. Shape into six oval patties; place in a shallow 1-1/2-qt. microwave-safe dish.

Cover and microwave on high for 5-6 minutes; drain. Turn patties, moving the ones in the center to the outside of dish. Pour consomme mixture over patties. Cover and microwave on high for 8-10 minutes or until meat is no longer pink. Let stand for 5 minutes. Serve with potatoes or noodles.

Yield: 6 servings.

Editor's Note: This recipe was tested with an 850-watt microwave.

Salisbury Steak Substitutions

Beef consomme is a stronger-flavored stock than broth because it has been simmered longer. It is readily available in cans, but regular beef broth can be substituted.

We've paired the salisbury steak with mashed potatoes, but it would be equally delicious served over hot cooked noodles.

Garden Skillet

Prep/Total Time: 30 min.

    2 pounds ground beef
    3 medium zucchini, julienned
    4 medium carrots, julienned
    1 can (15 ounces) canned bean sprouts, drained
    1 medium onion, cut into thin wedges
  3/4 cup julienned green pepper
    1 garlic clove, minced
    1 medium tomato, cut into wedges
    1 teaspoon salt
    1 teaspoon ground cumin

In a large skillet, cook beef over medium heat until no longer pink; drain. Add the zucchini, carrots, bean sprouts, onion, green pepper and garlic. Cook and stir for 3-4 minutes or until crisp-tender. Add the tomato, salt and cumin. Cook 2 minutes longer or until heated through.

Yield: 6-8 servings.

Add "Pep" to Skillet Dish

To give Garden Skillet a little more heat, toss in strips of jalapeno pepper and drizzle with taco sauce before serving.

Chili peppers, like jalapenos, contain a skin irritant called capsaicin. When handling chili peppers, wear rubber or plastic gloves and avoid touching your eyes or face to prevent burning. Wash hands and cutting surface thoroughly with hot, soapy water when finished.

Oriental Beef Noodle Toss

Prep/Total Time: 30 min.

1 **pound ground beef**
2 **packages (3 ounces** *each***) Oriental-flavored ramen noodles**
1 **package (16 ounces) frozen Oriental vegetable blend**
2 **cups water**
4 **to 5 tablespoons soy sauce**
1/4 **teaspoon ground ginger**
3 **tablespoons thinly sliced green onions**

In a large skillet, cook beef over medium heat until no longer pink; drain. Stir in contents of one noodle seasoning packet; set aside and keep warm.

Break the noodles; place in a large saucepan. Add the contents of second seasoning packet, vegetables, water, soy sauce and ginger. Bring to a boil. Reduce heat; cover and simmer for 6-10 minutes or until vegetables and noodles are tender. Stir in beef and onions.

Yield: 4-6 servings.

About Ramen Noodles

Ramen noodles are Asian instant-style, deep-fried noodles that are usually sold in cellophane packages, sometimes with bits of dehydrated vegetables and broth mix.

In this easy recipe, the seasoning packet that comes with the noodles provides the Oriental flavor. No additional seasoning, except for a little ground ginger and soy sauce, is needed.

Speedy **Ground Beef**

Soupy Joes

Prep/Total Time: 20 min.

1 pound ground beef
1 medium onion, chopped
1 can (10-1/2 ounces) condensed vegetable soup, undiluted
1 tablespoon ketchup
1 teaspoon prepared mustard
1/2 teaspoon salt
1/4 teaspoon pepper
6 hamburger buns, split and toasted

In a large saucepan, cook beef and onion over medium heat until meat is no longer pink; drain. Stir in the soup, ketchup, mustard, salt and pepper. Simmer, uncovered, for 5-10 minutes. Serve on buns.

Yield: 6 servings.

Souped-Up Sandwiches

Ground beef is tasty, inexpensive and can be used in a variety of ways. Best of all, it cooks quickly so meal preparation is a breeze. No wonder it's a mainstay in homes across the country!

Here, a simple can of vegetable soup turns ground beef into family-pleasing Soupy Joes. The quick-to-fix sandwiches are great for a hot lunch or a fast dinner served with potato chips and carrot and celery sticks.

Ground Beef Gyros

Prep/Total Time: 30 min.

☑ Uses less fat, sugar or salt. Includes Nutrition Facts and Diabetic Exchanges.

- 1 carton (8 ounces) plain yogurt
- 1/3 cup chopped seeded cucumber
- 2 tablespoons finely chopped onion
- 1 garlic clove, minced
- 1 teaspoon sugar

FILLING:
- 1-1/2 teaspoons dried oregano
- 1 teaspoon garlic powder
- 1 teaspoon onion powder
- 1 teaspoon salt, optional
- 3/4 teaspoon pepper
- 1 pound ground beef
- 4 pita breads (6 inches), halved, warmed
- 3 cups shredded lettuce
- 1 large tomato, chopped
- 1 small onion, sliced

In a small bowl, combine the first five ingredients; chill. In a large bowl, combine oregano, garlic powder, onion powder, salt if desired and pepper. Crumble beef over mixture and mix well. Shape into four patties. Grill patties, covered, over medium-hot heat for 6-7 minutes on each side or until a meat thermometer reads 160°. Cut patties into thin slices; stuff into pita halves. Add lettuce, tomato and onion. Serve with the cucumber-yogurt sauce.

Yield: 4 servings.

Nutrition Facts: 1 gyro (prepared with fat-free yogurt and lean ground beef and without salt) equals 422 calories, 11 g fat (0 saturated fat), 42 mg cholesterol, 453 mg sodium, 45 g carbohydrate, 3 g fiber, 33 g protein. **Diabetic Exchanges:** 3-1/2 meat, 3 starch.

A Course in Cucumbers

A cucumber-yogurt sauce adds an authentic finishing touch to these Greek gyros made with ground beef instead of the more traditional lamb.

Choose cucumbers with smooth, brightly colored skin and store in a plastic bag in the refrigerator. Wash thoroughly just before using. The thin skin, unless waxed, does not require peeling. To seed a cucumber, cut it in half lengthwise, then use a teaspoon to scrape out the seeds.

Beef Stroganoff Melt

Prep/Total Time: 30 min.

2   **pounds ground beef**
1   **cup sliced fresh mushrooms**
1   **medium onion, chopped**
1   **teaspoon salt**
1/2 **teaspoon garlic powder**
1/2 **teaspoon pepper**
2   **cups (16 ounces) sour cream**
1   **loaf (1 pound) unsliced French bread**
3   **tablespoons butter, softened**
3   **cups (12 ounces) shredded Swiss cheese**
1   **medium green pepper, thinly sliced**
2   **medium tomatoes, thinly sliced**

Stroganoff Made Simple

Piled with ground beef, mushrooms, green peppers and tomatoes, this open-faced sandwich is an easy way to feed your gang beef stroganoff. It has all the traditional flavor without all the timely work!

When shopping for ground beef, select meat that is bright red in color and is in a tightly sealed package. Purchase all ground beef before the "sell by" date.

In a large skillet, cook the beef, mushrooms and onion over medium heat until meat is no longer pink; drain. Stir in the salt, garlic powder and pepper. Remove from the heat; stir in sour cream.

Cut French bread in half lengthwise. Place on an ungreased baking sheet. Spread butter over cut halves; top with meat mixture and half of the cheese.

Arrange green pepper and tomatoes on top. Sprinkle with the remaining cheese. Bake at 375° for 15 minutes or until cheese is melted.

Yield: 8 servings.

Beef Hash Brown Pizza

Prep/Total Time: 30 min.

   5   **cups frozen shredded hash brown potatoes, thawed**
   1   **can (10-3/4 ounces) condensed cheddar cheese soup, undiluted**
   1   **egg, lightly beaten**
1/2   **teaspoon salt**
1/4   **teaspoon pepper**
   2   **pounds ground beef**
   1   **medium onion, chopped**
   1   **can (4 ounces) mushroom stems and pieces, drained**
   1   **can (15 ounces) pizza sauce**
   4   **cups (16 ounces) shredded pizza cheese blend, *divided***

Try Other Toppers

You can prepare this recipe exactly as directed, or you can top the change-of-pace potato-crust pizza with any of your family's favorite toppings. That's the great thing about pizza—the possibilities are endless!

To quickly thaw frozen hash browns, place them in a microwave-safe dish. Cover and defrost for 5 to 8 minutes, stirring once or twice, until thawed.

In a large bowl, combine the potatoes, soup, egg, salt and pepper. Spread mixture into a greased 15-in. x 10-in. x 1-in. baking pan. Bake at 400° for 20-25 minutes or until lightly browned.

Meanwhile, in a large skillet over medium heat, cook the beef, onion and mushrooms until meat is no longer pink; drain. Stir in pizza sauce and keep warm.

Sprinkle 2 cups cheese over hot crust. Spread beef mixture over the top; sprinkle with remaining cheese. Bake 5-10 minutes longer or until the cheese is melted.

Yield: 6-8 servings.

Dagwood Burgers

Prep/Total Time: 25 min.

1 pound ground beef
1/4 cup prepared coleslaw
    salad dressing
4 thick slices bread, toasted
4 bacon strips, cooked and
    drained
4 slices Swiss cheese
4 slices tomato
4 slices onion
8 slices unpeeled cucumber
4 slices dill pickle
4 pitted jumbo ripe olives
1/4 cup salad dressing of your
    choice, optional

Shape beef into four patties. Broil 4-6 in. from the heat for 6-8 minutes on each side, or cook in a large skillet over medium heat until no longer pink; drain.

Spread coleslaw dressing over bread. Top each slice with a beef patty, bacon, cheese, tomato, onion, two cucumber slices, pickle and olive. Secure with a toothpick. Serve with salad dressing of your choice if desired.

Yield: 4 servings.

Simple Burger Substitutions

You definitely need a knife and fork to dig into these piled-high, open-faced hamburgers. Vary their flavor by combining different salad dressings and cheese. For example, pair Thousand Island with Swiss, ranch with American or creamy Italian with mozzarella.

Cook ground beef burgers to 160°. To test for doneness, use tongs to hold burger while inserting instant-read thermometer from a side. Make sure thermometer is far enough in to read temperature in center.

Skillet Shepherd's Pie

Prep/Total Time: 30 min.

1　pound ground beef
1　cup chopped onion
2　cups frozen corn, thawed
2　cups frozen peas, thawed
2　tablespoons ketchup
1　tablespoon
　　Worcestershire sauce
2　teaspoons minced garlic
1　teaspoon beef bouillon
　　granules
1/2　cup boiling water
1　tablespoon cornstarch
1/2　cup sour cream
3-1/2　cups mashed potatoes (prepared with milk
　　and butter)
3/4　cup shredded cheddar cheese

In a large skillet, cook beef and onion over medium heat until meat is no longer pink; drain. Stir in the corn, peas, ketchup, Worcestershire sauce and garlic. Reduce heat; cover and simmer for 5 minutes.

Meanwhile, in a small bowl, dissolve bouillon in boiling water. Combine cornstarch and sour cream until smooth; stir into beef mixture until blended. Add bouillon mixture. Bring to a boil. Reduce heat; cook and stir until thickened.

Spread mashed potatoes over the top; sprinkle with cheese. Cover and cook until the potatoes are heated through and the cheese is melted.

Yield: 6 servings.

Meat-and-Potato Mainstay

You'll come to rely on Skillet Shepherd's Pie, which is very quick to make. And you should have most—if not all—of the ingredients already on hand. Served with a bowl of fresh or canned fruit on the side, it's a complete meat-and-potato meal.

To liven up the mashed potatoes on top, add fresh herbs or mix in shredded Swiss or cheddar cheese.

Tortellini Soup

Prep/Total Time: 30 min.

        1   **pound ground beef**
    3-1/2   **cups water**
        1   **can (28 ounces) diced tomatoes, undrained**
        1   **can (10-1/2 ounces) condensed French onion soup, undiluted**
        1   **package (9 ounces) frozen cut green beans**
        1   **package (9 ounces) refrigerated cheese tortellini**
        1   **medium zucchini, chopped**
        1   **teaspoon dried basil**

In a large saucepan, cook beef over medium heat until no longer pink; drain. Add the remaining ingredients; bring to a boil. Cook, uncovered, for 5 minutes or until heated through.

Yield: 6-8 servings.

Too-Easy Soup

Not only is this soup delicious...it's also unbelievably fast to make, going from stove to dinner table in just 30 minutes! Every steaming bowlful is brimming with ground beef, tomatoes, green beans, zucchini and cheese tortellini. A loaf of Italian or garlic bread would make a nice accompaniment.

For a creamy variation, substitute cream of mushroom soup for the French onion soup. If there happens to be any soup left over, it tastes even better the next day.

Grandma's Rice Dish

Prep: 20 min. **Bake:** 15 min.

- 1 **pound ground beef**
- 1/3 **cup chopped onion**
- 1/2 **cup chopped green pepper**
- 2 **cups cooked long grain rice**
- 1 **can (14-1/2 ounces) diced tomatoes, undrained**
- 1 **can (11 ounces) whole kernel corn, drained**
- 1 **can (2-1/4 ounces) sliced ripe olives, drained**
- 6 **bacon strips, cooked and crumbled**
- 2 **teaspoons chili powder**
- 1 **teaspoon garlic powder**
- 1/2 **teaspoon salt**
- 1-1/2 **cups (6 ounces) shredded cheddar cheese, *divided***
- 1/2 **cup dry bread crumbs**
- 1 **tablespoon butter, melted**

In a large skillet, cook the beef, onion and green pepper over medium heat until meat is no longer pink; drain. Stir in the rice, tomatoes, corn, olives, bacon, chili powder, garlic powder and salt. Bring to a boil; remove from the heat. Add 1 cup of cheese; stir until melted.

Transfer to a greased 11-in. x 7-in. x 2-in. baking dish. Sprinkle with remaining cheese. Toss bread crumbs with butter; sprinkle over top. Bake, uncovered, at 350° for 15-20 minutes or until cheese is melted.

Yield: 4 servings.

Rice Is Still Nice

Based on a recipe Grandma used to make years ago, this updated dish is pleasing hungry families today. It deliciously proves that casseroles can be put together in a hurry (and bake just as quickly), plus it's a great way to put leftover rice to use.

Don't have 2 cups cooked long grain rice left in the fridge? Bring 1-1/3 cups water, 1/4 teaspoon salt if desired and 2 teaspoons butter if desired to a boil in a 2-qt. saucepan. Stir in 2/3 cup rice; return to a boil. Cover and reduce heat to a simmer. Cook for 12 to 15 minutes or until tender.

Beef Quesadillas

Prep/Total Time: 30 min.

3/4 pound ground beef
1/2 cup refried beans
  1 can (4 ounces) chopped
     green chilies, drained
1/2 teaspoon dried oregano
1/2 teaspoon ground cumin
1/4 teaspoon salt
  4 flour tortillas (8 inches)
  2 tablespoons butter,
     softened
1-1/3 cups shredded taco cheese
Paprika

In a large skillet, cook the beef over medium heat until no longer pink; drain. Stir in the beans, chilies, oregano, cumin and salt. Cook over medium-low heat for 3-4 minutes or until heated through.

Spread one side of each tortilla with butter. Spoon 1/2 cup of the meat mixture over half of the unbuttered side. Sprinkle with 1/3 cup cheese; fold in half.

Place on a lightly greased baking sheet. Sprinkle with paprika. Bake at 475° for 10 minutes or until crisp and golden brown. Cut into wedges.

Yield: 4 servings.

Treat Them Like Tacos

Try serving these Beef Quesadillas with your favorite taco toppings, such as sour cream, salsa, guacamole, chopped tomatoes, shredded lettuce and even sliced olives.

Quesadillas are very versatile. Fillings can include any type of shredded cheese and cooked meat, refried beans and more. Have fun letting family members come up with their own combinations!

Hamburger Supper

Prep/Total Time: 30 min.

1 **pound ground beef**
1-1/2 **cups water**
1/2 **teaspoon poultry seasoning**
1/4 **teaspoon pepper**
1 **envelope brown gravy mix**
1 **medium onion, sliced and separated into rings**
1 **medium carrot, sliced**
2 **medium potatoes, sliced**
1 **cup (4 ounces) shredded cheddar cheese**

In a large skillet, cook beef over medium heat until no longer pink; drain. Stir in the water, poultry seasoning and pepper. Bring to a boil. Stir in gravy mix. Cook and stir for 2 minutes or until slightly thickened.

Arrange the onion, carrot and potatoes over beef. Reduce heat; cover and simmer for 10-15 minutes or until vegetables are tender. Sprinkle with cheese. Cover and cook 3-5 minutes longer or until the cheese is melted.

Yield: 4 servings.

Stir Together a Sauce

When cooking ground beef, cook over medium heat and stir often to break apart large pieces. Use a colander to drain fat and blot the meat with crumpled paper towel.

Instead of sprinkling this meal-in-one with shredded cheddar cheese, you could create a cheese sauce on the stove to drizzle over the top. Simply heat some process cheese (Velveeta) and milk on low until the cheese is melted and the mixture is smooth.

Minestrone Macaroni

Prep/Total Time: 25 min.

1 pound ground beef
2 cans (14-1/2 ounces *each*) Italian diced tomatoes, undrained
2-1/4 cups water
1-1/2 cups uncooked elbow macaroni
2 beef bouillon cubes
1 can (16 ounces) kidney beans, rinsed and drained
1 can (15 ounces) garbanzo beans, rinsed and drained
1 can (14-1/2 ounces) cut green beans, rinsed and drained

In a large skillet, cook beef over medium heat until no longer pink; drain. Add tomatoes, water, macaroni and bouillon; bring to a boil. Reduce heat; cover and simmer for 12-15 minutes or until macaroni is tender. Stir in beans and cook until heated through.

Yield: 6 servings.

Dig into Minestrone

Traditional minestrone is an Italian soup made with fresh vegetables, pasta and beans. With the addition of ground beef, this recipe has all the flavor of the popular soup but is a thicker, heartier, one-skillet meal meant to be eaten with a fork, not a spoon!

The pasta cooks right with the other ingredients, so there's no need to boil it in a separate saucepan. The canned beans called for can be stored in their original, sealed cans for up to 1 year.

Meatball Cabbage Rolls

Prep: 25 min. **Cook:** 8 hours

1 large head cabbage, cored
2 cans (one 8 ounces, one 15 ounces) tomato sauce, *divided*
1 small onion, chopped
1/3 cup uncooked long grain rice
2 tablespoons chili powder
Salt and garlic powder to taste
1 pound ground beef

In a Dutch oven, cook cabbage in boiling water just until leaves fall off head. Set aside 14-16 large leaves for rolls (refrigerate remaining cabbage for another use). Cut out the thick vein from the bottom of each reserved leaf, making a V-shaped cut.

In a large bowl, combine 8 oz. of tomato sauce, onion, rice, chili powder, salt and garlic powder. Crumble beef over mixture and mix well. Shape into 2-in. balls. Place one meatball on each cabbage leaf; overlap cut ends of leaf. Fold in sides, beginning from the cut end. Roll up completely to enclose meatball. Secure with toothpicks.

Place in a 5-qt. slow cooker. Pour remaining tomato sauce over cabbage rolls. Cover and cook on low for 8 hours or until meat is no longer pink and cabbage is tender. Discard toothpicks before serving.

Yield: 4-6 servings.

Slow Cooking Supper

Mouth-watering meatballs tucked inside make these stand out from other cabbage rolls. Plus, they're made in a slow cooker. Cutting the thick vein from each leaf after the cabbage has been boiled makes for easier rolling.

Slow cookers provide unbeatable fix-it-and-forget-it convenience, so you can offer from-scratch fare even on your most hurried days. Just fill your slow cooker early in the day, turn it on and head out the door. When you come home, you'll be greeted with the wonderful aroma of supper.

Mashed Potato Hot Dish

Prep: 15 min. **Bake:** 20 min.

- 1 **pound ground beef**
- 1 **can (10-3/4 ounces) condensed cream of chicken soup, undiluted**
- 2 **cups frozen French-style green beans**
- 2 **cups hot mashed potatoes (prepared with milk and butter)**
- 1/2 **cup shredded cheddar cheese**

In a large skillet, cook beef over medium heat until no longer pink; drain. Stir in soup and beans. Transfer to a greased 2-qt. baking dish. Top with mashed potatoes; sprinkle with cheese. Bake, uncovered, at 350° for 20-25 minutes or until bubbly and cheese is melted.

Yield: 4 servings.

Make Extra Mashed Potatoes

Whenever you're making homemade mashed potatoes, throw in a few extra spuds so you can make this hot dish for supper the next night. One large potato will yield about 1 cup mashed potatoes.

To cook potatoes for mashing, peel and cut into chunks. Then place in a saucepan and cover with water. Bring to a boil; cover and cook for 15 to 30 minutes or until tender. Drain well and mash. Add milk and butter; mash until the potatoes are light and fluffy.

Upside-Down Meat Pie

Prep/Total Time: 30 min.

1 pound ground beef
1/2 cup chopped celery
1/2 cup chopped onion
1/4 cup chopped green pepper
1 can (10-3/4 ounces) condensed tomato soup, undiluted
1 teaspoon prepared mustard
1-1/2 cups biscuit/baking mix
1/3 cup water
3 slices process American cheese, halved diagonally
Green pepper rings, optional

In a large skillet, cook the beef, celery, onion and green pepper over medium heat until meat is no longer pink; drain. Stir in soup and mustard. Transfer to a greased 9-in. pie plate.

Meanwhile, in a large bowl, combine dry baking mix and water until a soft dough forms. Turn onto a lightly floured surface; roll into a 9-in. circle. Place over meat mixture. Bake at 425° for 20 minutes or until golden brown. Cool for 5 minutes.

Run a knife around edge to loosen biscuit; invert onto a serving platter. Arrange cheese slices in a pinwheel pattern on top. Garnish with green pepper rings if desired.

Yield: 6 servings.

Make Your Own Mix

Thanks to the pleasing sloppy joe flavor, kids will dig right into this meat pie...and so will adults. The "crust" is made with biscuit/baking mix, which you can buy, or save money and make your own at home. Just follow this simple recipe.

In a large bowl, combine 9 cups all-purpose flour, 1/4 cup baking powder and 1 tablespoon salt. Cut in 2 cups shortening until the mixture resembles coarse crumbs. Store in an airtight container in a cool, dry place or in the freezer for up to 8 months. The recipe yields 12 cups.

Italian Hamburgers

Prep/Total Time: 25 min.

      6 tablespoons dry bread crumbs
    1/3 cup chopped onion
    1/3 cup chopped green pepper
      1 garlic clove, minced
    3/4 teaspoon dried oregano
    1/4 to 1/2 teaspoon salt
    1/4 to 1/2 teaspoon pepper
      1 pound ground beef
      6 tablespoons grated Parmesan cheese, *divided*
      1 can (15 ounces) tomato sauce
    3/4 teaspoon Italian seasoning
Hot cooked spaghetti

Combine the first seven ingredients. Crumble beef over mixture and sprinkle with 3 tablespoons Parmesan cheese; mix well. Shape into six patties.

In a large skillet, cook patties for 2 minutes on each side or until lightly browned. Combine the tomato sauce and Italian seasoning; pour over patties. Bring to a boil. Reduce heat; cover and simmer for 10-15 minutes or until meat is no longer pink. Sprinkle with remaining cheese. Serve patties and sauce over spaghetti.

Yield: 6 servings.

Gently Handle Hamburgers

Italian Hamburgers make a super supper that takes only minutes to prepare but still leaves the impression that you've spent a lot of time cooking.

Use a measuring cup or ice cream scoop to make equal-size hamburgers. Gently form each portion into a patty. For moist, light-textured burgers, be careful not to overmix or overhandle meat mixture.

Spaghetti Skillet

Prep/Total Time: 25 min.

1/2 **pound ground beef**
1/4 **pound bulk Italian sausage**
   1 **can (15 ounces) tomato sauce**
   1 **can (14-1/2 ounces) stewed tomatoes**
   1 **cup water**
   1 **can (4 ounces) mushroom stems and pieces, drained**
   2 **celery ribs, sliced**
   4 **ounces uncooked spaghetti, broken in half**
1/4 **teaspoon dried oregano**
Salt and pepper to taste

In a large skillet, cook beef and sausage over medium heat until no longer pink; drain. Add the remaining ingredients. Bring to a boil. Reduce heat; cover and simmer for 14-16 minutes or until spaghetti is tender.

Yield: 4-6 servings.

Canned Tomato Tips

What makes this dish so quick is that the spaghetti cooks right with the other ingredients—it's truly a one-skillet meal with little cleanup!

Italian stewed tomatoes can be used in place of the plain stewed tomatoes for added flavor. And keep extra cans of tomato sauce in the pantry. Tomato sauce is a thin tomato puree, often with seasonings and other flavorings added so that it is ready to use in various dishes or as a base for other sauces.

Mozzarella Beef Roll-Ups

Prep/Total Time: 30 min.

    1 pound ground beef
    1 medium green pepper,
       chopped
  1/3 cup chopped onion
    1 can (8 ounces) pizza sauce
   28 slices pepperoni
  1/2 teaspoon dried oregano
    6 flour tortillas (10 inches),
       warmed
    6 pieces (1 ounce *each*)
       string cheese

In a large skillet, cook the beef, green pepper and onion over medium heat until meat is no longer pink; drain. Stir in the pizza sauce, pepperoni and oregano.

Spoon about 1/2 cup beef mixture off-center on each tortilla; top with a piece of string cheese. Fold one side of tortilla over filling and roll up from the opposite side. Place seam side down on an ungreased baking sheet. Bake at 350° for 10 minutes or until heated through and cheese is melted.

Yield: 6 servings.

Try Other Tortillas

Pizza-flavored Mozzarella Beef Roll-Ups are sure to be popular at your table. The sandwiches are easy to assemble because each tortilla is simply wrapped around a portion of hearty meat filling and a piece of string cheese.

The recipe calls for plain flour tortillas, but you could also use the tomato- or spinach-flavored variety.

You don't have to wait for the weekend to cook beef. These recipes use quick-cooking cuts for hearty meals in minutes!

Vegetable Beef Stew (p. 74)

Quick & Easy Beef

Sirloin Squash Shish Kabobs (p. 68)

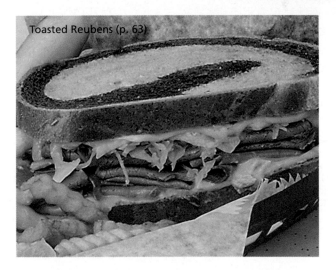

Toasted Reubens (p. 63)

Apricot Beef Stir-Fry

Prep/Total Time: 20 min.

✓ Uses less fat, sugar or salt. Includes Nutrition Facts and Diabetic Exchanges.

- 1 can (15 ounces) apricot halves
- 2 tablespoons cornstarch
- 3/4 cup beef broth
- 2 tablespoons soy sauce
- 1-1/2 pounds boneless beef top round *or* beef sirloin steak, cut into thin strips
- 1 tablespoon canola oil
- 2 cups fresh broccoli florets
- 1/2 cup chopped onion
- 1 cup cherry tomatoes

Hot cooked rice, optional

Drain apricots, reserving 1/4 cup juice. Cut apricots in quarters and set aside. In a small bowl, whisk the cornstarch, broth, soy sauce and reserved juice until smooth; set aside.

In a large skillet or wok, stir-fry beef in oil for 3 minutes. Add broccoli and onion; stir-fry 2-3 minutes longer or until vegetables are crisp-tender. Stir sauce and add to the pan. Bring to a boil; cook and stir for 2 minutes or until thickened. Add tomatoes and reserved apricots; cook until heated through. Serve over rice if desired.

Yield: 6 servings.

Nutrition Facts: 1 cup (prepared with unsweetened apricots, reduced-sodium beef broth and reduced-sodium soy sauce; calculated without rice) equals 249 calories, 10 g fat (3 g saturated fat), 72 mg cholesterol, 324 mg sodium, 10 g carbohydrate, 2 g fiber, 28 g protein. **Diabetic Exchanges:** 3 lean meat, 2 vegetable, 1 fat.

A Word on Woks

You don't have to own a wok to stir-fry—any large, deep skillet will do. The important thing is to have enough room to rapidly stir ingredients as they cook. If you do buy a wok, consider the type of stove you have.

If you have an electric range, a flat-bottom wok is best for even heat distribution. Gas ranges can accommodate either flat- or round-bottom woks.

Regardless of the wok or skillet used, tender items, such as the apricots in this recipe, should be added at the end of the cooking time and simply heated through.

Pepper Steak Sandwiches

Prep/Total Time: 20 min.

1 medium onion, thinly sliced
1 medium green pepper, thinly sliced
1 medium sweet red pepper, thinly sliced
1/2 cup mayonnaise, *divided*
1/4 cup Italian salad dressing
3/4 pound thinly sliced deli roast beef
5 sandwich rolls, split
3/4 cup shredded part-skim mozzarella cheese

In a large skillet, saute the onion and peppers in 2 tablespoons of mayonnaise until crisp-tender. Remove vegetables and keep warm. Reduce heat. Add the Italian dressing, roast beef and remaining mayonnaise to the skillet. Cook and stir for 4-5 minutes or until heated through. Place beef and vegetables on rolls; top with mozzarella cheese.

Yield: 5 servings.

Cheese Steak Story

Your family will love these warm sandwiches that dress up sliced deli roast beef with sauteed peppers and onion, mozzarella cheese and Italian salad dressing. Simply heat a package of frozen French fries and your meal is set!

It's said the authentic cheese steak sandwich was invented by an Italian immigrant in South Philadelphia in the 1930s. Many versions exist across the country, but they all feature thinly sliced beef on a hoagie roll.

Orange Beef Teriyaki

Prep/Total Time: 20 min.

1 can (11 ounces) mandarin oranges
1 tablespoon cornstarch
1-1/2 pounds boneless beef sirloin steak, thinly sliced
2 tablespoons vegetable oil
1/2 cup soy sauce
2 tablespoons honey
1-1/2 teaspoons ground ginger
1 garlic clove, minced
Hot cooked rice
Green onion and orange peel curls, optional

Drain oranges, reserving juice; set oranges aside. In a small bowl, combine cornstarch and 2 tablespoons reserved juice until smooth; set aside.

In a large skillet or wok, stir-fry beef in oil. Add the soy sauce, honey, ginger, garlic and remaining juice. Cover and cook over medium heat for 5-10 minutes or until meat is tender.

Stir cornstarch mixture; stir into beef mixture. Bring to a boil; cook and stir for 2 minutes or until thickened. Stir in the oranges. Serve with rice. Garnish with green onions and orange peel if desired.

Yield: 4-6 servings.

Citrus-Flavored Stir-Fry

Orange Beef Teriyaki is great for weeknight family suppers as well as for get-togethers with friends. The recipe works well made with chicken or pork, too.

Canned mandarin oranges are peeled, sectioned and placed in a light syrup. They are less acidic than regular oranges and are generally sweeter. Store an unopened can in a cool, dry place up to 6 months.

For even more fruity flavor, you could add pineapple tidbits along with the mandarin oranges. Or try sprinkling some crispy Chinese noodles on top to add a bit of crunch.

Italian Pepper Steak

Prep/Total Time: 25 min.

✓ Uses less fat, sugar or salt. Includes Nutrition Facts and Diabetic Exchanges.

  1   teaspoon Italian
       seasoning, *divided*
1/2   teaspoon salt, *divided*
1/2   teaspoon pepper, *divided*
  1   pound boneless beef
       sirloin steak, trimmed
  1   medium sweet red
       pepper, julienned
  1   medium sweet yellow pepper, julienned
  1   medium onion, julienned
  6   garlic cloves, peeled and thinly sliced
  1   tablespoon olive oil
  1   can (14-1/2 ounces) diced tomatoes, drained
  1   teaspoon balsamic vinegar

In a small bowl, combine 1/2 teaspoon Italian seasoning, 1/4 teaspoon salt and 1/4 teaspoon pepper. Rub mixture over both sides of steak; set aside. In a large nonstick skillet, saute peppers, onion and garlic in oil until vegetables are crisp-tender. Stir in the tomatoes and remaining Italian seasoning, salt and pepper. Reduce heat; cover and simmer for 5 minutes. Remove from heat. Stir in vinegar; keep warm.

Place steak on a broiler pan coated with nonstick cooking spray. Broil 4-6 in. from the heat for 4-8 minutes on each side or until the meat reaches desired doneness (for medium-rare, a meat thermometer should read 145°; medium, 160°; well-done, 170°). Let stand for 5 minutes before slicing; serve with vegetable mixture.

Yield: 4 servings.

Nutrition Facts: 3 ounces cooked beef with 1/2 cup vegetables equals 244 calories, 10 g fat (3 g saturated fat), 67 mg cholesterol, 500 mg sodium, 12 g carbohydrate, 3 g fiber, 26 g protein. **Diabetic Exchanges:** 3 lean meat, 2 vegetable, 1 fat.

Steak Done Light

Thin, tender strips of sirloin steak are served with sauteed sweet peppers, onion and tomato in this filling entree. Serve the steak with steamed sugar snap peas and a salad—you won't believe you're eating light!

Sweet red and yellow peppers are much easier to cut if you cut from the flesh, not skin, side. Place halved, seeded peppers skin side down on a cutting board then cut them into julienne strips.

Beef and Asparagus Stir-Fry

Prep/Total Time: 30 min.

- 1 **pound boneless beef top round steak (3/4 inch thick)**
- 2 **tablespoons cornstarch**
- 2 **tablespoons plus 1/2 cup water, *divided***
- 1/2 **teaspoon salt**
- 1/4 **teaspoon pepper**
- 1/8 **teaspoon hot pepper sauce**
- 3 **tablespoons vegetable oil, *divided***
- 2 **cups fresh asparagus pieces *or* fresh broccoli florets**
- 1 **cup sliced cauliflower**
- 1 **small sweet red *or* green pepper, julienned**
- 1 **small onion, cut into 1/4-inch wedges**
- 2 **teaspoons beef bouillon granules**
- 1 **tablespoon soy sauce**
- 1 **tablespoon ketchup**
- 1 **teaspoon red wine vinegar**

Hot cooked rice, optional

Slice beef into thin 3-in. strips. In a large resealable plastic bag, combine the cornstarch, 2 tablespoons water, salt, pepper and hot pepper sauce; add the beef. Seal bag and turn to coat.

In a large skillet or wok, stir-fry half of the beef in 1 tablespoon oil until no longer pink; remove from the skillet and keep warm. Repeat with remaining beef and 1 tablespoon oil.

Stir-fry the asparagus and cauliflower in remaining oil for 4 minutes. Add red pepper and onion; stir-fry for 2 minutes. Return beef to skillet. In a small bowl, combine the bouillon, soy sauce, ketchup, vinegar and remaining water; add to the skillet. Cook and stir for 2 minutes or until heated through. Serve with rice if desired.

Yield: 6 servings.

Do the Work Ahead

With tender slices of beef and fresh colorful vegetables, this mouth-watering stir-fry will soon become a weeknight mainstay, since it's also so quick to make.

Cut and prepare all the ingredients before you begin to stir-fry, including the tangy sauce that is added at the end of cooking. You could even chop and refrigerate the ingredients in separate resealable plastic bags the night before.

Shredded French Dip

Prep: 5 min. **Cook:** 6 hours

- 1 boneless beef chuck roast (3 pounds), trimmed
- 1 can (10-1/2 ounces) condensed French onion soup, undiluted
- 1 can (10-1/2 ounces) condensed beef consomme, undiluted
- 1 can (10-1/2 ounces) condensed beef broth, undiluted
- 1 teaspoon beef bouillon granules
- 8 to 10 French *or* Italian rolls, split

Halve roast and place in a 3-qt. slow cooker. Combine the soup, consomme, broth and bouillon; pour over roast. Cover and cook on low for 6-8 hours or until meat is tender.

Remove meat and shred with two forks. Serve on rolls. Skim fat from cooking juices and serve as a dipping sauce.

Yield: 10 servings.

Slow-Cooked Sandwiches

A chuck roast slow-simmered all day in a beefy broth is delicious when shredded and spooned onto rolls. Serve the cooking juices in individual cups for dipping.

Cut roasts over 3 pounds in half to ensure proper and even cooking.

The roast is done when a long-handled fork can be inserted into the thickest part of the roast easily. If the roast is cooked until it falls apart, the meat is actually overcooked and will be stringy, tough and dry.

Marinated Rib Eyes

Prep: 10 min. + marinating **Grill:** 10 min.

1/2 cup butter, melted
1/4 cup lemon juice
1/4 cup ketchup
2 tablespoons Worcestershire sauce
2 tablespoons cider vinegar
2 tablespoons olive oil
4 garlic cloves, minced
1 teaspoon salt
1 teaspoon sugar
1/2 teaspoon hot pepper sauce
Dash cayenne pepper
6 beef rib eye steaks (about 1 inch thick and 12 ounces *each*)

In a large resealable plastic bag, combine the first 11 ingredients. Add the steaks. Seal bag and turn to coat; refrigerate for 6 hours or overnight.

Drain and discard the marinade. Grill steaks, uncovered, over medium-hot heat for 4-5 minutes on each side or until the meat reaches desired doneness (for medium-rare, a meat thermometer should read 145°; medium, 160°; well-done, 170°).

Yield: 6 servings.

How Marinades Work

Marinades add flavor and can also tenderize meat. However, marinades only penetrate about 1/2 inch deep, so the flavor is on the outer surface of the food. Meat and poultry need at least 1 to 4 hours to marinate; many cuts can be marinated overnight, like these rib eyes.

Make up the marinade one evening and marinate the food until the next night, or add the food in the morning and marinate in the refrigerator until you are ready to cook that night.

Asian Beef Noodles

Prep/Total Time: 30 min.

- 1 package (3 ounces) beef-flavored ramen noodles
- 1 pound boneless beef sirloin steak (3/4 inch thick)
- 1 jalapeno pepper, seeded and finely chopped
- 1 tablespoon vegetable oil
- 2 tablespoons water
- 1 tablespoon steak sauce
- 1 medium carrot, shredded
- 2 tablespoons sliced green onion
- 1/4 cup peanut halves

Set aside seasoning packet from noodles. Prepare noodles according to package directions; drain and set aside.

Cut steak into 3-in. x 1/2-in. strips. In a large skillet, stir-fry the beef and jalapeno in oil for 1-2 minutes or until meat is no longer pink. Remove and keep warm.

In the same skillet, combine the noodles, water, steak sauce, carrot, onion and contents of seasoning packet. Cook and stir until heated through. Return beef to the pan. Sprinkle with peanuts. Serve immediately.

Yield: 4 servings.

Editor's Note: When cutting or seeding hot peppers, use rubber or plastic gloves to protect your hands. Avoid touching your face.

Cooking with Peanuts

Take your family's taste buds on a trip by serving them this tasty Asian-style stir-fry, teaming with strips of sirloin, shredded carrots, sliced green onions, beef-flavored ramen noodles and peanut halves.

Peanuts aren't just for snacking, as this main-dish recipe deliciously proves. They're also great tossed in salads, stirred in muffins or to top off cooked vegetables, such as carrots.

Meat 'n' Potato Kabobs

Prep/Total Time: 30 min.

✓ Uses less fat, sugar or salt. Includes Nutrition Facts and Diabetic Exchanges.

- 1 **pound boneless beef sirloin steak, cut into 1-inch cubes**
- 1-1/2 **teaspoons steak seasoning,** *divided*
- 1 **teaspoon minced garlic**
- 1 **cup cola**
- 3 **small red potatoes, cubed**
- 1 **tablespoon water**
- 1 **cup cherry tomatoes**
- 1 **sweet orange pepper, cut into 1-inch pieces**
- 1 **teaspoon canola oil**
- 1 **cup pineapple chunks**

Sprinkle beef cubes with 1 teaspoon steak seasoning and garlic; place in a large resealable plastic bag. Add cola. Seal bag and turn to coat; set aside. Place the potatoes and water in a microwave-safe dish; cover and microwave on high for 4 minutes or until tender. Drain. Add the tomatoes, orange pepper, oil and remaining steak seasoning; toss gently to coat.

Drain and discard marinade. Alternately thread the beef, vegetables and pineapple onto eight metal or soaked wooden skewers. Grill, covered, over medium-hot heat or broil 4-6 in. from the heat for 4 minutes on each side or until meat reaches desired doneness (for medium-rare, a meat thermometer should read 145°; medium, 160°; well-done, 170°).

Yield: 4 servings.

Editor's Note: This recipe was tested in a 1,100-watt microwave.

Nutrition Facts: 1 kabob (prepared with diet cola) equals 251 calories, 7 g fat (2 g saturated fat), 63 mg cholesterol, 311 mg sodium, 23 g carbohydrate, 3 g fiber, 24 g protein. **Diabetic Exchanges:** 3 lean meat, 1 starch, 1/2 fruit.

Dinner on a Stick

Your family is sure to enjoy these mildly seasoned skewers featuring steak and a bright mix of vegetables. You'll love that they come together quickly.

Make Parmesan couscous as a side. In a small saucepan, bring 1 cup water and 1 tablespoon butter to a boil. Stir in 3/4 cup uncooked couscous. Cover; remove from the heat. Let stand 5 minutes. Fluff with a fork. Stir in 1/4 cup grated Parmesan cheese, 2 tablespoons chopped green onion, 1 tablespoon diced pimiento, 1 teaspoon minced garlic, 1/4 teaspoon pepper and 1/8 teaspoon salt. Serves four.

Toasted Reubens

Prep/Total Time: 15 min.

- 1/2 cup mayonnaise
- 3 tablespoons ketchup
- 2 tablespoons sweet pickle relish
- 1 tablespoon prepared horseradish
- 4 teaspoons prepared mustard
- 8 slices rye bread
- 1 pound thinly sliced deli corned beef
- 4 slices Swiss cheese
- 1 can (8 ounces) sauerkraut, rinsed and well drained
- 2 tablespoons butter

In a small bowl, combine the mayonnaise, ketchup, pickle relish and horseradish; set aside. Spread mustard on one side of four slices of bread, then layer with the corned beef, cheese, sauerkraut and mayonnaise mixture; top with remaining bread.

In a large skillet, melt butter over medium heat. Add sandwiches; cover and cook on both sides until bread is lightly toasted and cheese is melted.

Yield: 4 servings.

Super Sandwich For Supper

This classic grilled sandwich is made with generous layers of corned beef, Swiss cheese and sauerkraut on rye bread. Sauerkraut is made by combining shredded cabbage, salt and spices, and allowing the mixture to ferment.

Precooked sauerkraut is available in jars and cans on supermarket shelves. Unopened cans can be stored in a cool, dark place for up to 6 months. To reduce sauerkraut's briny flavor, put it in a sieve and rinse it well under cold running water. Drain well before using.

Mushroom Beef Tenderloin

Prep/Total Time: 20 min.

3/4   pound fresh mushrooms, sliced
5   tablespoons butter, *divided*
2   teaspoons all-purpose flour
1   teaspoon salt
1/4   teaspoon pepper
1   cup heavy whipping cream
1   tablespoon minced fresh parsley
6   beef tenderloin steaks (1-1/2 inches thick and 4 ounces *each*)

In a large skillet, saute mushrooms in 3 tablespoons butter for 6-8 minutes or until tender. Stir in the flour, salt and pepper until blended. Gradually add the cream. Bring to a gentle boil; cook and stir for 1-2 minutes or until thickened. Stir in parsley; set aside and keep warm.

Meanwhile, in another large skillet, heat the remaining butter over medium-high heat. Cook steaks for 6-7 minutes on each side or until meat reaches desired doneness (for medium-rare, a meat thermometer should read 145°; medium, 160°; well-done, 170°). Serve with the mushroom sauce.

Yield: 6 servings.

Shopping for Mushrooms

Ready to serve in just 20 minutes, this main dish is quick to fix but seems special. A delightful mushroom sauce perfectly complements the juicy beef tenderloin.

Mushrooms add an earthy, nutty flavor to recipes. Select mushrooms with fresh, firm, smooth caps with closed gills. Avoid those with cracks, brown spots or blemishes and ones that are shriveled or moist. Gently remove dirt by rubbing with a mushroom brush or wipe mushrooms with a damp paper towel.

Beef Gyros

Prep/Total Time: 30 min.

- 1 cup ranch salad dressing
- 1/2 cup chopped seeded peeled cucumber
- 1 pound boneless beef sirloin steak, cut into thin strips
- 2 tablespoons olive oil
- 5 whole gyro-style pitas (6 inches)
- 1 medium tomato, chopped
- 1 can (2-1/4 ounces) sliced ripe olives, drained
- 1/2 small onion, thinly sliced
- 1 carton (4 ounces) crumbled feta cheese
- 2-1/2 cups shredded lettuce

In a small bowl, combine the salad dressing and cucumber; set aside. In a large skillet, cook beef in oil over medium heat until no longer pink.

Layer half of each pita with the steak, tomato, olives, onion, feta cheese, lettuce and dressing mixture. Bring edges of each pita over filling and secure with a toothpick.

Yield: 5 servings.

Stay Home for Gyros

Why go out for Greek food when you can easily whip up these gyros in your kitchen? Simply stir together the dressing, which is made with just two ingredients, and cook the beef. Then set out the fixings in small separate bowls so everyone can assemble their own gyro.

It's easier to slice beef cuts like sirloin and round steak if you do so while the beef is still partially frozen.

Microwave Stir-Fry

Prep/Total Time: 30 min.

1/4 cup all-purpose flour
 2 teaspoons salt
1/4 teaspoon pepper
1/4 teaspoon ground cumin
 1 pound boneless beef sirloin steak, cut into 1/8-inch strips
 1 tablespoon vegetable oil
 1 can (14-1/2 ounces) diced tomatoes
 3 medium carrots, julienned
1/2 cup finely chopped onion
1/2 teaspoon dried basil
1/4 teaspoon dried oregano
 1 cup julienned zucchini
1-1/2 cups sliced fresh mushrooms
Hot cooked rice, optional

In a resealable plastic bag, combine the first four ingredients; add meat. Seal bag and turn to coat.

Pour oil into a shallow 2-qt. microwave-safe dish; arrange meat evenly in dish. Cover and microwave at 50% power for 6 minutes, stirring once; set aside. Drain tomatoes, reserving juice; set tomatoes aside.

In a microwave-safe bowl, combine tomato juice, carrots, onion, basil and oregano. Cover and microwave on high for 4 minutes, stirring once. Pour over meat; add the tomatoes, zucchini and mushrooms. Cover and microwave at 50% power for 12 minutes, stirring several times. Let stand for 3 minutes. Serve with rice if desired.

Yield: 5 servings.

Make It in the Microwave

Coming home after a busy day, you can rely on this fast-to-fix stir-fry that's made in the microwave.

To allow for variances in microwave oven wattage, always check food for doneness at the minimum cooking time given in a recipe. And don't omit the standing time called for in some recipes, like the one here. Standing time is always important because it allows heat conduction to finish the job of cooking.

Spicy Grilled Steaks

Prep/Total Time: 20 min.

- 1   tablespoon paprika
- 2   teaspoons dried thyme
- 1   teaspoon onion powder
- 1   teaspoon garlic powder
- 1/2 teaspoon rubbed sage
- 1/2 teaspoon salt
- 1/2 teaspoon pepper
- 1/2 teaspoon cayenne pepper
- 4   boneless beef top loin steaks (about 12 ounces *each*)

In a small bowl, combine the first eight ingredients. Rub about 1 teaspoon of spice mixture over each side of steaks.

Grill, covered, over medium heat for 6-8 minutes on each side or until meat reaches desired doneness (for medium-rare, a meat thermometer should read 145°; medium, 160°; well-done, 170°).

Yield: 4 servings.

Rely on Rubs For Flavor

Dry rubs are a combination of herbs and spices that are rubbed onto meat, fish or poultry. They are quick to make and an easy way to add a flavor boost to a plain piece of meat without adding any fat. Meat lovers will be in their glory when they see—and smell—these herb-rubbed steaks sizzling on the grill.

Avoid grilling at too high a temperature, which will char the outside of the steak before the inside reaches the desired doneness. Grill steaks to at least medium-rare, 145°, but don't overcook.

Sirloin Squash Shish Kabobs

Prep: 10 min. + marinating **Grill:** 10 min.

1 cup packed brown sugar

1 cup soy sauce

1 teaspoon *each* garlic powder, ground mustard and ground ginger

1 pound boneless beef sirloin steak, cut into 1-inch pieces

1 medium zucchini, cut into 1/4-inch slices

1 medium yellow summer squash, cut into 1/4-inch slices

1 medium sweet red pepper, cut into 1-inch pieces

1 medium red onion, cut into eight wedges, optional

In a small bowl, combine the brown sugar, soy sauce, garlic powder, mustard and ginger. Place beef in a large resealable plastic bag; add 1 cup marinade. Seal bag and toss to coat. Place zucchini, yellow squash, red pepper and onion if desired in another resealable plastic bag; add remaining marinade and toss to coat. Refrigerate beef and vegetables for at least 4 hours, turning occasionally.

Drain and discard marinade. On eight metal or soaked wooden skewers, alternately thread beef and vegetables. Grill, covered, over medium-hot heat or broil 4-6 in. from the heat for 10 minutes or until meat is no longer pink, turning occasionally.

Yield: 4 servings.

Colorful Beef and Veggie Kabobs

The soy sauce marinade used in this recipe can also marinate six pork chops or a large round steak cut into serving-size pieces. Meat cut into smaller pieces absorbs more marinade, which helps tenderize it and increase flavor.

Select firm, plump zucchini and squash with bright green and yellow skin. Wash but do not peel. Remove the stem and blossom ends and cut into 1/4-inch slices. The tender flesh has a high water content, a mild flavor and does not require long cooking.

Beef Potpie with Biscuits

Prep: 15 min. **Bake:** 35 min.

1-1/2   pounds boneless beef top
      round steak, cut into
      1/2-inch cubes
  2   cups frozen peas and
      carrots, thawed
  1   large potato, peeled,
      cooked and diced
  1   medium onion, chopped
  1   jar (18 ounces) beef gravy
1/2   teaspoon dried thyme
1/4   teaspoon pepper
  1   tube (12 ounces)
      refrigerated buttermilk biscuits

In a large skillet, cook beef over medium heat until no longer pink; drain. Stir in the vegetables, gravy, thyme and pepper. Transfer to a greased 9-in. deep-dish pie plate or 11-in. x 7-in. x 2-in. baking dish. Bake, uncovered, at 400° for 25 minutes.

Place the biscuits in a single layer over meat mixture. Bake 10-15 minutes longer or until biscuits are golden brown.

Yield: 6 8 servings.

Use Up Those Leftovers!

Casseroles are a great way to finish leftovers by giving them a different look and flavor. This recipe calls for boneless beef top round steak that's been cut into cubes and describes how to cook it. But you could stir in any leftover beef you have. Same with the peas, carrots and potatoes.

Don't have a deep-dish pie plate or 11-in. x 7-in. x 2-in. baking dish? Any 2-quart baking dish will work just as well.

Beef Soup Spuds

Prep/Total Time: 20 min.

4 medium baking potatoes
1 can (18.8 ounces) chunky
   vegetable beef soup
2 cups cooked fresh broccoli
   florets
1/8 teaspoon pepper
1 cup (4 ounces) shredded
   cheddar cheese
Chopped green onions, optional

Scrub and pierce the potatoes; place on a microwave-safe plate. Microwave, uncovered, on high for 6-7 minutes on each side or until tender. Meanwhile, in a large saucepan, combine the soup, broccoli and pepper; cook until heated through.

With a sharp knife, cut an X in the top of each potato; fluff pulp with a fork. Top with soup mixture, cheese and onions if desired.

Yield: 4 servings.

Can't Top These Spuds!

Canned vegetable soup is the convenient base for this tater topper. As the potatoes are cooked in the microwave, the chunky soup—along with broccoli for extra color and flavor— is heated in a snap on the stovetop. Shredded cheddar cheese and chopped green onions sprinkled on top make this filling meat-and-potato dish even more appealing.

Cool-as-a-Cucumber Salad (p. 282), pictured with the piled-high potatoes, is a refreshing side dish.

Beef Broccoli Stir-Fry

Prep/Total Time: 25 min.

   3 tablespoons cornstarch, *divided*
   2 tablespoons plus 1/2 cup water, *divided*
1/2 teaspoon garlic powder
   1 pound boneless beef top round steak, cut into thin 3-inch strips
   2 tablespoons vegetable oil, *divided*
   4 cups fresh broccoli florets
   1 small onion, cut into wedges
1/3 cup soy sauce
   2 tablespoons brown sugar
   1 teaspoon ground ginger
Hot cooked rice

In a large resealable plastic bag, combine 2 tablespoons cornstarch, 2 tablespoons water and garlic powder; add beef. Seal bag and turn to coat.

In a large skillet or wok over medium-high heat, stir-fry beef in 1 tablespoon oil until meat is no longer pink; remove and keep warm. Stir-fry broccoli and onion in remaining oil for 4-5 minutes. Return beef to pan.

In a small bowl, combine the soy sauce, brown sugar, ginger, remaining cornstarch and water until smooth; add to the pan. Cook and stir for 2 minutes or until thickened. Serve with rice.

Yield: 4 servings.

Broccoli in Brief

This tasty stir-fry combines tender beef strips, nutritious broccoli and wholesome rice in one dish, making it a well-rounded meal by itself.

Select firm but tender stalks of broccoli with compact, dark green or slightly purplish florets. Wash the broccoli. For florets, cut 1/4 to 1/2 inch below the heads; discard the stalks. One and one-quarter pounds of broccoli will yield the 4 cups florets needed for this recipe.

Herbed Beef Tenderloin

Prep/Total Time: 30 min.

    2   tablespoons seasoned bread crumbs
    1/2 teaspoon garlic salt
    1/2 teaspoon *each* dried basil, oregano and thyme
    1/4 teaspoon fennel seed, crushed
    1/4 teaspoon pepper
    4   beef tenderloin steaks (1 inch thick)

In a small bowl, combine bread crumbs and seasonings. Rub on both sides of steaks. Place steaks in an ungreased 13-in. x 9-in. x 2-in. baking pan.

Bake, uncovered, at 425° for 25-28 minutes or until meat reaches desired doneness (for medium-rare, a meat thermometer should read 145°; medium, 160°; well-done, 170°).

Yield: 4 servings.

Great for Grilling, Too

When warm weather allows, grill Herbed Beef Tenderloin instead. Bread crumbs and seasonings seal in the meat's juices with wonderful results.

Bow tie pasta makes a fuss-free side dish. Cook 2 cups pasta according to package directions; drain. Transfer to a serving bowl. Add 1/4 cup zesty Italian salad dressing, 1/4 cup shredded Parmesan cheese and 1 tablespoon minced fresh parsley; toss to coat. Serves four.

Three-Step Stroganoff

Prep/Total Time: 30 min.

✓ Uses less fat, sugar or salt. Includes Nutrition Facts and Diabetic Exchanges.

1-1/2 **pounds boneless beef top round steak, thinly sliced**

1 **tablespoon vegetable oil**

1 **can (10-3/4 ounces) condensed cream of mushroom soup, undiluted**

1/2 **cup water**

1 **envelope onion soup mix**

1/2 **cup sour cream**

Hot cooked noodles

Minced fresh parsley, optional

In a large skillet, cook beef over medium-hot heat in oil until no longer pink; drain. Stir in soup, water and onion soup mix. Reduce heat; cover and simmer for 20 minutes. Stir in sour cream; cook until heated through (do not boil). Serve with noodles; sprinkle with parsley if desired.

Yield: 6 servings.

Nutrition Facts: 1 cup (prepared with reduced fat cream of mushroom soup, reduced-sodium onion soup mix and reduced-fat sour cream; calculated without noodles) equals 250 calories, 9 g fat (0 saturated fat), 81 mg cholesterol, 521 mg sodium, 10 g carbohydrate, 0 fiber, 29 g protein. **Diabetic Exchanges:** 3-1/2 lean meat, 1 starch.

All About Stroganoff

Named after 19th century Russian diplomat Count Paul Stroganov, stroganoff consists of thin slices of beef, onions and sliced mushrooms, all quickly sauteed in butter and combined with a comforting sour cream sauce.

An envelope of onion soup mix adds the speedy seasoning to Three-Step Stroganoff, a quick version of the traditional entree. Canned cream of mushroom soup replaces the fresh mushrooms.

We've paired the dish with hot cooked noodles, but it would be equally delicious over rice pilaf.

Vegetable Beef Stew

Prep: 20 min. **Cook:** 8-1/2 hours

5   medium red potatoes, peeled and cut into 1/2-inch chunks
2-1/2   cups sliced fresh mushrooms
4   medium carrots, sliced
2   celery ribs, thinly sliced
3   bacon strips, diced
1/4   cup all-purpose flour
3/4   teaspoon pepper, *divided*
1/2   teaspoon salt, *divided*
2   pounds beef stew meat, cut into 3/4-inch cubes
1   large onion, chopped
2   garlic cloves, minced
1   tablespoon vegetable oil
1   can (14-1/2 ounces) beef broth
1/2   cup dry red wine *or* additional beef broth
1   bay leaf
1/8   teaspoon dried thyme
1   can (10-3/4 ounces) condensed tomato soup, undiluted
1/3   cup water
2   tablespoons cornstarch
3   tablespoons cold water

Fast Flavor Boost

Here's a beef- and vegetable-packed slow-cooked stew that simmers all day in a mouth-watering gravy.

Add more flavor to the gravy by first browning the beef in a skillet. Then scrape all of the browned bits from the bottom of the skillet and add to the slow cooker along with the meat.

Place the first four ingredients in a 5-qt. slow cooker. In a large skillet, cook bacon over medium heat until crisp. Drain on paper towels. Reserve drippings. In a large resealable plastic bag, combine the flour, 1/4 teaspoon pepper and 1/4 teaspoon salt. Add meat; seal bag and shake to coat. Brown the beef, onion and garlic in drippings and oil. Transfer to slow cooker. Stir in broth, wine or additional broth, bay leaf, thyme, reserved bacon and remaining salt and pepper. Cover and cook on low for 8-9 hours or until tender. Discard bay leaf.

Combine soup and water; add to slow cooker. Cover and cook on high for 30 minutes. Combine cornstarch and cold water; stir into slow cooker. Cover and cook for 30-40 minutes or until slightly thickened.

Yield: 7-8 servings.

Tomato Steak Sandwiches

Prep/Total Time: 15 min.

- 3 plain bagels, split
- 6 tablespoons cream cheese, softened
- 1 pound boneless beef sirloin steak, cut into thin strips
- 2 teaspoons vegetable oil
- 1/8 teaspoon salt
- Dash pepper
- 6 thick slices tomato
- 6 slices part-skim mozzarella cheese

Place bagel halves on an ungreased baking sheet; spread with cream cheese and set aside. In a large skillet, cook and stir beef over medium heat in oil for 3-5 minutes or until no longer pink; drain. Season with salt and pepper.

Using a slotted spoon, place beef on bagels. Top with tomato and mozzarella cheese. Broil 4-6 in. from the heat for 3-5 minutes or until cheese is melted and lightly browned.

Yield: 6 servings.

Shopping for Beef

When purchasing the boneless beef sirloin steak for these open-faced sandwiches, you'll want to select meat with a bright, cherry-red color and without any gray or brown patches.

Make sure the package is cold and free of tears or holes. Also make sure the package doesn't have excessive liquid, as this might indicate that the meat was subjected to improper temperatures. Purchase before the "sell by" date on the packaging for best quality.

Chicken-Fried Steaks

Prep/Total Time: 25 min.

2-1/4 cups all-purpose flour, *divided*
   2 teaspoons baking powder
  3/4 teaspoon *each* salt, onion powder,
       garlic powder, chili powder and pepper
   2 eggs, lightly beaten
1-2/3 cups buttermilk, *divided*
   4 beef cube steaks (1 pound)
Oil for deep-fat frying
1-1/2 cups milk

In a shallow bowl, combine 2 cups flour, baking powder and seasonings. In another shallow bowl, combine eggs and 1 cup buttermilk. Dip each cube steak in buttermilk mixture, then roll in flour mixture. Let stand for 5 minutes.

In a large skillet, heat 1/2 in. of oil on medium-high. Fry steaks for 5-7 minutes. Turn carefully; cook 5 minutes longer or until coating is crisp and meat is no longer pink. Remove steaks and keep warm.

Drain, reserving 1/3 cup drippings; stir remaining flour into drippings until smooth. Cook and stir over medium heat for 2 minutes. Gradually whisk in milk and remaining buttermilk. Bring to a boil; cook and stir for 2 minutes or until thickened. Serve with steaks.

Yield: 4 servings (2 cups gravy).

Beef or Chicken?

Associated with Southern cuisine, Chicken-Fried Steak is actually a piece of beef coated and fried like a piece of fried chicken. Cube steak, which is tenderized by the pounding of a meat mallet or electric tenderizer, is the most common cut of beef used to make it.

This recipe produces lots of rich buttermilk gravy to ladle over everyone's steak. Serve mac 'n' cheese and a vegetable alongside for a true down-home meal.

Spinach Steak Pinwheels

Prep/Total Time: 20 min.

1-1/2   pounds boneless beef
         sirloin steak
     8   bacon strips, cooked and
         drained
     1   package (10 ounces)
         frozen chopped spinach,
         thawed and squeezed dry
   1/4   cup grated Parmesan
         cheese
   1/2   teaspoon salt
   1/8   teaspoon cayenne pepper

Make diagonal cuts in steak at 1-in. intervals to within 1/2 in. of bottom of meat. Repeat cuts in opposite direction. Pound to 1/2-in. thickness. Place bacon down the center of the meat.

In a large bowl, combine the spinach, Parmesan cheese, salt and cayenne; spoon over bacon. Roll up and secure with toothpicks. Cut into six slices.

Grill, uncovered, over medium heat for 6 minutes on each side or until meat reaches desired doneness (for medium-rare, a meat thermometer should read 145°; medium, 160°; well-done, 170°). Discard toothpicks.

Yield: 6 servings.

Tricks to Tenderize Beef

Bacon and spinach bring plenty of flavor to these sirloin steak spirals. It's an easy dish to make and great to grill at your next backyard cookout.

Making the diagonal cuts at 1-inch intervals partially tenderizes the meat and makes it more flexible for rolling.

To pound the steak, place it between two pieces of waxed paper. Starting in the center and working out to the edges, pound lightly with a meat mallet's flat side until the steak is even in thickness.

Corned Beef Potato Dinner

Prep/Total Time: 30 min.

1 pound red potatoes, cut into small wedges
1-1/2 cups water
1 large onion, thinly sliced and separated into rings
4 cups coleslaw mix
8 ounces thinly sliced deli corned beef, cut into 1/4-inch strips
1 tablespoon vegetable oil
1/3 cup red wine vinegar
4 teaspoons spicy brown mustard
1 teaspoon sugar
1 teaspoon caraway seeds
1/2 teaspoon garlic powder
1/2 teaspoon salt
1/2 teaspoon pepper

Place potatoes and water in a 3-qt. microwave-safe bowl. Cover; microwave on high for 4-5 minutes or until potatoes are crisp-tender. Add the onion; cover and cook for 1-2 minutes or until onions are tender. Stir in the coleslaw mix. Cover and cook 2-3 minutes longer or until potatoes are tender; drain.

In a large skillet, saute corned beef in oil for 3-4 minutes; drain. Stir in the remaining ingredients. Cook and stir for 1 minute or until heated through. Add to the potato mixture; toss to combine. Cover and microwave for 1-2 minutes or until heated through.

Yield: 4 servings.

Editor's Note: This recipe was tested in a 1,100-watt microwave.

Not Just for St. Patrick's Day

This dish takes less time to make than other corned beef dinners because it's prepared in the microwave. It also calls for thinly sliced deli corned beef and coleslaw mix, so you don't have the chore of shredding cabbage.

According to the USDA, corned beef and cabbage was a traditional Easter Sunday dinner in Ireland. During the winter, the beef was preserved. It was then enjoyed after the long, meatless Lenten fast.

Breaded Sirloin

Prep/Total Time: 25 min.

        2 eggs
    1/2 cup milk
        1 cup seasoned bread crumbs
        3 tablespoons grated Parmesan cheese
        2 tablespoons minced fresh parsley
        2 garlic cloves, minced
    1/4 teaspoon salt
    1/8 teaspoon pepper
        2 pounds boneless beef sirloin steak (1-1/2 inches thick), cut into eight pieces
    1/4 cup vegetable oil
        4 medium ripe tomatoes, sliced
        8 slices part-skim mozzarella cheese
Lemon wedges

In a shallow bowl, whisk the eggs and milk. In another shallow bowl, combine the bread crumbs, Parmesan cheese, parsley, garlic, salt and pepper. Dip steak in egg mixture, then roll in crumb mixture.

In a large skillet, cook steaks in oil in batches over medium-high heat for 2-3 minutes on each side or until no longer pink. Drain on paper towels.

Transfer to an ungreased baking sheet. Top beef with tomato and cheese slices. Broil 4-6 in. from the heat for 1-2 minutes or until cheese is melted. Serve with lemon.

Yield: 8 servings.

Savory Beef Steaks

This quick recipe calls for thin beef steaks to be dipped in an egg mixture, then coated in a combination of seasoned bread crumbs, Parmesan cheese, parsley, garlic, salt and pepper. After the steaks are pan-fried to perfection, they are topped with tomato and cheese slices and put under the broiler. The recipe works with boneless pork chops, too.

Breaded Sirloin is nice served with mashed potatoes, gravy and a fresh salad. Leftover meat slices are terrific in sandwiches.

Tangy Barbecued Beef

Prep/Total Time: 30 min.

1-1/2   cups ketchup
  1/2   cup water
    2   tablespoons brown sugar
    2   tablespoons chopped onion
    2   tablespoons lemon juice
    1   tablespoon cider vinegar
    1   tablespoon Worcestershire sauce
  1/2   teaspoon minced garlic
  1/4   teaspoon ground mustard
  1/4   to 1/2 teaspoon hot pepper sauce
Dash pepper
    3   cups thinly sliced deli roast beef, cut into strips
    6   sandwich rolls, split

In a large saucepan, combine the first 11 ingredients; bring to a boil. Reduce heat; cover and simmer for 14-15 minutes or until heated through, stirring occasionally. Stir in beef; cover and simmer 5-10 minutes longer or until heated through. Serve on rolls.

Yield: 6 servings.

Supper Couldn't Be Simpler

Families are sure to enjoy these Tangy Barbecued Beef sandwiches. Convenient deli roast beef is jazzed up with a flavorful sauce that simmers swiftly on the stovetop.

Store-bought bean or potato salad and chips are simple side dish ideas. For dessert, buy brownies or cookies from the supermarket's bakery.

Hearty Fajitas

Prep/Total Time: 30 min.

✓ Uses less fat, sugar or salt.
Includes Nutrition Facts.

- 1/2   pound boneless beef top round steak, cut into strips
- 1/4   pound boneless skinless chicken breast, cut into strips
- 2   to 3 tablespoons canola oil
- 1/2   pound uncooked medium shrimp, peeled and deveined
- 1   medium green pepper, thinly sliced
- 1   medium sweet red pepper, thinly sliced
- 2   small onions, thinly sliced
- 2   to 3 medium tomatoes, cut into wedges
- 2   teaspoons chili powder
- 1   teaspoon salt
- 1   can (16 ounces) refried beans
- 1/2   cup shredded part-skim mozzarella cheese
- 14   flour tortillas (8 inches), warmed

In a large skillet, stir-fry steak and chicken in oil. Add the shrimp, peppers, onions, tomatoes, chili powder and salt; cook until chicken juices run clear and vegetables are crisp-tender.

Meanwhile, in a large saucepan, cook the refried beans and cheese until cheese is melted. Spoon over tortillas; top with meat mixture.

Yield: 14 fajitas.

Nutrition Facts: 1 fajita (prepared with 2 tablespoons oil and fat-free refried beans) equals 409 calories, 10 g fat (2 g saturated fat), 82 mg cholesterol, 788 mg sodium, 49 g carbohydrate, 7 g fiber, 31 g protein.

Fajitas Are Fast to Fix

When you need to get dinner on the table quickly, fix these filling fajitas. Featuring beef, chicken, shrimp and bell peppers cooked together in one skillet, they'll satisfy everyone's tastes. The hearty mixture is wonderful rolled up in warm flour tortillas with Spanish rice on the side.

To warm tortillas, put a tortilla on a microwave-safe plate and cover with a damp paper towel. Continue to alternate tortillas with paper towels. Microwave for 30 seconds to 1 minute or until warm.

Cube Steak Diane

4 beef cube steaks
1/4 cup butter, cubed
1/2 cup white grape juice
2 tablespoons
   Worcestershire sauce
4 teaspoons Dijon mustard
Salt and pepper to taste

In a large skillet, saute steaks in butter for 2 minutes on each side or until meat is no longer pink; drain.

In a small bowl, combine the grape juice, Worcestershire sauce and mustard; stir into cooking juices. Bring to a boil; cook for 1 minute. Remove steaks and keep warm. Cook the sauce 1-2 minutes longer or until thickened. Season with salt and pepper. Serve over cube steaks.

Yield: 4 servings.

Quick Cube Steak Recipes

Dijon mustard and grape juice combine in a flavorful sauce in this recipe for Cube Steak Diane. Here are two more easy ways to dress up cube steak:

Flour cube steaks and brown in a skillet. Add a can of mushroom soup, a little water and some fresh mushrooms; simmer.

Season cube steaks with cumin and green pepper and onion slices. Top with a jar of salsa before baking.

Steak Tortillas

Prep/Total Time: 15 min.

  2 cups thinly sliced cooked beef rib eye steak (about 3/4 pound)
  1 small onion, chopped
  1/4 cup salsa
  1/2 teaspoon ground cumin
  1/2 teaspoon chili powder
  1/4 teaspoon garlic powder
  1-1/2 teaspoons all-purpose flour
  1/2 cup cold water
  6 flour tortillas (8 inches), warmed
Shredded cheese, chopped lettuce and tomatoes, optional
Additional salsa, optional

In a large nonstick skillet, saute the steak and onion until meat is no longer pink; drain. Stir in the salsa, cumin, chili powder and garlic powder.

In a small bowl, combine flour and water until smooth; gradually add to the skillet. Bring to a boil; cook and stir for 1-2 minutes or until thickened. Place on tortillas; top with cheese, lettuce, tomatoes and additional salsa if desired. Fold in sides.

Yield: 6 servings.

New Look For Leftovers

When you're having steak for dinner, grill one extra so you'll have leftovers to make these delicious Steak Tortillas. The steak strips are seasoned with salsa, chili powder and cumin, then tucked inside soft flour tortillas with cheese, lettuce, tomatoes and additional salsa.

You can substitute picante sauce for the salsa. It comes in a variety of heat levels, which will affect the spiciness of the tortillas. Choose a variety that suits your family's tastes.

Busy cooks can depend on chicken when they want to offer their families a flavorful variety of entrees throughout the year.

Chicken Rice Skillet (p. 87)

Baked Chimichangas

Prep/Total Time: 30 min.

☑ Uses less fat, sugar or salt.
Includes Nutrition Facts.

2-1/2 cups shredded cooked
  chicken breast
1 cup salsa
1 small onion, chopped
3/4 teaspoon ground cumin
1/2 teaspoon dried oregano
6 flour tortillas (10 inches),
  warmed
3/4 cup shredded reduced-fat cheddar cheese
1 cup reduced-sodium chicken broth
2 teaspoons chicken bouillon granules
1/8 teaspoon pepper
1/4 cup all-purpose flour
1 cup fat-free half-and-half cream
1 can (4 ounces) chopped green chilies

In a nonstick skillet, simmer chicken, salsa, onion, cumin and oregano until heated through and most of liquid has evaporated.

Place 1/2 cup chicken mixture down the center of each tortilla; top with 2 tablespoons cheese. Fold sides and ends over filling and roll up. Place seam side down in a 13-in. x 9-in. x 2-in. baking dish coated with nonstick cooking spray. Bake, uncovered, at 425° for 15 minutes or until lightly browned.

Meanwhile, in a small saucepan, combine the broth, bouillon and pepper. Cook until bouillon is dissolved. In a small bowl, combine flour and cream until smooth; gradually stir into broth. Bring to a boil; cook and stir for 2 minutes or until thickened. Stir in chilies; cook until heated through. To serve, cut chimichangas in half; top with sauce.

Yield: 6 servings.

Nutrition Facts: 1 chimichanga with 1/4 cup sauce equals 423 calories, 9 g fat (3 g saturated fat), 57 mg cholesterol, 1,326 mg sodium, 47 g carbohydrate, 7 g fiber, 32 g protein.

On the Lighter Side

Usually chimichangas are deep-fried, so this baked version is healthier as well as delicious. To serve, simply fill tortillas with salsa-coated shredded chicken and cheddar cheese, bake, then top with a thick, full-flavored sauce. You can also substitute ground beef for the chicken.

Buying skinned and deboned chicken breasts can cut minutes off cooking time. Save money by buying large packages, then rewrap individually and freeze.

Chicken Rice Skillet

Prep/Total Time: 30 min.

4 boneless skinless chicken breast halves
(4 ounces *each*)
2 tablespoons vegetable oil
2 celery ribs, chopped
4 green onions, thinly sliced
1/2 cup chopped sweet red pepper
1/2 cup chopped sweet yellow pepper
2 cups frozen green beans, thawed
1 jar (4-1/2 ounces) sliced mushrooms, drained
1 can (14-1/2 ounces) chicken broth
1/4 cup water
3 garlic cloves, minced
1/2 teaspoon salt
1/4 teaspoon lemon-pepper seasoning
1/8 teaspoon garlic powder
1/8 teaspoon pepper
2 cups uncooked instant rice

Rice in an Instant

Pleasant seasonings and plenty of vegetables highlight this traditional chicken and rice pairing.

Instant rice has been fully or partially cooked before being dehydrated and packaged. It takes only a few minutes to prepare. Fluffing just-cooked rice with a fork shortly before serving lets the steam escape, which helps keep the grains separate.

In a large skillet, cook chicken over medium heat in oil for 3-4 minutes on each side or until almost tender. Add celery, onions and peppers; cook until vegetables are crisp-tender. Stir in the beans and mushrooms; cook until chicken juices run clear.

Stir in the broth, water and seasonings. Bring to a boil. Stir in rice; cover and remove from the heat. Let stand for 5 minutes or until rice is tender; fluff rice with a fork.

Yield: 4 servings.

Chunky Chicken Noodle Soup

Prep/Total Time: 20 min.

- 1/2   cup diced carrot
- 1/4   cup diced celery
- 1/4   cup chopped onion
-   1   teaspoon butter
-   6   cups chicken broth
- 1-1/2   cups diced cooked chicken
-   1   teaspoon salt
- 1/2   teaspoon dried marjoram
- 1/2   teaspoon dried thyme
- 1/8   teaspoon pepper
- 1-1/4   cups uncooked medium egg noodles
-   1   tablespoon minced fresh parsley

In a large saucepan, saute the carrot, celery and onion in butter until tender. Stir in the broth, chicken and seasonings; bring to a boil. Reduce heat. Add noodles; cook for 10 minutes or until noodles are tender. Sprinkle with parsley.

Yield: 6 servings.

Simple Soup Substitutions

Marjoram and thyme come through nicely in this old-fashioned soup that tastes just like Grandma used to make—although hers simmered all day and this version takes just 20 minutes!

One 10-ounce can of chunk white chicken is equivalent to 1-1/2 cups cubed cooked chicken. Either can be used in this speedy soup. You can also modify the recipe to include other vegetables your family enjoys.

Chicken Salad Clubs

Prep/Total Time: 10 min.

- 8 bacon strips
- 4 lettuce leaves
- 8 slices rye *or* pumpernickel bread
- 1 pound prepared chicken salad
- 4 slices Swiss cheese
- 8 slices tomato
- 1/3 cup honey mustard salad dressing

In a skillet or microwave, cook bacon until crisp; drain on paper towels. Place lettuce on four slices of bread; layer each with chicken salad, two bacon strips, one cheese slice and two tomato slices. Spread salad dressing on one side of remaining bread; place on tomatoes.

Yield: 4 servings.

From-Scratch Chicken Salad

Stop by the grocery store on the way home to pick up the 1 pound of prepared chicken salad called for in this recipe. While you're there, buy a bag of potato chips to serve alongside the sandwiches.

You can also make the sandwich spread from scratch using leftover chicken. Combine 2 cups diced cooked chicken, 1 diced celery rib, 2 chopped hard-cooked eggs, 1 small diced cucumber, 1/3 cup mayonnaise, 1/4 teaspoon salt, 1/8 teaspoon ground mustard and 1/8 teaspoon white pepper.

Chicken Caesar Salad Pizza

Prep/Total Time: 30 min.

✓ Uses less fat, sugar or salt. Includes Nutrition Facts and Diabetic Exchanges.

- 1 tube (10 ounces) refrigerated pizza crust
- 3/4 pound boneless skinless chicken breasts, cut into strips
- 2 teaspoons canola oil
- 1/2 cup fat-free Caesar salad dressing
- 1/2 cup shredded Parmesan cheese, *divided*
- 1 teaspoon salt-free lemon-pepper seasoning
- 1 garlic clove, minced
- 1 package (8 ounces) fat-free cream cheese, cubed
- 4 cups thinly sliced romaine
- 1/2 cup diced sweet red pepper
- 1 can (2-1/4 ounces) sliced ripe olives, drained

Unroll pizza crust onto a 12-in. pizza pan coated with nonstick cooking spray; flatten dough and build up edges slightly. Prick with a fork. Bake at 400° for 11 minutes or until lightly browned. Cool on a wire rack.

In a nonstick skillet, cook chicken in oil over medium heat until no longer pink; cool. In a small bowl, combine the dressing, 1/4 cup Parmesan, lemon-pepper and garlic. Combine cream cheese and half of the dressing mixture until well blended.

Combine romaine, red pepper and olives. Add remaining dressing; toss. Spread cream cheese mixture over crust. Top with romaine mixture, chicken and remaining Parmesan.

Yield: 6 servings.

Nutrition Facts: 1 serving equals 280 calories, 6 g fat (1 g saturated fat), 43 mg cholesterol, 952 mg sodium, 28 g carbohydrate, 2 g fiber, 25 g protein. **Diabetic Exchanges:** 2 lean meat, 1-1/2 starch, 1 vegetable, 1/2 fat.

Cutting Chicken Into Strips

This delectable cold pizza proves that you can eat well even when you're eating healthy. A tube of refrigerated pizza crust is baked, spread with some seasoned cream cheese and topped with nicely dressed salad fixings and moist chicken.

When cutting the chicken, be sure to make strips of uniform size. For easier slicing, cut the chicken before it is completely thawed. And use a kitchen shears instead of a knife. After handling raw chicken, wash the scissors, cutting board, countertop and your hands thoroughly with hot, soapy water.

Chicken Spaghetti Toss

Prep/Total Time: 30 min.

5	green onions, chopped
2	garlic cloves, minced
2	tablespoons butter
2	tablespoons olive oil
1-1/2	pounds boneless skinless chicken breasts, cubed
3	tablespoons lemon juice
3	tablespoons minced fresh parsley
1	teaspoon seasoned salt
1/2	teaspoon lemon-pepper seasoning
1	package (7 ounces) angel hair pasta

In a large skillet, saute onions and garlic in butter and oil until tender. Stir in the chicken, lemon juice, parsley, seasoned salt and lemon-pepper. Saute for 15-20 minutes or until chicken juices run clear.

Meanwhile, cook spaghetti according to package directions; drain. Add to chicken mixture and toss to coat.

Yield: 4 servings.

Appealing Side Dish

Roasted tarragon asparagus would make an eye-appealing accompaniment to the Chicken Spaghetti Toss.

Place 1-1/2 pounds fresh trimmed asparagus in a shallow baking dish coated with nonstick cooking spray. Drizzle with 2 to 3 tablespoons olive oil; sprinkle with 1/2 teaspoon coarsely ground pepper and 1/8 teaspoon salt. Toss to coat.

Bake, uncovered, at 450° for 13 to 15 minutes or until crisp-tender, turning occasionally. Sprinkle with 1-1/2 teaspoons minced fresh tarragon or 1/2 teaspoon of dried tarragon. Serves six.

Corny Chicken Wraps

Prep/Total Time: 15 min.

✓ Uses less fat, sugar or salt. Includes
Nutrition Facts and Diabetic Exchanges.

- **1 pound boneless skinless chicken breasts, cut into strips**
- **1/2 cup chopped green pepper**
- **1/4 cup chopped green onions**
- **2 teaspoons canola oil**
- **1-1/2 cups frozen whole kernel corn, thawed**
- **1-1/2 cups salsa**
- **1/4 cup sliced ripe olives**
- **1/2 teaspoon chili powder**
- **6 flour tortillas (8 inches), warmed**
- **1 cup (4 ounces) shredded reduced-fat cheddar cheese**

In a nonstick skillet, saute the chicken, green pepper and onions in oil for 3-4 minutes or until chicken juices run clear; drain. Stir in the corn, salsa, olives and chili powder. Cook and stir over medium heat for 3-4 minutes or until heated through.

Spoon about 1/2 cup chicken mixture over one side of each tortilla. Sprinkle with cheese; roll up and secure with toothpicks.

Yield: 6 servings.

Nutrition Facts: 1 wrap equals 363 calories, 11 g fat (4 g saturated fat), 55 mg cholesterol, 740 mg sodium, 38 g carbohydrate, 4 g fiber, 26 g protein. **Diabetic Exchanges:** 3 lean meat, 2-1/2 starch.

Treat Your Gang To Tex-Mex

These zippy Tex-Mex wraps are a speedy alternative to traditional tacos. To increase the spicy flavor, use a medium or hot salsa.

Stir up salsa red beans 'n' rice as a quick side dish. In a large nonstick skillet, saute 1 chopped green pepper, 1/4 cup chopped red onion, 3 finely chopped green onions and 4 minced garlic cloves in 1 tablespoon olive oil until tender.

Stir in 5 cups cooked brown rice, 1-1/4 cups salsa, a 16-ounce can of kidney beans and 1/2 teaspoon salt. Bring to a boil. Reduce heat; simmer, uncovered, for 2 to 3 minutes or until heated through. Serves eight.

Citrus Chicken Kabobs

Prep/Total Time: 25 min.

✓ Uses less fat, sugar or salt. Includes Nutrition Facts and Diabetic Exchanges.

- 1 **pound fresh broccoli, broken into florets**
- 2 **large navel oranges**
- 1 **pound boneless skinless chicken breasts, cut into 1-inch cubes**
- 4 **plum tomatoes, quartered**
- 1 **large onion, cut into wedges**

GLAZE:
- 1/4 **cup barbecue sauce**
- 2 **tablespoons lemon juice**
- 2 **tablespoons reduced-sodium soy sauce**
- 2 **tablespoons honey**

Place 1 in. of water in a large saucepan; add broccoli. Bring to a boil. Reduce heat; cover and simmer for 3-4 minutes or until crisp-tender. Drain.

Cut each orange into eight wedges. On eight metal or soaked wooden skewers, alternately thread chicken, vegetables and oranges. In a small bowl, combine the glaze ingredients.

If grilling the kabobs, coat grill rack with nonstick cooking spray before starting the grill. Grill kabobs, uncovered, over medium heat or broil 4-6 in. from the heat for 5-7 minutes on each side or until chicken juices run clear, basting frequently with glaze.

Yield: 4 servings.

Nutrition Facts: One kabob equals 278 calories, 3 g fat (1 g saturated fat), 63 mg cholesterol, 568 mg sodium, 38 g carbohydrate, 8 g fiber, 28 g protein. **Diabetic Exchanges:** 3 very lean meat, 3 vegetable, 1-1/2 fruit.

Cooking Food On Skewers

You and your family won't believe how fresh and light these appealing kabobs taste! Navel orange wedges are threaded onto the skewers along with chicken and veggies, while a simple glaze containing lemon juice is used for basting. You'll love the citrus flavor!

Soak wooden skewers for at least 15 minutes in cold water before using to prevent them from burning on the grill. Leave a little space between pieces of food as you thread them onto the skewers to promote thorough cooking.

Nostalgic Chicken and Dumplings

Prep: 20 min. **Cook:** 4 hours 50 min.

6   bone-in chicken breast halves
     (10 ounces *each*), skin removed
2   whole cloves
12 pearl onions, *divided*
1   bay leaf
1   garlic clove, minced
1/2 teaspoon *each* salt, dried thyme
     and marjoram
1/4 teaspoon pepper
1/2 cup chicken broth
1/2 cup white wine *or* additional
     chicken broth
3   tablespoons cornstarch
1/4 cup cold water
1/2 teaspoon browning sauce, optional
1   cup biscuit/baking mix
6   tablespoons milk
1   tablespoon minced fresh parsley

Place the chicken in a 5-qt. slow cooker. Insert cloves into one onion; add to slow cooker. Add bay leaf and remaining onions. Sprinkle chicken with the garlic, salt, thyme, marjoram and pepper. Pour broth and wine or additional broth over chicken mixture. Cover and cook on low for 4-1/2 to 5 hours or until chicken juices run clear and a meat thermometer reads 170°.

Remove chicken to a platter; keep warm. Discard cloves and bay leaf. Increase temperature to high. Combine cornstarch, water and browning sauce if desired until smooth. Stir into slow cooker.

The Key to Light Dumplings

Enjoy old-fashioned goodness without all the fuss when you fix this supper in your slow cooker. It features tender chicken, wonderful dumplings and a full-flavored sauce.

For light and fluffy dumplings, keep the lid on the slow cooker until the cooking time is almost complete. Sudden drafts affect the temperature and can deflate the dumplings.

In another small bowl, combine the biscuit mix, milk and parsley. Drop by tablespoonfuls onto simmering liquid. Cover and cook on low for 20-25 minutes or until a toothpick inserted into dumplings comes out clean (do not lift cover while simmering). Serve dumplings and gravy with chicken.

Yield: 6 servings.

Creamy Tomato Chicken

Prep/Total Time: 20 min.

- 6 boneless skinless chicken breast halves (4 ounces *each*)
- 2 tablespoons vegetable oil
- 1 can (14-1/2 ounces) Italian diced tomatoes, undrained
- 1 can (10-3/4 ounces) condensed cream of chicken soup, undiluted
- 1/8 teaspoon ground cinnamon
- 6 slices part-skim mozzarella cheese

Hot cooked noodles

In a large skillet, cook chicken over medium heat in oil until chicken juices run clear. Remove and keep warm.

In a large bowl, combine the tomatoes, soup and cinnamon; add to the skillet. Cook and stir until heated through. Return chicken to skillet; top with cheese. Cover and cook until the cheese is melted. Serve over noodles.

Yield: 6 servings.

Shopping for Chicken

Served over hot cooked noodles, this effortless entree is great for weeknight meals yet tastes special enough for weekend company. Plus, it's so simple to whip up!

When shopping for chicken, make sure the package is cold and has no holes or tears. Place the package in a plastic bag to prevent it from leaking onto other groceries. Purchase chicken before the "sell by" date on the packaging for the best quality.

Fiesta Chicken 'n' Stuffing

Prep/Total Time: 20 min.

3   eggs
3/4   cup milk
2   cups crushed stuffing mix
1-1/2   cups cubed cooked chicken
1   large tomato, chopped
3   tablespoons chopped green chilies
3   tablespoons chopped green onions
Sour cream and salsa, optional

In a large bowl, combine eggs and milk. Stir in the stuffing mix, chicken, tomato, chilies and onions. Transfer to a greased microwave-safe 9-in. pie plate. Cover with waxed paper.

Microwave on high for 3 minutes; stir. Microwave for another 3 minutes; stir. Cook 2-3 minutes longer or until set and a meat thermometer reads 160°. Let stand for 5 minutes before serving. Garnish with sour cream and salsa if desired.

Yield: 4 servings.

Editor's Note: This recipe was tested with an 850-watt microwave.

Uses for Leftover Chicken

A microwave oven makes quick work of this mouth-watering casserole. Pick either chicken-flavored or corn bread stuffing mix to prepare it.

Leftover cooked chicken breasts can be cut into strips or cubes and then frozen. Kept on hand in the freezer, they're ready for future use in casseroles like this one or in stir-fries, soups and salads.

Honey Mustard Chicken

Prep/Total Time: 30 min.

☑ Uses less fat, sugar or salt. Includes Nutrition Facts and Diabetic Exchanges.

4 **boneless skinless chicken breast halves (4 ounces** *each***)**
1 **jar (12 ounces) chicken gravy**
4 **teaspoons Dijon mustard**
2 **to 3 teaspoons honey**
Hot cooked rice, optional

In a large skillet coated with nonstick cooking spray, cook chicken over medium-high heat for 5 minutes on each side. Combine the gravy, mustard and honey; pour over chicken. Bring to a boil. Reduce heat; cover and simmer for 8-12 minutes or until chicken juices run clear. Serve over rice if desired.

Yield: 4 servings.

Nutrition Facts: 1 serving (prepared with fat-free gravy and 2 teaspoons honey; calculated without rice) equals 165 calories, 2 g fat (trace saturated fat), 72 mg cholesterol, 717 mg sodium, 7 g carbohydrate, trace fiber, 28 g protein. **Diabetic Exchanges:** 3 very lean meat, 1/2 starch.

Honey of a Recipe

Your whole family will enjoy this saucy skillet chicken served over rice. It cooks up so tender and juicy. Fresh green beans and refrigerated buttermilk biscuits would deliciously round out the meal. But you could also serve the chicken on rolls with lettuce and tomato as a sandwich.

When measuring sticky liquids like honey, spray the measuring spoon or cup with nonstick cooking spray before adding the liquid. This will make it easier to pour out the liquid…and clean the measuring utensil! Honey is available in liquid and whipped form. This recipe should be made with liquid honey.

Vegetable Chicken Stir-Fry

Prep/Total Time: 20 min.

✓ Uses less fat, sugar or salt. Includes Nutrition Facts and Diabetic Exchanges.

- 1 **tablespoon cornstarch**
- 1 **cup reduced-sodium chicken broth**
- 1/4 **cup reduced-sodium soy sauce**
- 1 **pound boneless skinless chicken breasts, cut into strips**
- 3 **garlic cloves, minced**

Dash ground ginger

- 2 **tablespoons olive oil, *divided***
- 2 **cups fresh broccoli florets**
- 1 **cup fresh cauliflowerets**
- 1 **cup sliced fresh carrots**
- 1 **cup fresh *or* frozen snow peas**
- 1 **teaspoon sesame seeds, toasted**

In a small bowl, combine the cornstarch, broth and soy sauce until smooth; set aside. In a large nonstick skillet, stir-fry the chicken, garlic and ginger in hot oil for 4-5 minutes or until chicken is no longer pink. Remove and keep warm.

In a large skillet, stir-fry broccoli, cauliflower and carrots in the remaining oil for 4 minutes or until crisp-tender. Add snow peas; stir-fry for 2 minutes. Stir broth mixture; add to pan. Bring to a boil; cook and stir for 1 minute or until thickened. Add chicken; cook until heated through. Top with sesame seeds.

Yield: 4 servings.

Nutrition Facts: 1-1/2 cups equals 256 calories, 9 g fat (1 g saturated fat), 66 mg cholesterol, 862 mg sodium, 13 g carbohydrate, 2 g fiber, 31 g protein. **Diabetic Exchanges:** 3 lean meat, 2 vegetable, 1 fat.

Simple to Toss Together

Toss together this light, lively stir-fry for the perfect mix of good taste and nutrition. It calls for a bounty of crisp vegetables, including broccoli, carrots, cauliflower and snow peas, but you can use any combination of vegetables that you choose.

The stir-fry is topped with toasted sesame seeds. Sesame seed is versatile and can be used in many of the same ways as nuts. The seed has a nutty, slightly sweet flavor. Toasting sesame seeds will intensify their flavor.

Dilly Chicken Sandwiches

Prep/Total Time: 30 min.

 4 boneless skinless chicken breast halves
   (4 ounces *each*)
 1 garlic clove, minced
3/4 teaspoon dill weed, *divided*
 6 tablespoons butter, *divided*
 8 slices French bread (1/2 inch thick)
1/4 cup cream cheese, softened
 2 teaspoons lemon juice
 4 lettuce leaves
 8 slices tomato

Flatten chicken to 1/4-in. thickness; set aside. In a large skillet, saute garlic and dill in 3 tablespoons butter. Add chicken; cook over medium heat until chicken juices run clear. Remove and keep warm.

Spread both sides of bread with remaining butter. In a skillet or griddle, grill bread on both sides until golden brown. Meanwhile, in a small bowl, combine the cream cheese, lemon juice and remaining dill; spread on one side of grilled bread. Place lettuce, chicken and tomato on four slices of bread; top with remaining bread.

Yield: 4 servings.

Help with Dried Herbs

A creamy lemon-dill spread adds summery flavor to tender chicken served between slices of grilled French bread in this recipe. Thought by 1st century Romans to be a good luck symbol, dill has been around for thousands of years.

Dried herbs available in supermarkets have a stronger, more concentrated flavor than fresh herbs but can quickly lose their pungency. Store dried herbs in a cool, dark place no longer than 6 months. The more airtight the storage container—glass, screw-top containers are best—the longer dried herbs will last.

Italian Chicken

Prep/Total Time: 30 min.

☑ Uses less fat, sugar or salt. Includes Nutrition Facts and Diabetic Exchanges.

- **4 boneless skinless chicken breast halves (4 ounces *each*)**
- **1 cup Italian salad dressing**
- **2 tablespoons grated Parmesan cheese**
- **1/4 teaspoon salt, optional**

Minced fresh parsley

Place chicken in a greased 9-in. square baking dish. Drizzle with salad dressing; sprinkle with Parmesan cheese and salt if desired. Bake, uncovered, at 375° for 20-25 minutes or until chicken juices run clear. Sprinkle with parsley.

Yield: 4 servings.

Nutrition Facts: 1 chicken breast half (prepared with fat-free salad dressing; calculated without salt) equals 177 calories, 3 g fat (1 g saturated fat), 70 mg cholesterol, 980 mg sodium, 7 g carbohydrate, trace fiber, 28 g protein. **Diabetic Exchanges:** 3 lean meat, 1 starch.

From-Scratch Salad Dressing

Want to make this chicken dish for your family tonight but don't have a bottle of Italian salad dressing on hand? Try this recipe to make 1 cup from scratch using pantry staples.

In a jar with a tight-fitting lid, combine 1/2 cup olive oil, 4 tablespoons red wine vinegar, 4 tablespoons water, 1 teaspoon sugar, 1 teaspoon Italian seasoning, 1/2 teaspoon salt and 1/2 teaspoon coarsely ground black pepper; shake well.

Lattice-Top Chicken Stew

Prep: 10 min. **Bake:** 35 min.

- 1 package (16 ounces) frozen California-blend vegetables, thawed and drained
- 2 cups cubed cooked chicken
- 1 can (10-3/4 ounces) condensed cream of potato soup, undiluted
- 1 cup milk
- 1/2 cup shredded cheddar cheese
- 1/2 cup french-fried onions
- 1/2 teaspoon seasoned salt
- 1 tube (8 ounces) refrigerated crescent rolls

In a large bowl, combine the vegetables, chicken, soup, milk, cheese, onions and seasoned salt. Transfer to a greased 13-in. x 9-in. x 2-in. baking dish. Bake, uncovered, at 350° for 20 minutes.

Meanwhile, separate crescent dough into two rectangles. Seal perforations; cut each rectangle lengthwise into four strips. Working quickly, weave strips over warm filling, forming a lattice crust. Bake 15 minutes longer or until crust is golden brown.

Yield: 6-8 servings.

Creating a Lattice Top

Convenient crescent roll dough turns into the pretty topping on this creamy casserole filled with chicken and vegetables.

To make the lattice crust, lay strips in rows about 1/2 to 3/4 in. apart; fold every other strip halfway back. Starting at the center, add strips at right angles, lifting every other strip as the cross strips are put down. Continue to add strips, lifting and weaving until the lattice top is completed.

Creamed Chicken 'n' Biscuits

Prep/Total Time: 25 min.

BISCUITS:

      2 cups all-purpose flour
      1 tablespoon baking
         powder
      1 teaspoon salt
    2/3 cup milk
    1/3 cup vegetable oil

CREAMED CHICKEN:

    1/4 cup finely chopped onion
    1/4 cup butter
    1/4 cup all-purpose flour
    1/4 to 1/2 teaspoon salt
    1/8 teaspoon pepper
      2 cups milk *or* chicken broth
      2 cups chopped cooked chicken

Minced fresh parsley

In a large bowl, combine the flour, baking powder and salt; add milk and oil. Stir until the dough forms a ball. On a lightly floured surface, knead 8-10 times or until smooth.

Roll or pat dough into a 6-in. square about 1 in. thick. Cut into six rectangles. Place on a lightly greased baking sheet. Bake at 450° for 10-12 minutes or until golden brown.

Meanwhile, in a large skillet, saute onion in butter until tender. Stir in flour, salt and pepper until blended. Gradually add milk; bring to a boil. Reduce heat; cook and stir for 1-2 minutes or until thickened. Stir in chicken and parsley; cook until heated through. Split biscuits; top with the creamed chicken.

Yield: 6 servings.

Comfort Food...Fast!

Using leftover chicken, you can whip up this down-home dinner in minutes. To save even more time, you could bake a tube of refrigerated buttermilk biscuits instead of making them from scratch. Or serve the creamed chicken mixture on bread or rolls you already have on hand.

When a recipe calls for cooked chicken and you don't have any leftovers, stop by your grocer's deli and pick up a rotisserie chicken. One chicken usually yields 2 to 3 cups chopped meat.

Kung Pao Wings

Prep/Total Time: 30 min.

8	whole chicken wings (about 1-1/2 pounds)
2	tablespoons sugar
2	teaspoons cornstarch
1/4	cup water
1/4	cup soy sauce
2	tablespoons lemon juice
1/4	teaspoon crushed red pepper flakes
1	tablespoon vegetable oil
1	small sweet red pepper, diced
1/2	cup diced onion
1	to 2 garlic cloves, minced
1/3	cup peanuts

Hot cooked rice

Cut chicken wings into three sections; discard wing tip section. Set the wings aside. In a small bowl, combine the sugar, cornstarch, water, soy sauce, lemon juice and crushed red pepper flakes until blended; set aside.

In a large skillet, cook chicken wings, uncovered, over medium-high heat for 10-15 minutes or until chicken juices run clear, turning occasionally.

Add the red pepper, onion and garlic; cook, uncovered, for 3-5 minutes or until vegetables are crisp-tender. Stir cornstarch mixture; gradually add to skillet. Bring to a boil; cook and stir for 2 minutes or until sauce is thickened and the vegetables are tender. Sprinkle with peanuts. Serve with rice.

Yield: 4 servings.

Add Some "Pow" To Supper

Served as an entree over hot cooked rice, these delicious drummettes have plenty of personality—with sweet red pepper for color, red pepper flakes for zip and peanuts for crunch. They're quick and easy to fix, too.

When making Kung Pao Wings, you can substitute 1-1/2 pounds of uncooked chicken wing sections (wingettes) for the eight whole chicken wings called for. Just omit the first step of the recipe.

Italian Chicken Pockets

Prep/Total Time: 15 min.

3/4   **pound boneless skinless chicken breast, cubed**
2   **tablespoons olive oil**
1   **medium green pepper, chopped**
1   **cup sliced fresh mushrooms**
1   **package (3-1/2 ounces) sliced pepperoni**
1   **cup spaghetti sauce**
3   **pita breads (6 inches), halved and warmed**
Grated Parmesan cheese, optional

In a large skillet, cook chicken over medium heat in oil until chicken juices run clear. Add green pepper and mushrooms; cook until tender, stirring occasionally. Stir in pepperoni; cook until heated through. Drain. Stir in spaghetti sauce; cook until heated through. Spoon into pita bread halves. Sprinkle with Parmesan cheese if desired.

Yield: 6 servings.

Put Pitas to Good Use

These pita sandwiches are stuffed with chicken, green pepper, mushrooms and pepperoni smothered with spaghetti sauce and topped with Parmesan cheese.

Pita bread, also called pocket bread, is a flat, round bread made from white or whole wheat flour. The bread has a variety of uses. It's hearty enough to hold hamburgers and barbecued meats...perfect for packed lunches since it doesn't get soggy as some breads do...good cut into wedges and served with dips...and makes a great pizza base.

Lemon Chicken Soup

Prep/Total Time: 10 min.

1 can (11-1/2 ounces) condensed chicken with rice soup, undiluted
1 can (10-3/4 ounces) condensed cream of chicken soup, undiluted
2-1/4 cups water
1 cup diced cooked chicken
1 to 2 tablespoons lemon juice
Pepper to taste
Minced fresh parsley, optional

In a large saucepan, combine soups and water; cook until heated through. Add the chicken, lemon juice and pepper. Garnish with parsley if desired.

Yield: 4-5 servings.

Soup and Sandwich Combo

Your family won't have to wait long to hear "Soup's on!" when you stir together this simple recipe...only 10 minutes, to be exact. Just add diced, cooked chicken and lemon juice to cans of cream of chicken and chicken with rice soup, then heat. It's that easy!

Grilled ham and cheese sandwiches are the perfect accompaniment to the hassle-free soup. Place a bowl of assorted fresh fruit on the table to top off the meal.

Apple Chicken Quesadillas

Prep/Total Time: 25 min.

✓ Uses less fat, sugar or salt. Includes Nutrition Facts and Diabetic Exchanges.

- 2 **medium tart apples, sliced**
- 1 **cup diced cooked chicken breast**
- 1/2 **cup shredded fat-free cheddar cheese**
- 1/2 **cup shredded part-skim mozzarella cheese**
- 1/2 **cup fresh *or* frozen corn, thawed**
- 1/2 **cup chopped fresh tomatoes**
- 1/2 **cup chopped onion**
- 1/4 **teaspoon salt**
- 6 **flour tortillas (8 inches), warmed**
- 3/4 **cup shredded lettuce**
- 3/4 **cup salsa**
- 6 **tablespoons fat-free sour cream**

In a large bowl, combine the first eight ingredients. Place about 3/4 cup on half of each tortilla. Fold tortilla in half over filling and secure with toothpicks.

Place on a baking sheet coated with nonstick cooking spray. Bake at 400° for 8-10 minutes or until golden brown. Carefully turn quesadillas over; bake 5-8 minutes longer or until golden brown. Discard toothpicks. Cut each quesadilla into three wedges. Serve with lettuce, salsa and sour cream.

Yield: 6 servings.

Nutrition Facts: 3 wedges equals 289 calories, 6 g fat (2 g saturated fat), 28 mg cholesterol, 629 mg sodium, 40 g carbohydrate, 3 g fiber, 18 g protein. **Diabetic Exchanges:** 2 lean meat, 1-1/2 starch, 1 vegetable, 1/2 fruit.

Unusually Delicious

Your family may be surprised by the combination of chicken, apples, tomatoes and corn inside the crispy tortillas, but they'll love it!

Granny Smith apples are a great choice for this recipe. They're available year-round and have a nice tart flavor and crisp texture. Wash before using.

Lemonade Chicken

Prep: 15 min. + marinating **Grill:** 20 min.

1   can (12 ounces) frozen lemonade concentrate, thawed
2   tablespoons brown sugar
2   tablespoons soy sauce
1   teaspoon garlic powder
1   teaspoon minced fresh mint *or* 1/4 teaspoon dried mint flakes
6   bone-in chicken breast halves (about 4 pounds)

In a large resealable plastic bag, combine the first five ingredients. Remove half of the marinade to a small bowl; cover and refrigerate. Add chicken to the bag; seal and turn to coat. Refrigerate overnight, turning occasionally

Drain and discard marinade. Grill, covered, over medium heat for 10 minutes on each side, basting occasionally with reserved marinade. Grill 5-10 minutes longer or until chicken juices run clear, basting and turning several times.

Yield: 6 servings.

Don't Re-Use Marinades

It doesn't take a seasoned cook to prepare this eye-appealing entree. Served with your favorite salad, it makes a wonderful summer supper. Try it with limeade or orange juice concentrate in place of the lemonade.

For food safety reasons, if you want to use some of the marinade for basting, like in this recipe, set aside some of the fresh marinade for this purpose. Any marinade that comes in contact with uncooked meat, poultry or seafood should be discarded.

Mushroom Chicken Pizza

Prep/Total Time: 30 min.

☑ Uses less fat, sugar or salt. Includes
Nutrition Facts and Diabetic Exchanges.

- **1** tube (10 ounces) refrigerated pizza crust
- **1** can (6 ounces) Italian tomato paste
- **1-1/2** cups cubed cooked chicken breast
- **2** cups grape tomatoes, halved
- **1/2** cup sliced fresh mushrooms
- **1/4** cup sliced ripe olives
- **1/8** teaspoon garlic salt
- **1/8** teaspoon salt
- **1/8** teaspoon pepper
- **1** tablespoon olive oil
- **1-1/2** cups (6 ounces) shredded part-skim mozzarella cheese

Press dough onto the bottom of a 15-in. x 10-in. x 1-in. baking pan coated with nonstick cooking spray. Prick crust with a fork. Bake at 400° for 5 minutes.

Spread tomato paste over crust to within 1/2 in. of edges. Top with the chicken, tomatoes, mushrooms, olives, garlic salt, salt and pepper. Drizzle with oil. Sprinkle with cheese. Bake 13-16 minutes longer or until cheese is melted.

Yield: 6 servings.

Nutrition Facts: 1 piece equals 319 calories, 10 g fat (4 g saturated fat), 46 mg cholesterol, 618 mg sodium, 32 g carbohydrate, 3 g fiber, 23 g protein. **Diabetic Exchanges:** 2 lean meat, 1-1/2 starch, 1 vegetable, 1/2 fat.

Keep the Crust Crisp

Who doesn't like pizza? The one here is a light and tasty alternative to greasier frozen and home-delivered versions, and its crispy crust and fresh toppings are such to be a hit with kids of all ages.

Baking the pizza crust for 5 minutes prevents a soggy crust once the sauce and toppings are added.

For the crispest crust, put a thin layer of cheese under the sauce and toppings, then top with more cheese. The bottom cheese layer will provide a buffer between the crust and the moist toppings.

Nutty Chicken Fingers

Prep/Total Time: 30 min.

1/2   cup finely chopped pecans

1/3   cup crushed cornflakes

   1   tablespoon dried parsley
      flakes

1/8   teaspoon garlic powder

1/8   teaspoon salt

   2   tablespoons milk

3/4   pound boneless skinless
      chicken breasts, cut into
      1-inch strips

In a shallow bowl, combine the first five ingredients. Place milk in another shallow bowl. Dip chicken in milk, then roll in pecan mixture.

Place in a single layer in an ungreased 15-in. x 10-in. x 1-in. baking pan. Bake, uncovered, at 400° for 12-15 minutes or until juices run clear.

Yield: about 2 dozen.

Chicken Fingers In a Snap

Watch the room light up with smiles when you bring this fun dish to the table. Your kids will love the crunchy nut coating on the chicken strips, and with only a handful of ingredients, preparation is a snap.

You can chop the pecans yourself, but the nuts are also available prechopped in the baking aisle of your grocery store.

To crush cornflakes with little mess, put the flakes in a resealable plastic bag before crushing. You'll need 1 cup of whole flakes to yield 1/3 cup crushed.

Pasta with Chicken and Squash

Prep/Total Time: 25 min.

1 package (16 ounces) spiral pasta
2 cups heavy whipping cream
1 tablespoon butter
2 cups (8 ounces) shredded Mexican cheese blend
1 small onion, chopped
1 garlic clove, minced
5 tablespoons olive oil, *divided*
2 medium zucchini, julienned
2 medium yellow summer squash, julienned
1-1/4 teaspoons salt, *divided*
1/8 teaspoon pepper
1 pound boneless skinless chicken breasts, sliced
1/4 teaspoon *each* dried basil, marjoram and savory
1/4 teaspoon dried rosemary, crushed
1/8 teaspoon rubbed sage

Cook pasta according to package directions. Meanwhile, in a large saucepan, add cream and butter; cook until butter is melted. Stir until smooth. Add cheese; cook and stir until cheese is melted. Rinse and drain pasta; add to cheese mixture. Cover and keep warm.

In a large skillet, saute onion and garlic in 3 tablespoons oil until onion is tender. Add squash; cook until tender. Add 1 teaspoon of salt and pepper; remove and keep warm.

Add remaining oil to skillet; cook chicken with herbs and remaining salt until juices run clear. Place pasta on a serving platter; top with chicken and squash.

Yield: 8 servings.

How to Julienne Veggies

In this special dish, a bed of noodles is covered with a creamy cheese sauce, tender squash and strips of chicken that've been stir-fried with flavorful herbs. It's delicious and pretty, too!

To julienne the squash, use a utility knife to cut a thin strip from one side. Turn so the flat side is down. Cut widthwise into 2-inch lengths, then cut each piece lengthwise into thin strips. Stack the strips and carefully cut lengthwise into thinner strips.

String Bean Chicken Skillet

Prep/Total Time: 30 min.

1/2 pound fresh green beans, cut into 2-inch pieces
1/2 pound fresh wax beans, cut into 2-inch pieces
3 boneless skinless chicken breast halves
(4 ounces *each*)
2 tablespoons vegetable oil
2 tablespoons plus 1-1/2 teaspoons cornstarch
3 tablespoons soy sauce
1 can (8 ounces) pineapple chunks
1 medium sweet red pepper, julienned
1 small onion, thinly sliced
1/4 teaspoon salt
1/4 teaspoon ground ginger
Hot cooked rice

Place beans in a saucepan and cover with water; bring to a boil. Cook, uncovered, for 3 minutes; drain and set aside. Meanwhile, flatten chicken to 1/4-in. thickness; cut into 1/2-in. strips. In a large skillet, stir-fry chicken in oil for 3-4 minutes or until no longer pink. Remove with a slotted spoon.

In a small bowl, combine cornstarch and soy sauce until smooth. Drain the pineapple, reserving juice; set pineapple aside. Stir the juice into the soy sauce mixture; set aside.

In the same skillet, stir-fry red pepper and onion for 5 minutes. Add the chicken, beans, pineapple, salt and ginger. Gradually stir in the soy sauce mixture. Bring to a boil; cook and stir for 2 minutes or until thickened. Serve with rice.

Yield: 6 servings.

String Beans in Brief

Many stir-fries feature snow peas, but this one stars string beans instead, along with chicken, pineapple and sweet red pepper.

String beans are actually just green and wax beans, which may be used interchangeably in recipes and are known for their mild flavor and general appeal.

Green and wax beans are available year-round; peak season is from July through October. Select brightly colored, straight, smooth pods that are unblemished. Beans should be crisp and have a firm, velvety feel.

Spicy Chicken Linguine

Prep/Total Time: 30 min.

1/4 cup butter, cubed
3 tablespoons all-purpose flour
2 teaspoons garlic powder
1 teaspoon pepper
2-1/2 cups milk
1 package (8 ounces) cream cheese, cubed
1 cup (4 ounces) shredded Parmesan cheese
12 ounces uncooked linguine
3 cups cubed cooked chicken
1 can (4 ounces) diced green chilies

In a large saucepan, melt butter. Stir in flour, garlic powder and pepper until blended. Gradually add milk. Bring to a boil; cook and stir for 2 minutes or until thickened. Reduce heat; add cream cheese and Parmesan cheese. Cook and stir for 8-10 minutes or until cheese is melted.

Meanwhile, cook linguine according to package directions. Add chicken and chilies to cheese sauce; cook 5 minutes longer or until heated through. Drain linguine; top with chicken mixture.

Yield: 6 servings.

Pasta Dish Packs a Punch

A can of diced green chilies is what makes the cheese sauce in this recipe "spicy." If your palate doesn't like such a punch, just leave the chilies out.

We used linguine to prepare this chicken and pasta specialty, but the sauce is also excellent served with spaghetti or even fettuccine noodles.

Almond Orange Chicken

Prep/Total Time: 30 min.

2 tablespoons plus 1/2 cup all-purpose flour, *divided*
2 eggs, lightly beaten
3/4 cup ground almonds
6 boneless skinless chicken breast halves (4 ounces *each*)
4 tablespoons butter, *divided*
1/3 cup chopped onion
1-1/2 cups milk
1/4 teaspoon poultry seasoning
1/3 cup orange marmalade
1/4 cup orange juice
1/2 teaspoon grated orange peel
1 teaspoon salt
1/4 teaspoon pepper
Hot cooked rice, optional

Place 1/2 cup flour, eggs and almonds in separate shallow bowls. Roll chicken in flour, then dip in eggs and roll in almonds. In a large skillet, cook chicken over medium-high heat in 2 tablespoons butter for 4-5 minutes on each side or until chicken juices run clear. Remove and keep warm.

In the same skillet, saute onion in remaining butter until tender. In a small bowl, combine the milk, poultry seasoning and remaining flour. Gradually stir into pan. Bring to a boil; cook and stir for 2 minutes or until thickened. Remove from the heat; stir in the orange marmalade, orange juice and peel, salt and pepper. Pour over chicken. Serve with rice if desired.

Yield: 6 servings.

Keep Chicken Juicy

You can cook this succulent, nut-coated chicken with a mild orange sauce in mere minutes. It's wonderful for a weeknight supper but is also special enough to serve to company.

When placing chicken pieces in a skillet and when turning, use tongs or a spatula. Piercing the chicken with a fork allows the juices to escape. Cook chicken only until it tests done. Overcooking the chicken will make it dry.

Pineapple Chicken Lo Mein

Prep/Total Time: 30 min.

1 can (20 ounces)
  unsweetened pineapple
  chunks
1 pound boneless skinless
  chicken breasts, cut into
  1-inch cubes
2 garlic cloves, minced
3/4 teaspoon ground ginger
  or 1 tablespoon minced
  fresh gingerroot
3 tablespoons vegetable oil,
  divided
2 medium carrots, julienned
1 medium green pepper, julienned
4 ounces spaghetti, cooked and drained
3 green onions, sliced
1 tablespoon cornstarch
1/3 cup soy sauce

Drain pineapple, reserving 1/3 cup juice (discard remaining juice or save for another use); set pineapple aside.

In a large skillet, cook the chicken, garlic and ginger over medium heat in 2 tablespoons oil for 6 minutes or until the chicken juices run clean. Stir in the carrots, green pepper and pineapple. Cover and cook for 2-3 minutes or until vegetables are crisp-tender. Stir in spaghetti and onions.

In a small bowl, combine the cornstarch, soy sauce, reserved pineapple juice and remaining oil until smooth. Gradually add to chicken mixture. Bring to a boil; cook and stir for 2 minutes or until thickened.

Yield: 4 servings.

Lowdown on Lo Mein

The perfect supper to serve on busy weeknights, this speedy lo mein combines tender chicken and colorful veggies with a tangy sauce. Quick-cooking spaghetti and canned pineapple make it a cinch to throw together when time is short.

Get creative when cooking lo mein. In fact, you don't even have to follow a recipe! Simply select a variety of stir-fry ingredients, such as chicken, beef or pork and your family's favorite vegetables. After cooking them, stir in cooked noodles and a stir-fry sauce—which you can find bottled at the grocery store—and heat through.

Pecan Parmesan Chicken

Prep/Total Time: 30 min.

✓ Uses less fat, sugar or salt. Includes Nutrition Facts and Diabetic Exchanges.

    6 boneless skinless chicken breast halves
       (4 ounces *each*)
  1/2 cup soft bread crumbs
  1/3 cup grated Parmesan cheese
  1/3 cup ground pecans
    1 teaspoon dried oregano
  1/2 teaspoon seasoned salt
  1/2 teaspoon dried basil
  1/4 teaspoon pepper
    2 egg whites
    2 teaspoons cornstarch
    1 tablespoon olive oil

Flatten chicken to 1/2-in. thickness. In a shallow bowl, combine the bread crumbs, Parmesan cheese, pecans, oregano, salt, basil and pepper. In another shallow bowl, whisk egg whites and cornstarch until smooth. Dip chicken into egg white mixture, then roll in crumb mixture.

In a large nonstick skillet, cook chicken over medium heat in oil for 3-5 minutes on each side or until browned. Transfer to an ungreased 15-in. x 10-in. x 1-in. baking pan. Bake, uncovered, at 450° for 8-10 minutes or until juices run clear.

Yield: 6 servings.

Nutrition Facts: 1 chicken breast half equals 238 calories, 10 g fat (2 g saturated fat), 66 mg cholesterol, 342 mg sodium, 8 g carbohydrate, 1 g fiber, 27 g protein. **Diabetic Exchanges:** 3 lean meat, 1/2 fat, 1/2 starch.

Dress Up Frozen Vegetables

Treat moist chicken breasts to a crunchy coating of pecans, Parmesan cheese, basil and oregano. Italian mixed vegetables is an ideal accompaniment to the chicken entree.

In a large nonstick skillet, bring a 24-ounce package frozen California blend vegetables and 1/4 cup water to a boil. Cover and cook for 10 to 12 minutes or until vegetables are crisp-tender. Uncover; cook and stir until liquid is reduced. Add 1/4 cup Italian salad dressing, 1/4 teaspoon salt, 1/4 teaspoon dried basil and 1/8 teaspoon dried oregano. Cook and stir until heated through. Serves six.

Swiss Mushroom Chicken

Prep/Total Time: 30 min.

4   **boneless skinless chicken breast halves (4 ounces *each*)**
1   **egg**
1   **cup crushed butter-flavored crackers (about 25 crackers)**
3/4 **teaspoon salt**
1/2 **pound fresh mushrooms, sliced**
2   **tablespoons butter, *divided***
4   **slices deli ham *or* thinly sliced hard salami**
4   **slices Swiss cheese**

Flatten chicken to 1/4-in. thickness. In a shallow bowl, lightly beat the egg. Combine cracker crumbs and salt in another shallow bowl. Dip chicken in egg, then roll in crumbs; set aside.

In a large ovenproof skillet, saute mushrooms in 1 tablespoon butter until tender; remove and set aside. In the same skillet, cook chicken over medium heat in remaining butter for 3-4 minutes on each side or until juices run clear.

Top each chicken breast half with a ham slice, mushrooms and a cheese slice. Broil 4-6 in. from the heat for 1-2 minutes or until cheese is melted.

Yield: 4 servings.

Fancy But Fuss-Free

Cooked red potatoes sprinkled with parsley would make an elegant accompaniment, along with broccoli drizzled with a no-fuss mustard sauce.

To make the sauce, melt 1 tablespoon butter in a saucepan. Stir in 1 tablespoon flour until smooth. Gradually stir in 1/2 cup plus 2 tablespoons milk. Bring to a boil; cook and stir for 2 minutes or until thickened. Stir in 1-1/2 teaspoons prepared mustard, 1/4 teaspoon dill weed and 1/4 teaspoon salt. Drizzle over 4 cups cooked broccoli florets. Serves four.

Broccoli Chicken Stir-Fry

Prep/Total Time: 30 min.

✓ Uses less fat, sugar or salt.
Includes Nutrition Facts.

- 1 pound boneless skinless chicken breasts, cut into 1-inch pieces
- 1 tablespoon canola oil
- 2 cups fresh broccoli florets
- 1 small sweet red pepper, julienned
- 1 can (8 ounces) sliced water chestnuts, drained
- 1 package (6 ounces) frozen snow peas, thawed
- 1 small onion, cut into thin wedges
- 2 garlic cloves, minced
- 1 teaspoon Chinese Five Spice
- 1 can (14-1/2 ounces) chicken broth
- 2 tablespoons cornstarch
- 2 tablespoons cold water
- 4 cups hot cooked rice

In a nonstick skillet or wok, stir-fry chicken in oil for 8 minutes or until lightly browned and juices run clear. Remove and keep warm. In same skillet, stir-fry broccoli, red pepper, water chestnuts, snow peas, onion and garlic for 6-8 minutes or until crisp-tender.

Return chicken to the pan; sprinkle with Chinese Five Spice. Stir in broth; bring to a boil. Combine cornstarch and cold water until smooth; gradually stir into skillet. Cook and stir for 2 minutes or until thickened. Serve with rice.

Yield: 4 servings.

Nutrition Facts: 1-1/2 cups stir-fry with 1 cup rice equals 459 calories, 6 g fat (1 g saturated fat), 66 mg cholesterol, 504 mg sodium, 65 g carbohydrate, 6 g fiber, 35 g protein.

Grind Your Own Seasoning

Chinese Five Spice is the key ingredient in this colorful chicken stir-fry. It can be purchased in Asian markets and at some grocery stores, but can also easily be made at home, using these simple instructions.

In a spice grinder or with a mortar and pestle, combine 2 tablespoons each aniseed, fennel seed, ground cinnamon, whole cloves and whole peppercorns. Grind until the mixture becomes a fine powder. Store in an airtight container for up to 6 months. Yields about 1/2 cup.

Szechuan Chicken Noodle Toss

Prep/Total Time: 20 min.

✓ Uses less fat, sugar or salt. Includes Nutrition Facts and Diabetic Exchanges.

- 4 quarts water
- 6 ounces uncooked thin spaghetti
- 1 package (16 ounces) frozen Oriental vegetables
- 1 tablespoon reduced-fat stick margarine
- 1 pound boneless skinless chicken breasts, cut into 2-inch strips
- 2 garlic cloves, minced
- 1/8 teaspoon crushed red pepper flakes
- 1 tablespoon canola oil
- 1/3 cup stir-fry sauce
- 3 green onions, chopped

In a Dutch oven, bring water to a boil. Add spaghetti; cook for 4 minutes. Add vegetables; cook 3-4 minutes longer or until spaghetti and vegetables are tender. Drain. Toss with margarine; set aside and keep warm.

In a nonstick skillet, stir-fry chicken, garlic and red pepper flakes in oil until chicken is no longer pink. Add stir-fry sauce; heat through. Add onions and spaghetti mixture; toss to coat.

Yield: 4 servings.

Editor's Note: This recipe was tested with Parkay Light stick margarine.

Nutrition Facts: 1-1/2 cups equals 394 calories, 7 g fat (1 g saturated fat), 66 mg cholesterol, 831 mg sodium, 44 g carbohydrate, 5 g fiber, 35 g protein. **Diabetic Exchanges:** 3 lean meat, 2-1/2 starch, 1 vegetable.

Some Like It Hot

If your family loves Chinese food, they'll enjoy this chicken stir-fry that's equally delicious made with pork or beef strips. Szechuan cuisine is primarily known for its hot and spicy dishes. Dried peppers are frequently used; this recipe calls for crushed red pepper flakes.

Know the expression "Oil and water don't mix?" It's true, which is why drinking water doesn't help combat the effects of spicy foods. Since most spices are oily, the water just rolls over the spice. Eat rice instead—it absorbs the oil. Drinking milk also helps.

Breaded Chicken Patties

Prep/Total Time: 20 min.

1/4 cup finely chopped onion
1/4 cup finely chopped celery
  6 tablespoons butter, *divided*
  3 tablespoons all-purpose flour
1-1/3 cups milk, *divided*
  2 tablespoons minced fresh parsley
  1 teaspoon salt
  1 teaspoon onion salt
1/2 teaspoon celery salt
1/4 teaspoon pepper
  2 cups finely chopped cooked chicken
  1 cup dry bread crumbs
Sandwich rolls, split
Lettuce leaves and tomato slices, optional

In a large saucepan, saute onion and celery in 3 tablespoons butter until tender. Combine flour and 1 cup milk. Gradually add to pan. Bring to a boil; cook and stir for 2 minutes or until thickened. Add parsley, seasonings and chicken. Remove from the heat. Chill until completely cooled.

Shape chicken mixture into six patties, using about 1/3 cup mixture for each patty. Place crumbs and remaining milk in separate shallow bowls. Roll patties in crumbs, then dip into milk; roll again in crumbs.

In a large skillet, cook patties in remaining butter for 3 minutes on each side or until golden brown. Serve on rolls with lettuce and tomato if desired.

Yield: 6 servings.

Freeze the Patties

Breaded Chicken Patties may be frozen for up to 3 months. Place the uncooked patties on a baking sheet and put them in the freezer until frozen. Then place in a large resealable freezer bag. The patties won't stick together, so you can take out any number at a time you want.

To prepare the frozen patties, cook in butter for 5 to 6 minutes on each side or until they are golden and heated through.

Chicken Pasta Primavera

Prep/Total Time: 30 min.

2   cups uncooked spiral pasta
1   pound boneless skinless chicken breasts, cubed
2   garlic cloves, minced
2   tablespoons butter
1   package (16 ounces) frozen broccoli-cauliflower blend, thawed
3/4 cup heavy whipping cream
3/4 cup grated Parmesan cheese
1   teaspoon salt
1/4 teaspoon pepper

Cook pasta according to package directions. Meanwhile, in a large skillet, saute chicken and garlic in butter until chicken is no longer pink. Add the vegetables and cream; cook until vegetables are tender. Drain pasta. Add the pasta, Parmesan cheese, salt and pepper to the skillet; cook and stir until heated through.

Yield: 4 servings.

Pleasing Pasta Dish

This colorful combination of chicken, pasta and vegetables coated in a creamy white sauce is sure to be popular at your house. Your family will enjoy its garden-fresh flavor; you'll appreciate that it can be made in just 30 minutes!

Pasta should be cooked until al dente, which means firm yet tender. Test often while cooking to avoid overcooking, which would cause a soft or mushy texture. As soon as the pasta tests done, pour into a large colander to drain, minding the steam as you pour.

Bow Tie Lemon Chicken

Prep/Total Time: 30 min.

✓ Uses less fat, sugar or salt. Includes Nutrition Facts and Diabetic Exchanges.

- 4-2/3 **cups uncooked bow tie pasta**
- 12 **ounces boneless skinless chicken breasts, cut into 1-inch strips**
- 1/2 **teaspoon salt-free lemon-pepper seasoning**
- 2 **garlic cloves, minced**
- 1 **tablespoon canola oil**
- 1 **cup chicken broth**
- 1 **cup frozen peas, thawed**
- 2/3 **cup shredded carrots**
- 1/4 **cup cubed reduced-fat cream cheese**
- 2 **teaspoons lemon juice**
- 1/2 **teaspoon salt**
- 1/3 **cup shredded Parmesan cheese**

Cook pasta according to package directions. Meanwhile, sprinkle chicken with lemon-pepper. In a large nonstick skillet, stir-fry chicken and garlic in oil until chicken juices run clear.

Remove and keep warm. Add broth, peas, carrots, cream cheese and lemon juice to the skillet; cook and stir until cheese is melted. Drain pasta. Add pasta, chicken and salt to vegetable mixture; cook until heated through. Sprinkle with Parmesan cheese.

Yield: 4 servings.

Nutrition Facts: 1-1/2 cups equals 399 calories, 11 g fat (4 g saturated fat), 64 mg cholesterol, 824 mg sodium, 42 g carbohydrate, 4 g fiber, 33 g protein. **Diabetic Exchanges:** 3 lean meat, 2 starch, 1 vegetable, 1 fat.

Use a Fresh Lemon

The zesty flavor of lemon brightens every bite of this creamy chicken and pasta dish. Try fresh lemon juice. It will enhance the flavor of this recipe more than bottled juice.

You'll be able to get more juice out of a room temperature lemon. If you're working with a cold lemon, microwave it for a few seconds or roll it on the countertop with your hand a few times.

Cashew Chicken

Prep: 5 min. **Bake:** 45 min.

- 1 pound boneless skinless chicken breasts, cut into 1-inch cubes
- 1 medium onion, chopped
- 2 cups frozen broccoli cuts
- 1-3/4 cups boiling water
- 1 cup uncooked long grain rice
- 1 jar (6 ounces) sliced mushrooms, drained
- 1 tablespoon chicken bouillon granules
- 1/2 to 1 teaspoon ground ginger

Pepper to taste

- 3/4 cup salted cashews, *divided*

In a large bowl, combine the first nine ingredients. Transfer to a greased shallow 1-1/2-qt. baking dish. Cover and bake at 375° for 45-55 minutes or until rice is tender and chicken is no longer pink. Stir in 1/2 cup of cashews. Sprinkle with remaining cashews.

Yield: 4 servings.

Onion Advice

Five minutes is all you need to get this chicken casserole into the oven! The only prep work is to cut the chicken breasts into cubes and chop the onion. When there's no time to chop onions, substitute 1 tablespoon of onion powder for the medium chopped onion.

When you have free time, peel a bag of onions, chop some and freeze them in freezer bags in the amounts called for in some of your favorite recipes. Also freeze some whole for soups and stews.

Chicken Avocado Melt

Prep/Total Time: 30 min.

   4 boneless skinless chicken breast halves
      (4 ounces *each*)
 1/3 cup cornstarch
   1 teaspoon ground cumin
   1 teaspoon garlic powder
   1 teaspoon salt
 1/8 teaspoon cayenne pepper
   1 egg
   2 tablespoons water
 1/2 cup cornmeal
 1/4 cup vegetable oil
   1 medium avocado, thinly sliced
   2 cups (8 ounces) shredded Monterey Jack cheese
Sour cream, salsa and sliced green onions, optional

Flatten chicken to 1/4-in. thickness; set aside. In a shallow bowl, combine cornstarch, cumin, garlic powder, salt and cayenne. In another shallow bowl, beat egg and water. Dip chicken into egg, then roll in the cornstarch mixture and cornmeal.

In a large skillet, cook chicken over medium heat in oil until golden brown on both sides. Place in a greased 13-in. x 9-in. x 2-in. baking dish; arrange avocado evenly on top.

Bake, uncovered, at 350° for 10-15 minutes or until chicken juices run clear. Sprinkle with cheese. Serve with sour cream, salsa and green onions if desired.

Yield: 4 servings.

Taste of the Southwest

Avocado gives this chicken dish Southwestern flair. Ripe avocados yield to gentle palm pressure, but you'll most likely find firm, unripe ones in the supermarket. Select those that are unblemished and heavy for their size.

To speed the ripening process, place several avocados in a paper bag and set aside at room temperature for 2 to 4 days. Ripe avocados can be stored in the refrigerator for up to 1 week.

Chicken a la King

Prep: 10 min. **Cook:** 7-1/2 hours

✓ Uses less fat, sugar or salt. Includes Nutrition Facts and Diabetic Exchanges.

- 1 can (10-3/4 ounces) condensed cream of chicken soup, undiluted
- 3 tablespoons all-purpose flour
- 1/4 teaspoon pepper

Dash cayenne pepper

- 1 pound boneless skinless chicken breasts, cut into cubes
- 1 celery rib, chopped
- 1/2 cup chopped green pepper
- 1/4 cup chopped onion
- 1 package (10 ounces) frozen peas, thawed
- 2 tablespoons diced pimientos, drained

Hot cooked rice, optional

In a 3-qt. slow cooker, combine soup, flour, pepper and cayenne until smooth. Stir in chicken, celery, green pepper and onion. Cover and cook on low for 7-8 hours or until meat juices run clear. Stir in peas and pimientos. Cook 30 minutes longer or until heated through. Serve with rice if desired.

Yield: 6 servings.

Nutrition Facts: 1 cup (prepared with reduced-fat soup; calculated without rice) equals 183 calories, 3 g fat (0 saturated fat), 52 mg cholesterol, 284 mg sodium, 16 g carbohydrate, 0 fiber, 22 g protein. **Diabetic Exchanges:** 2-1/2 very lean meat, 1 starch.

All About Pimientos

"A la King" refers to a dish of cubed chicken or turkey in a rich cream sauce containing pimientos, green peppers and mushrooms. This tasty version, that conveniently cooks in the slow cooker, calls for peas in place of the mushrooms.

A pimiento is a large, red, heart-shaped sweet pepper that measures 3 to 4 inches long. The flesh is sweet, succulent and more aromatic than that of the red bell pepper. An unopened jar of pimientos can be stored in a cool, dark place for up to 1 year; once opened, refrigerated for up to 2 weeks.

Chicken Enchiladas

Prep/Total Time: 30 min.

- 2 tablespoons butter
- 1/4 cup all-purpose flour
- 2-1/2 cups chicken broth
- 1 teaspoon dried coriander
- 1 can (4 ounces) chopped green chilies, *divided*
- 2 cups cubed cooked chicken
- 1 cup (4 ounces) shredded Monterey Jack cheese
- 8 flour tortillas (8 inches), warmed
- 1 cup (4 ounces) shredded cheddar cheese

Melt butter in a large saucepan. Stir in flour until smooth. Gradually add broth. Bring to a boil; cook and stir for 2 minutes or until thickened. Stir in coriander and half of the chilies. In a large bowl, combine the chicken, Monterey Jack cheese and remaining chilies.

Spoon 1/3 cup chicken mixture onto each tortilla; roll up. Place seam side down in an ungreased 13-in. x 9-in. x 2-in. baking dish. Pour sauce over enchiladas. Sprinkle with cheddar cheese. Bake, uncovered, at 375° for 15-18 minutes or until heated through and cheese is melted.

Yield: 4 servings.

Roll Up
Supper in a Flash

These rolled tortillas are filled with a hearty mixture of Monterey Jack cheese, chicken and green chilies, then topped with a creamy sauce and cheddar cheese. If you have leftover turkey, you could substitute it for the chicken.

Peanut butter cashew sundaes would make a cool finale to the spicy meal. In a small bowl, combine 1/3 cup light corn syrup and 1/4 cup peanut butter until blended. Place a scoop of vanilla ice cream in four individual bowls; serve sauce over ice cream. Sprinkle with salted cashews.

Apricot Salsa Chicken

Prep/Total Time: 30 min.

1/2 cup all-purpose flour
1 teaspoon salt
1/4 teaspoon pepper
1/4 teaspoon paprika
6 boneless skinless chicken breast halves (4 ounces *each*)
3 tablespoons vegetable oil
1 jar (16 ounces) salsa
1 jar (12 ounces) apricot preserves
1/2 cup apricot nectar
Hot cooked rice

In a large resealable plastic bag, combine the first four ingredients; add chicken in batches. Seal bag and turn to coat.

In a large skillet, cook chicken over medium heat in oil until browned on each side; drain. Stir in the salsa, preserves and nectar; bring to a boil. Reduce heat; simmer, uncovered, for 15 minutes or until the sauce thickens and meat juices run clear. Serve with rice.

Yield: 6 servings.

Testing Chicken For Doneness

Apricot preserves and salsa combine to make a sweet-and-spicy sauce that smothers pieces of chicken in this recipe. Peach preserves could be used in place of the apricot.

To check if chicken is completely cooked through, make a small slit with the tip of a knife into the thickest part of the chicken and pry the slit open. The meat should be opaque with no signs of pink coloring. If the juices do not run clear, continue cooking.

Cookin' with **Chicken**

Cajun Chicken Club

Prep/Total Time: 15 min.

> 4 boneless skinless chicken breast halves (4 ounces *each*)
> 1/2 to 1 teaspoon Cajun seasoning
> 1 tablespoon vegetable oil
> 4 slices Swiss cheese
> 1/4 cup creamy Parmesan salad dressing
> 4 sandwich rolls, split and toasted
> 8 tomato slices
> 8 bacon strips, cooked

Flatten the chicken to 3/8-in. thickness; sprinkle with Cajun seasoning. In a large skillet, cook chicken in oil for 5 minutes on each side or until juices run clear. Place cheese over chicken. Remove from the heat; cover and let stand for 1 minute or until cheese begins to melt.

Spread dressing over both halves of rolls. Layer bottom halves with two slices of tomato, chicken and two strips of bacon; replace the tops.

Yield: 4 servings.

Flattening Chicken Breasts

Cajun seasoning gives these chicken club sandwiches a zippy flavor. There are many different varieties on the market today, but most contain garlic, onion, chilies, black pepper, mustard and celery.

To flatten the chicken, place boneless chicken breasts between two pieces of waxed paper or plastic wrap or in a resealable plastic bag. Starting in the center and working out to the edges, pound lightly with the flat side of a meat mallet until the chicken is even in thickness.

Chicken Divine

Prep/Total Time: 25 min.

6 **boneless skinless chicken breast halves (4 ounces** *each***)**
Dash pepper
1 **package (10 ounces) frozen chopped broccoli, thawed**
2 **medium carrots, julienned**
2 **tablespoons water**
1 **jar (16 ounces) Parmesan and mozzarella pasta sauce**
2 **tablespoons sherry** *or* **chicken broth**
1/8 **teaspoon ground nutmeg**
Hot cooked noodles

Place chicken in a greased 11-in. x 7-in. x 2-in. microwave-safe dish; sprinkle with pepper. Cover with waxed paper. Microwave on high for 6-7 minutes or until juices run clear.

In a microwave-safe bowl, combine the broccoli, carrots and water. Cover and microwave on high for 3-4 minutes or until crisp-tender; drain. Spoon over chicken.

In a small bowl, combine the pasta sauce, sherry and nutmeg; pour over chicken and vegetables. Cover and cook on high for 3 minutes or until heated through. Serve with noodles.

Yield: 6 servings.

Editor's Note: This recipe was tested with Ragu creamy pasta sauce with an 850-watt microwave.

Divinely Easy To Prepare

For this easy microwave recipe, simply dress up a jar of creamy white pasta sauce with sherry and nutmeg, then cook it with chicken, broccoli and carrots. Served over hot cooked noodles, the hearty combination is swift and satisfying.

You can find jars of prepared pasta sauce in grocery stores by the dried pasta and in the refrigerated section next to the fresh pasta.

Barley Chicken Chili

Prep/Total Time: 25 min.

1 cup chopped onion
1/2 cup chopped green
pepper
1 teaspoon olive oil
2-1/4 cups water
1 can (15 ounces) tomato
sauce
1 can (14-1/2 ounces)
chicken broth
1 can (10 ounces) diced
tomatoes and green
chilies, undrained
1 cup quick-cooking barley
1 tablespoon chili powder
1/2 teaspoon ground cumin
1/4 teaspoon garlic powder
3 cups cubed cooked chicken

In a large saucepan, saute onion and green pepper in oil until tender. Add the water, tomato sauce, broth, tomatoes, barley, chili powder, cumin and garlic powder; bring to a boil. Reduce heat; cover and simmer for 10 minutes. Add chicken. Cover and simmer 5 minutes longer or until barley is tender.

Yield: 9 servings (about 2 quarts).

Keep It in the Freezer

On a Saturday or Sunday afternoon, make a double batch of Barley Chicken Chili. Enjoy half for dinner that night, then freeze the rest for a weeknight meal later on.

You can rely on a variety of refrigerated breads to round out meals featuring chili, stew and soups. Keep tubes of biscuits, crescent rolls, corn bread twists, crusty French bread and dinner rolls on hand.

From down-home
dinners to
more elegant entrees,
turkey solves any
dining dilemma.

Veggie Turkey Casserole (p. 153)

Timeless **Turkey**

Apple-Walnut Turkey Sandwiches (p. 148)

Zesty Apricot Turkey (p. 155)

Marinated Turkey Tenderloins

Prep: 10 min. + marinating **Grill:** 20 min.

 1 cup lemon-lime soda
1/4 cup soy sauce
 2 tablespoons lemon juice
 2 garlic cloves, minced
 1 teaspoon prepared horseradish
1/2 teaspoon lemon-pepper
  seasoning
1/4 teaspoon curry powder
1/4 teaspoon ground ginger
1/4 teaspoon paprika
1/4 teaspoon crushed red pepper
  flakes
 2 pounds turkey breast
  tenderloins

In a large bowl, combine the first 10 ingredients. Pour 1 cup into a large resealable plastic bag; add turkey. Seal bag and turn to coat; refrigerate 8 hours or overnight, turning occasionally. Cover and refrigerate remaining marinade for serving.

Drain and discard marinade from turkey. Grill turkey, covered, over medium-hot heat for 10-12 minutes on each side or until a meat thermometer reads 170°. Serve with reserved marinade.

Yield: 8 servings.

Guide to Marinating

Lemon-lime soda, soy sauce, lemon juice and a handful of seasonings combine to make the fuss-free marinade that flavors turkey breast tenderloins in this grilled entree.

Always marinate meat in the refrigerator, turning several times to evenly coat. If a marinade is to be used later for basting or as a serving sauce, as in this recipe, reserve a portion before adding the meat.

Cordon Bleu Casserole

Prep: 15 min. **Bake:** 25 min.

2 cups cubed fully cooked ham
4 cups cubed cooked turkey
1 cup (4 ounces) shredded Swiss cheese
1 large onion, chopped
1/3 cup butter, cubed
1/3 cup all-purpose flour
1/8 teaspoon ground mustard
1/8 teaspoon ground nutmeg
1-3/4 cups milk
TOPPING:
1-1/2 cups soft bread crumbs
1/2 cup shredded Swiss cheese
1/4 cup butter, melted

In a large nonstick skillet, saute ham for 4-5 minutes or until browned; drain and pat dry. In a greased 2-qt. baking dish, layer the turkey, cheese and ham; set aside.

In a large saucepan, saute the onion in butter until tender. Stir in the flour, mustard and nutmeg until blended. Gradually stir in milk. Bring to a boil; cook and stir for 2 minutes or until thickened. Pour over the ham.

Combine topping ingredients; sprinkle over the top. Bake, uncovered, at 350° for 25-30 minutes or until golden brown and bubbly.

Yield: 6 servings.

Cordon Bleu In a Casserole

Featuring turkey, ham and Swiss cheese, this comforting casserole topped with bread crumbs is a convenient way to feed your family cordon bleu. It has all the traditional flavor without the timely work—just 15 minutes of prep work, in fact! Cobs of corn are an easy accompaniment.

Swiss cheese has a slightly nutty flavor. It is easier to grate, either by hand or in a food processor, if it's cold. Cleanup after grating cheese will be a breeze if you spray the grating disk or metal blade with nonstick spray first.

Cajun Sausage Pasta

Prep/Total Time: 30 min.

1 large onion, chopped
3 garlic cloves, minced
2 tablespoons olive oil
1 cup reduced-sodium chicken broth
2 cups dry white wine *or* additional reduced-sodium chicken broth
1 can (14-1/2 ounces) diced tomatoes, undrained
1 can (6 ounces) tomato paste
2 tablespoons sugar
1 teaspoon ground cumin
1/4 teaspoon cayenne pepper
1/4 teaspoon pepper
1 pound turkey Italian sausage links, sliced
1 medium green pepper, julienned
1 medium sweet red pepper, julienned
5 cups hot cooked penne pasta

In a large saucepan, saute onion and garlic in oil until tender. Add broth and wine or additional broth. Bring to a boil; cook, uncovered, until liquid is reduced to 1 cup. Reduce heat. Stir in the tomatoes, tomato paste, sugar, cumin, cayenne and pepper. Cover and simmer for 15-20 minutes.

Meanwhile, in a nonstick skillet, cook sausage and peppers over medium heat until sausage is no longer pink and peppers are tender; drain. Stir in the tomato mixture. Serve over pasta.

Yield: 5 servings.

"Kick" It Up a Notch

If you can stand a little heat, cook this zesty Cajun entree. Cumin and cayenne give the dish "kick," while turkey sausage and red and green peppers perk up its flavor.

With a nice combination of herbs and spices, turkey Italian sausage usually contains half the fat of pork sausage. For variety, make the dish with chicken.

Hot Turkey Salad

Prep/Total Time: 30 min.

    4 cups cubed cooked turkey
    2 cups diced celery
    1 cup slivered almonds, toasted
    1 teaspoon salt
  1/2 teaspoon dried thyme
  1/4 teaspoon pepper
1-1/2 cups mayonnaise
    1 cup (4 ounces) shredded cheddar cheese
    1 cup crushed potato chips

In a greased 2-qt. baking dish, combine the first eight ingredients. Top with potato chips. Bake, uncovered, at 450° for 15 minutes or until bubbly.

Yield: 4-6 servings.

Try It Different Ways

Hot Turkey Salad is quite versatile. It can be served plain by the scoopful—cooked carrots and refrigerated breadsticks are simple sides. To dress it up a little, spoon it into baked puff pastry shells. Or serve it on hamburger buns as a hot sandwich. Plus, it tastes as terrific made with chicken. Whichever way you choose, your family is sure to "gobble" it up!

Cranberry-Orange Turkey Cutlets

Prep/Total Time: 20 min.

✓ Uses less fat, sugar or salt. Includes Nutrition Facts and Diabetic Exchanges.

- **1 pound turkey breast cutlets**
- **1 cup dry bread crumbs**
- **1 egg white**
- **1 tablespoon fat-free milk**
- **1/2 teaspoon salt**
- **3/4 cup cranberry-orange *or* whole-berry cranberry sauce**
- **1 tablespoon olive oil**

Flatten turkey to 1/4-in. thickness. Place bread crumbs in a shallow bowl. In another bowl, beat the egg white, milk and salt. Dip turkey into egg white mixture, then coat with crumbs. Refrigerate turkey, uncovered, for 10 minutes.

Meanwhile, in a small saucepan, heat cranberry-orange sauce. In a large nonstick skillet, cook turkey in oil for 3-4 minutes on each side or until juices run clear. Serve sauce over turkey.

Yield: 4 servings.

Editor's Note: This recipe was tested with Ocean Spray Cranberry-Orange sauce. Look for it in the canned fruit section of your grocery store.

Nutrition Facts: 4 ounces turkey with 3 tablespoons sauce equals 399 calories, 9 g fat (1 g saturated fat), 82 mg cholesterol, 609 mg sodium, 44 g carbohydrate, 1 g fiber, 34 g protein. **Diabetic Exchanges:** 3 lean meat, 1-1/2 starch, 1-1/2 fruit.

Cutlets Are a Cut Above

These turkey cutlets are easy to prepare but look elegant. They make a special weeknight meal but are also wonderful to serve to company on weekends. Serve cooked brussels sprouts as a side…or all the traditional turkey trimmings!

Turkey cutlets are small, thin steaks that are removed from the breast meat and pounded to flatten and tenderize them. They are available uncooked or fully cooked, unbreaded or breaded, and unflavored or seasoned with various herbs and spices.

Lemon Turkey Burgers

Prep/Total Time: 20 min.

✓ Uses less fat, sugar or salt. Includes Nutrition Facts and Diabetic Exchanges.

- 1 **egg, lightly beaten**
- 1/3 **cup finely chopped onion**
- 3 **tablespoons minced fresh parsley**
- 2 **tablespoons lemon juice**
- 1 **tablespoon grated lemon peel**
- 3 **garlic cloves, minced**
- 1 **teaspoon caraway seeds, crushed**
- 1 **teaspoon salt**
- 1/2 **teaspoon pepper**
- 1 **pound lean ground turkey**
- 1 **tablespoon olive oil**
- 6 **whole wheat sandwich rolls, split**
- 6 **lettuce leaves**
- 6 **thin tomato slices**

In a large bowl, combine the first nine ingredients. Crumble turkey over mixture and mix well. Shape into six patties.

In a large nonstick skillet, cook patties in oil in two batches over medium heat until a meat thermometer reads 165°. Serve on rolls with lettuce and tomato.

Yield: 6 servings.

Nutrition Facts: 1 sandwich equals 268 calories, 11 g fat (3 g saturated fat), 95 mg cholesterol, 680 mg sodium, 24 g carbohydrate, 4 g fiber, 18 g protein. **Diabetic Exchanges:** 2 lean meat, 1-1/2 starch, 1/2 fat.

Forget the Beef!

You'll never miss the beef in these full-flavored turkey burgers. Grated lemon peel and crushed caraway seeds pleasantly season the moist sandwiches.

When you come home from the grocery store with fresh ground turkey, assemble these burgers right away. Then freeze in a single layer in a resealable plastic freezer bag. The burgers can be frozen for up to 2 months. To use, thaw overnight in the refrigerator and cook as directed in the recipe.

Kidney Bean Sausage Supper

Prep/Total Time: 25 min.

✓ Uses less fat, sugar or salt. Includes Nutrition Facts and Diabetic Exchanges.

- 1 **pound turkey Italian sausage links, cut into 1/2-inch pieces**
- 1 **large green pepper, julienned**
- 1 **medium onion, sliced**
- 1/2 **cup reduced-sodium chicken broth**
- 1 **can (16 ounces) kidney beans, rinsed and drained**
- 1 **can (14-1/2 ounces) diced tomatoes and green chilies, undrained**

Hot cooked rice, optional

In a large nonstick skillet, cook sausage over medium heat until no longer pink; drain. Add the green pepper, onion and broth; cover and cook for 5 minutes or until vegetables are tender. Add beans and tomatoes; bring to a boil.

Reduce heat; cover and simmer for 10 minutes or until vegetables are tender. Serve in bowls over rice if desired.

Yield: 4 servings.

Nutrition Facts: 1 cup sausage mixture (calculated without rice) equals 337 calories, 11 g fat (3 g saturated fat), 61 mg cholesterol, 1,564 mg sodium, 33 g carbohydrate, 10 g fiber, 27 g protein. **Diabetic Exchanges:** 3 lean meat, 2 vegetable, 1-1/2 starch.

Spill the Beans On Beans

Looking for a nutritious and tasty meal that doesn't take a lot of time to prepare? This bean and turkey sausage dish is satisfying and quick...it can be on the table in only 25 minutes.

Rinse and drain canned kidney beans before using. Not only will you reduce the sodium content of the beans but also eliminate some of the sugars.

This medium-size bean has a dark red skin and cream-colored flesh. Its popularity can be attributed to its full-bodied flavor.

Pepperoni Pizza Supreme

Prep/Total Time: 30 min.

☑ Uses less fat, sugar or salt. Includes Nutrition Facts and Diabetic Exchanges.

- 1 **prebaked thin Italian bread shell crust (10 ounces)**
- 1 **can (8 ounces) pizza sauce**
- 1 **tablespoon grated Parmesan cheese**
- 1 **teaspoon Italian seasoning**
- 1/2 **teaspoon garlic powder**
- 1/2 **cup sliced fresh mushrooms**
- 1/2 **cup chopped fresh broccoli florets**
- 1/4 **cup chopped green pepper**
- 1/4 **cup chopped sweet red pepper**
- 1/2 **cup shredded reduced-fat cheddar cheese**
- 38 **slices turkey pepperoni**
- 1 **cup (4 ounces) shredded part-skim mozzarella cheese**

Place crust on an ungreased baking sheet. Spread with pizza sauce; sprinkle with the Parmesan cheese, Italian seasoning and garlic powder. Top with the mushrooms, broccoli and peppers.

Sprinkle with cheddar cheese. Top with pepperoni and mozzarella cheese. Bake at 400° for 14-18 minutes or until vegetables are crisp-tender and cheese is melted.

Yield: 6 slices.

Nutrition Facts: 1 slice equals 244 calories, 9 g fat (3 g saturated fat), 28 mg cholesterol, 698 mg sodium, 26 g carbohydrate, 1 g fiber, 17 g protein. **Diabetic Exchanges:** 1-1/2 starch, 1-1/2 lean meat, 1 fat.

Bread Shell Basics

Here's a in-a-hurry home-made alternative to typical restaurant or frozen pizza. Your family will love the crispy combination of fresh vegetables, and the lighter cheeses and turkey pepperoni. The only thing missing is the guilt!

Italian bread shell crusts come in original, thin and whole wheat. Select a shell that will please your whole gang's palate. Or feel free to substitute a refrigerated pizza crust, crust mix or any homemade variety.

Apricot Turkey Stir-Fry

Prep/Total Time: 20 min.

✓ Uses less fat, sugar or salt. Includes Nutrition Facts and Diabetic Exchanges.

- 1 **tablespoon cornstarch**
- 1/2 **cup apricot nectar**
- 3 **tablespoons reduced-sodium soy sauce**
- 2 **tablespoons white vinegar**
- 1/4 **teaspoon crushed red pepper flakes**
- 1/2 **cup dried apricot halves, cut in half lengthwise**
- 1 **pound turkey tenderloin, cut into thin slices**
- 1 **teaspoon canola oil**
- 1 **teaspoon sesame oil** *or* **additional canola oil**
- 2-1/2 **cups fresh snow peas**
- 1 **medium onion, chopped**
- 1 **medium sweet red** *or* **yellow pepper, cut into 1-inch pieces**

In a small bowl, combine the cornstarch, apricot nectar, soy sauce, vinegar and red pepper flakes until smooth. Add apricots; set aside. In a large nonstick skillet or wok, stir-fry turkey in canola and sesame oil until no longer pink. Add the peas, onion and red pepper; stir-fry until crisp-tender. Remove meat and vegetables with a slotted spoon; keep warm.

Stir cornstarch mixture and gradually add to pan. Bring to a boil; cook and stir for 1-2 minutes or until thickened. Return meat and vegetables to the pan; toss to coat. Heat through.

Yield: 4 servings.

Nutrition Facts: 1-1/2 cups stir-fry equals 270 calories, 3 g fat (1 g saturated fat), 82 mg cholesterol, 512 mg sodium, 27 g carbohydrate, 4 g fiber, 33 g protein. **Diabetic Exchanges:** 4 very lean meat, 2 vegetable, 1 fruit, 1/2 fat.

Get Clued in On Couscous

Tender slices of turkey, crunchy snow peas, red pepper and dried apricots make this easy stir-fry a standout. We served it over a bed of hot cooked couscous, but you could also spoon it over thin spaghetti or rice.

Couscous is a granular form of semolina, which is what pasta is made from. Packaged precooked couscous is available in some larger markets. Cooked, it can also be served with milk as a porridge, with dressing as a salad, or sweetened and mixed with fruits for dessert.

Tangy Turkey Kabobs

Prep/Total Time: 30 min.

1/2 cup honey mustard salad dressing
  2 teaspoons dried rosemary, crushed
 12 small red potatoes, cut in half
  1 pound turkey breast slices, cut into 1-inch strips
  2 unpeeled green apples, cut into 1-inch pieces

In a small bowl, combine salad dressing and rosemary; set aside. Place potatoes in a saucepan and cover with water; bring to a boil. Cook for 5 minutes; drain.

Fold turkey strips in thirds; thread onto metal or soaked wooden skewers alternately with potatoes and apples. Spoon half of the dressing over kabobs. Grill, uncovered, over medium-hot heat for 5-7 minutes on each side or until meat juices run clear, basting occasionally with remaining dressing.

Yield: 4 servings.

Great Grilled Fare

Grill some corn and pepper packets alongside the kabobs. In a bowl, combine 4 ears of corn cut into 2-inch chunks, 1 medium green pepper cut into 2-inch strips, 1 medium sweet red pepper cut into 2-inch strips, 2 table-spoons minced fresh parsley, 3/4 teaspoon garlic salt, 1/4 teaspoon celery seed and 1/4 teaspoon pepper. Place on a piece of heavy-duty foil. Drizzle with 1/4 cup melted butter.

Fold foil around vegetables and seal tightly. Grill, covered, over medium-hot heat for 10 to 12 minutes. Open foil carefully to allow steam to escape. Serves four.

Turkey 'n' Stuffing Pie

Prep/Total Time: 30 min.

1 egg, lightly beaten
1 cup chicken broth
1/3 cup butter, melted
5 cups seasoned stuffing cubes

FILLING:

1 can (4 ounces) mushroom stems and pieces, drained
1/2 cup chopped onion
1 tablespoon butter
1 tablespoon all-purpose flour
3 cups cubed cooked turkey
1 cup frozen peas
1 tablespoon minced fresh parsley
1 teaspoon Worcestershire sauce
1/2 teaspoon dried thyme
1 jar (12 ounces) turkey gravy
5 slices process American cheese, cut into strips

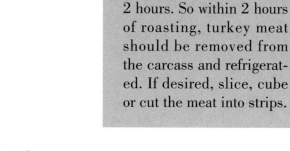

Tasty Treatment for Leftover Turkey

Stuffing forms the crust for this attractive cheese-latticed turkey pie. Try it the day after Thanksgiving or anytime you have leftover roast turkey.

Any perishable food should not stand at room temperature for longer than 2 hours. So within 2 hours of roasting, turkey meat should be removed from the carcass and refrigerated. If desired, slice, cube or cut the meat into strips.

In a large bowl, combine the egg, broth and butter. Stir in stuffing. Pat onto the bottom and up the sides of a greased 9-in. pie plate; set aside.

For filling, in a large skillet, saute mushrooms and onion in butter until tender. Sprinkle with flour until well blended. Stir in the turkey, peas, parsley, Worcestershire sauce and thyme. Stir in gravy. Bring to a boil; boil and stir for 2 minutes.

Spoon into crust. Bake at 375° for 20 minutes. Arrange cheese strips in a lattice pattern over filling. Bake 5-10 minutes longer or until cheese is melted.

Yield: 4-6 servings.

Turkey Florentine

Prep/Total Time: 30 min.

1 cup seasoned bread
   crumbs
8 slices uncooked turkey
   breast
2 tablespoons vegetable oil
4 slices Swiss cheese, cut in
   half
1 package (10 ounces)
   frozen chopped spinach,
   thawed and squeezed dry
3 cups meatless spaghetti
   sauce

Place the bread crumbs in a large resealable plastic bag; add turkey in batches and shake to coat. In a large skillet over medium heat, brown turkey in oil. Remove from the skillet.

Place half of a cheese slice and 2 tablespoons of spinach down the center of each turkey slice. Fold turkey over filling; secure with toothpicks.

Place in a greased 9-in. square baking dish. Top with spaghetti sauce. Bake, uncovered, at 400° for 12-15 minutes or until turkey juices run clear. Discard toothpicks.

Yield: 4 servings.

Squeeze Spinach Dry

For this main course, tuck Swiss cheese and spinach into skillet-browned turkey slices, then top them with store-bought spaghetti sauce before baking until they're heated through. Serve the roll-ups with pasta, steamed carrots and hot dinner rolls to round out the meal.

To remove excess moisture from frozen spinach that has been thawed, drain it in a colander. With clean hands, squeeze the water out of the spinach.

Ranch Turkey Pasta Dinner

Prep/Total Time: 20 min.

2-1/2 cups uncooked penne
      pasta
  6 to 8 tablespoons butter,
      cubed
  1 envelope ranch salad
      dressing mix
  1 cup frozen peas and
      carrots, thawed
  3 cups cubed cooked turkey

Cook pasta according to package directions. Meanwhile, in a large skillet, melt butter. Stir in salad dressing until smooth. Add peas and carrots; cook and stir for 2-3 minutes. Drain pasta and add to skillet. Stir in turkey; cook for 3-4 minutes or until heated through.

Yield: 4 servings.

Give Leftovers a Lift

This "second-time-around" dish is a great way to finish up a whole turkey roasted the day before. It's so simple to prepare and tastes delicious.

Leftover cooked turkey can be stored in the refrigerator for 1 to 2 days or in the freezer for up to 3 months. If you don't have any cooked turkey on hand, stop by the deli to pick up a large piece of turkey breast. Then take it home and cut it up. Or use leftover chicken if you have that instead.

Turkey Scallopini

Prep/Total Time: 20 min.

> 6 **turkey breast slices (about 1-1/2 pounds)**
> 1/4 **cup all-purpose flour**
> 1/8 **teaspoon salt**
> 1/8 **teaspoon pepper**
> 1 **egg**
> 2 **tablespoons water**
> 1 **cup soft bread crumbs**
> 1/2 **cup grated Parmesan cheese**
> 1/4 **cup butter**

Minced fresh parsley

Pound turkey to 1/4-in. thickness. In a shallow bowl, combine the flour, salt and pepper. In another bowl, beat egg and water. On a plate, combine the bread crumbs and Parmesan cheese. Dredge turkey in flour mixture, then dip in egg mixture and coat with crumbs. Let stand for 5 minutes.

Melt butter in a skillet over medium-high heat; cook turkey for 2-3 minutes on each side or until meat juices run clear and coating is golden brown. Sprinkle with parsley.

Yield: 6 servings.

Take a Look at Turkey

Quick-cooking turkey breast slices make this recipe a winner when you only have a few minutes to fix a satisfying meal. You can also used flattened boneless skinless chicken breast halves in place of the turkey.

Turkey cutlets and slices, tenderloins, boneless breasts and drumsticks are a delicious and economical way to enjoy the wonderful taste of turkey without preparing the whole bird.

Sweet 'n' Sour Turkey

Prep/Total Time: 20 min.

✓ Uses less fat, sugar or salt. Includes Nutrition Facts and Diabetic Exchanges.

- 2 **tablespoons cornstarch**
- 2 **tablespoons brown sugar**
- 1 **cup chicken broth**
- 2 **tablespoons soy sauce**
- 1 **tablespoon lemon juice**
- 2 **celery ribs, sliced**
- 2 **medium carrots, sliced**
- 1 **small onion, cut into thin wedges**
- 3 **tablespoons butter, cubed**
- 2 **cups julienned cooked turkey**
- 1 **can (14 ounces) unsweetened pineapple tidbits, undrained**
- 1/4 **cup slivered almonds, toasted**

Hot cooked rice, optional

In a small bowl, combine cornstarch and brown sugar. Stir in the broth, soy sauce and lemon juice until smooth; set aside.

In a large skillet or wok, stir-fry the celery, carrots and onion in butter for 3-4 minutes or until crisp-tender. Stir broth mixture; gradually add to pan. Bring to a boil; cook and stir for 2 minutes or until thickened. Add the turkey, pineapple and almonds; heat through. Serve over rice if desired.

Yield: 4 servings.

Nutrition Facts: 1-1/3 cups (prepared with reduced-sodium chicken broth, reduced-sodium soy sauce and reduced-fat margarine; calculated without rice) equals 327 calories, 11 g fat (2 g saturated fat), 48 mg cholesterol, 642 mg sodium, 32 g carbohydrate, 3 g fiber, 25 g protein. **Diabetic Exchanges:** 2-1/2 lean meat, 2 vegetable, 1-1/2 fruit, 1 fat.

Marinate with Pineapple Juice

If you're a sweet-and-sour lover, you'll have a lot to look forward to when you simmer up this saucy supper. Simply stir-fry leftover turkey, canned pineapple tidbits and veggies for the in-a-dash dinner.

Pineapple contains an enzyme that is a natural meat tenderizer, so add pineapple juice to marinades or just marinate meat in the juice alone. The pineapple flavor is particularly compatible with pork.

Turkey Sloppy Joes

Prep: 15 min. **Cook:** 4 hours

✓ Uses less fat, sugar or salt. Includes Nutrition Facts and Diabetic Exchanges.

- 1 **pound ground turkey breast**
- 1 **small onion, chopped**
- 1/2 **cup chopped celery**
- 1/4 **cup chopped green pepper**
- 1 **can (10-3/4 ounces) reduced-fat reduced-sodium condensed tomato soup, undiluted**
- 1/2 **cup ketchup**
- 1 **tablespoon brown sugar**
- 2 **tablespoons prepared mustard**
- 1/4 **teaspoon pepper**
- 8 **hamburger buns, split**

In a large saucepan coated with nonstick cooking spray, cook the turkey, onion, celery and green pepper over medium heat until meat is no longer pink; drain if necessary. Stir in the soup, ketchup, brown sugar, mustard and pepper. Transfer to a 3-qt. slow cooker. Cover and cook on low for 4 hours. Serve on buns.

Yield: 8 servings.

Nutrition Facts: 1 sandwich equals 247 calories, 7 g fat (2 g saturated fat), 45 mg cholesterol, 553 mg sodium, 32 g carbohydrate, 2 g fiber, 14 g protein. **Diabetic Exchanges:** 2 starch, 1-1/2 lean meat.

Simple Sandwiches And Slaw

This tangy turkey sandwich filling is so easy to prepare in the slow cooker. Serve the sloppy joes with fresh orange slices and brown rice slaw.

In a bowl, combine 2 cups coleslaw mix, 2 cups cooked brown rice and 1 chopped tart apple. In a small bowl, combine 1/3 cup orange juice concentrate, 1/3 cup fat-free mayonnaise, 1 teaspoon sugar and 1/4 teaspoon salt; pour over coleslaw mixture and toss to coat. Cover and refrigerate until serving. Stir in 1/4 cup chopped toasted pecans. Serves eight.

Apple-Walnut Turkey Sandwiches

Prep/Total Time: 15 min.

3/4 cup mayonnaise
1/4 cup chopped celery
1/4 cup raisins
1/4 cup chopped walnuts, toasted
  1 medium tart apple, chopped
3/4 pound sliced deli turkey
  8 slices sourdough bread
Lettuce leaves

In a large bowl, combine the mayonnaise, celery, raisins and walnuts. Stir in apple; set aside. Place turkey on four slices of bread. Top with apple mixture, lettuce and remaining bread.

Yield: 4 servings.

An Ap-peel-ing Sandwich

This turkey sandwich, with its cool Waldorf salad filling, is a breeze to prepare. You'll family will enjoy it so much, they'll ask you to make it frequently!

Waldorf salad was created at New York's Waldorf-Astoria Hotel in the 1890s. It contained apples, celery and mayonnaise; chopped walnuts later became an integral part of the dish. If you prefer, serve the salad on a bed of lettuce instead of using it as a filling in this sandwich.

Herb-Glazed Turkey Slices

Prep/Total Time: 20 min.

✓ Uses less fat, sugar or salt. Includes Nutrition Facts and Diabetic Exchanges.

- **1 package (1-1/4 pounds) turkey breast slices (1/4 inch thick)**
- **1 tablespoon vegetable oil**
- **1/2 cup chicken broth**
- **1/2 cup apple juice**
- **1 tablespoon honey**
- **1 tablespoon Dijon mustard**
- **1/2 teaspoon salt**
- **1/4 teaspoon *each* dried basil, dried rosemary, crushed and garlic powder**
- **1 tablespoon cornstarch**
- **1 tablespoon water**

In a large skillet, brown turkey slices on each side in oil. In a small bowl, combine the broth, apple juice, honey, mustard, salt, basil, rosemary and garlic powder; pour over turkey. Bring to a boil. Reduce heat; cover and simmer for 8 minutes or until the turkey is no longer pink.

Combine cornstarch and water until smooth; stir into skillet. Bring to a boil; cook and stir for 2 minutes or until thickened.

Yield: 4 servings.

Nutrition Facts: 1 serving equals 233 calories, 5 g fat (1 g saturated fat), 88 mg cholesterol, 577 mg sodium, 11 g carbohydrate, trace fiber, 35 g protein. **Diabetic Exchanges:** 3 very lean meat, 1 starch, 1 fat.

Turkey in a Hurry

In the mood for a taste of turkey, but don't have time to prepare a whole bird? Here's the perfect solution! These savory slices—and easy-to-prepare herb glaze —offer the goodness of turkey without the hassle. Serve with hot cooked brussels sprouts, carrots and rice pilaf if desired.

To boil whole brussels sprouts, remove any yellow outer leaves and trim ends; cut an X in the core end. Add 1 inch of water to a saucepan; add sprouts. Bring to a boil. Reduce heat; cover and simmer 10 to 12 minutes or until crisp-tender. Drain.

Turkey Bow Tie Skillet

Prep/Total Time: 30 min.

1/2 **pound ground turkey breast**
1-1/2 **teaspoons vegetable oil**
3/4 **cup chopped celery**
1/2 **cup chopped onion**
1/2 **cup chopped green
pepper**
1 **garlic clove, minced**
1 **can (14-1/2 ounces)
chicken broth**
2 **cups uncooked bow tie pasta**
1 **can (14-1/2 ounces) stewed
tomatoes**
1 **tablespoon white vinegar**
3/4 **teaspoon sugar**
1/2 **teaspoon chili powder**
1/2 **teaspoon garlic salt**
2 **tablespoons grated Parmesan cheese**
1 **tablespoon minced fresh parsley**

In a large skillet or Dutch oven, cook turkey in oil over medium heat until no longer pink. Add the celery, onion, green pepper and garlic; cook until vegetables are tender. Remove the turkey and vegetables with a slotted spoon and keep warm.

Add chicken broth to the pan; bring to a boil. Add bow tie pasta; cook for 10 minutes or until tender. Reduce heat; stir in the stewed tomatoes, vinegar, sugar, chili powder, garlic salt and turkey mixture. Simmer for 10 minutes or until heated through. Sprinkle with Parmesan cheese and fresh parsley.

Yield: 6 servings.

All About Ground Turkey

This stovetop recipe combines ground turkey, pasta, green pepper, tomatoes and more into one satisfying dish. It's a hearty meal in itself!

Just like beef cuts that are ground into hamburger, turkey can be ground and used in the same way. Ground turkey consists of white or dark turkey meat, or a combination of both. It contains less fat than ground beef.

Wild Rice Turkey Dinner

Prep: 10 min. **Cook:** 7 hours

3/4	cup uncooked wild rice
1	medium butternut squash, peeled, seeded and cut into 1-inch pieces
1	medium onion, cut into 1-inch pieces
2	turkey breast tenderloins (8 ounces *each*)
3	cups chicken broth
1/2	teaspoon salt
1/2	teaspoon pepper
1/2	teaspoon dried thyme
1/2	cup dried cranberries

In a 5-qt. slow cooker, layer the rice, squash, onion and turkey. Add broth; sprinkle with salt, pepper and thyme. Cover and cook on low for 7-8 hours or until turkey juices run clear.

Remove turkey; cut into slices. Stir cranberries into rice mixture; serve with a slotted spoon. Serve with turkey.

Yield: 4 servings.

Turkey Tenderloin Substitutions

Combine wild rice, squash and cranberries with turkey tenderloins for a complete and satisfying supper that cooks all day in the slow cooker.

Turkey tenderloins are boneless breast meat available in the meat case of most grocery stores. Use them as you would boneless skinless chicken breasts. Can't find turkey breast tenderloins? Turkey breast slices or strips can be used instead.

Turkey with Orange Sauce

Prep/Total Time: 15 min.

✓ Uses less fat, sugar or salt. Includes Nutrition Facts and Diabetic Exchanges.

> 1 **pound turkey breast tenderloins**
> 1/2 **teaspoon salt,** *divided*
> 1/4 **teaspoon pepper**
> 2 **teaspoons cornstarch**
> 1 **tablespoon brown sugar**
> 1 **cup orange juice**
> 1-1/2 **teaspoons lemon juice**
> 2 **teaspoons butter**

Sprinkle turkey with 1/4 teaspoon salt and pepper; place in a microwave-safe 11-in. x 7-in. x 2-in. dish. Cover, venting one corner, and microwave on high for 4 minutes. Turn turkey over; cover and microwave 1-2 minutes longer or until turkey is no longer pink and a meat thermometer reads 170°.

In a microwave-safe bowl, combine the cornstarch, brown sugar, orange juice, lemon juice, butter and remaining salt. Microwave, uncovered, on high for 1-2 minutes or until thickened; stir until smooth. Serve with turkey.

Yield: 4 servings.

Editor's Note: This recipe was tested with an 850-watt microwave.

Nutrition Facts: 4 ounces cooked turkey with 1/4 cup sauce equals 189 calories, 3 g fat (1 g saturated fat), 75 mg cholesterol, 370 mg sodium, 11 g carbohydrate, trace fiber, 28 g protein. **Diabetic Exchanges:** 4 very lean meat, 1 fruit.

Reach for the Fruit

Fill cantaloupe wedges with gelatin and fruit for a fun, refreshing dessert. Cut one melon in half lengthwise from bud to stem end; discard seeds. Cut a thin slice off the bottom of each half so melon sits level; pat dry.

In a bowl, dissolve 1 package (3 ounces) strawberry banana gelatin in 1 cup boiling water. Stir in 1/2 cup unsweetened applesauce and 1 cup sliced fresh strawberries. Pour into melon halves (discard any remaining gelatin mixture). Cover with plastic wrap and refrigerate overnight. Just before serving, slice each melon half into three wedges.

Veggie Turkey Casserole

Prep: 10 min. **Bake:** 30 min.

- 3 **cups cubed cooked turkey**
- 2 **cups frozen mixed vegetables**
- 2 **cups frozen broccoli florets**
- 1 **can (10-3/4 ounces) condensed cream of chicken soup, undiluted**
- 1 **can (10-3/4 ounces) condensed cream of mushroom soup, undiluted**
- 1/2 **cup chopped onion**
- 1/4 **teaspoon garlic powder**
- 1/4 **teaspoon celery seed**

In a large bowl, combine all the ingredients. Transfer to a greased 11-in. x 7-in. x 2-in. baking dish. Bake, uncovered, at 350° for 30-35 minutes or until heated through. Stir before serving.

Yield: 4 servings.

Keep Casserole On Hand

You can rely on canned goods, frozen vegetables and leftover turkey to hurry along the preparation of this creamy main dish. Serve the casserole with homemade or refrigerated biscuits for a down-home meal your family will surely love.

Cooked poultry casseroles can be refrigerated for 3 to 4 days or frozen for up to 6 months, so you can make the dish ahead and have it on hand for an especially busy weeknight.

Taste of Home's Weeknight Cooking Made Easy

Turkey Quesadillas

Prep/Total Time: 20 min.

✓ Uses less fat, sugar or salt. Includes Nutrition Facts and Diabetic Exchanges.

- **1 pound lean ground turkey**
- **1 cup chopped red onion**
- **1 to 2 garlic cloves, minced**
- **2 cups julienned zucchini**
- **1 cup salsa**
- **1 cup frozen corn**
- **1 cup julienned sweet red pepper**
- **1 can (4 ounces) chopped green chilies**
- **2 tablespoons minced fresh cilantro**
- **1/2 teaspoon dried oregano**
- **1/2 teaspoon ground cumin**
- **1/4 teaspoon salt**
- **1/8 teaspoon cayenne pepper**
- **8 flour tortillas (8 inches)**
- **2 cups (8 ounces) shredded reduced-fat Mexican cheese blend**

In a nonstick skillet, cook turkey, onion and garlic over medium heat until meat is no longer pink; drain. Add zucchini, salsa, corn, red pepper and chilies. Reduce heat; cover and simmer until vegetables are tender. Stir in seasonings.

For each quesadilla, place one tortilla in an ungreased nonstick skillet. Sprinkle with 1-1/2 cups turkey mixture and 1/4 cup cheese; cover with another tortilla. Cook over medium heat, carefully turning once, until lightly browned on both sides and cheese begins to melt. Cut into eight wedges.

Yield: 4 quesadillas (8 wedges each).

Nutrition Facts: 2 wedges equals 179 calories, 7 g fat (2 g saturated fat), 32 mg cholesterol, 388 mg sodium, 18 g carbohydrate, 1 g fiber, 12 g protein. **Diabetic Exchanges:** 2 starch, 2 lean meat, 1-1/2 fat.

Pleasing Mexican Specialty

These tasty wedges are chock-full of seasoned ground turkey, zucchini, corn, red pepper, green chilies and cheese. They're sure to be popular with your whole family. Plus, they're a snap to prepare on busy weeknights!

Feel free to use fresh corn for the frozen corn called for if you have it on hand. Cut the kernels from 2 medium ears of corn to equal 1 cup.

Fried rice would complement the quesadillas. So would sliced fresh tomatos and cucumbers drizzled with a light vinaigrette.

Zesty Apricot Turkey

Prep/Total Time: 20 min.

☑ Uses less fat, sugar or salt. Includes
Nutrition Facts and Diabetic Exchanges.

- 1/3 **cup reduced-sugar apricot preserves**
- 1 **tablespoon white wine vinegar**
- 1 **tablespoon honey**
- 1/2 **teaspoon grated lemon peel**
- 1 **garlic clove, minced**
- 1/8 **teaspoon hot pepper sauce**
- 1 **boneless skinless turkey breast half (1 pound)**

In a microwave-safe dish, combine the first six ingredients. Microwave, uncovered, on high for 1-2 minutes or until the preserves are melted. Stir to blend. Set aside half to serve with turkey.

Prepare grill for indirect heat. Grill turkey, covered, over indirect medium heat for 3 minutes on each side. Baste with 1 tablespoon reserved apricot sauce. Grill 7-10 minutes longer or until a meat thermometer reads 170°. Slice turkey; serve with reserved apricot sauce.

Yield: 4 servings.

Nutrition Facts: 4 ounces equals 193 calories, 1 g fat (1 g saturated fat), 70 mg cholesterol, 62 mg sodium, 17 g carbohydrate, 1 g fiber, 28 g protein. **Diabetic Exchanges:** 3 lean meat, 1/2 fruit.

How to Thaw Poultry

Zesty Apricot Turkey is bound to be the centerpiece of any backyard barbecue. The turkey's fruity coating gets a little kick from hot pepper sauce...and would be a nice complement to other meats, too.

Never defrost frozen poultry at room temperature. Thaw in the refrigerator, in cold water or in a microwave. Cold-water thawing is an option that takes less time than thawing in the refrigerator but requires more attention. The poultry must be in a leak-proof bag. Submerge the wrapped poultry in cold tap water. Change the water every 30 minutes until thawed.

Turkey Pasta Soup

Prep/Total Time: 30 min.

✓ Uses less fat, sugar or salt. Includes Nutrition Facts and Diabetic Exchanges.

- 1 **cup uncooked small pasta shells**
- 1 **pound lean ground turkey**
- 2 **medium onions, chopped**
- 2 **garlic cloves, minced**
- 3 **cans (14-1/2 ounces *each*) reduced-sodium chicken broth**
- 2 **cans (15 ounces *each*) white kidney *or* cannellini beans, rinsed and drained**
- 2 **cans (14-1/2 ounces *each*) Italian stewed tomatoes**
- 2 **teaspoons dried oregano**
- 2 **teaspoons dried basil**
- 1 **teaspoon fennel seed, crushed**
- 1 **teaspoon pepper**
- 1/2 **teaspoon salt**
- 1/4 **teaspoon crushed red pepper flakes**

Cook pasta according to package directions. Meanwhile, in a large soup kettle, cook the turkey, onions and garlic over medium heat until meat is no longer pink; drain. Stir in the broth, beans, tomatoes and seasonings. Bring to a boil. Reduce heat; simmer, uncovered, for 10 minutes. Drain pasta and add to the soup. Cook 5 minutes longer or until heated through.

Yield: 10 servings.

Nutrition Facts: 1-1/3 cups equals 211 calories, 4 g fat (1 g saturated fat), 36 mg cholesterol, 868 mg sodium, 28 g carbohydrate, 6 g fiber, 15 g protein. **Diabetic Exchanges:** 2 very lean meat, 2 vegetable, 1 starch.

Chop Extra Onions

Eating right on hectic weeknights just got a little easier, thanks to Turkey Pasta Soup. The low-fat turkey and high-protein beans make it as nutritious as it is filling.

The recipe calls for chopping two medium onions. Dice a few extra and spread them on a baking sheet. Cover the sheet and place it in your freezer. Once frozen, store the onions in a resealable storage bag in the freezer for up to 8 months. You can follow the same method for green and sweet red peppers as well as jalapenos.

Italian Turkey Burgers

Prep/Total Time: 25 min.

✓ Uses less fat, sugar or salt. Includes
Nutrition Facts and Diabetic Exchanges.

- 1/4 **cup canned crushed tomatoes**
- 2 **tablespoons grated Parmesan cheese**
- 1/2 **teaspoon garlic powder**
- 1/2 **teaspoon dried oregano**
- 1/4 **teaspoon salt**
- 1/4 **teaspoon pepper**
- 1 **pound lean ground turkey**
- 8 **slices Italian bread, toasted**
- 1/2 **cup meatless spaghetti sauce, warmed**

In a large bowl, combine the first six ingredients. Crumble turkey over mixture and mix well. Shape into four 3/4-in.-thick patties.

Coat grill rack with nonstick cooking spray before starting the grill. Grill patties, uncovered, over medium heat for 6-8 minutes on each side or until a meat thermometer reads 165°.

Place a patty on each of four slices of bread. Drizzle with spaghetti sauce; top with remaining bread.

Yield: 4 servings.

Nutrition Facts: One sandwich equals 306 calories, 12 g fat (3 g saturated fat), 92 mg cholesterol, 680 mg sodium, 24 g carbohydrate, 2 g fiber, 25 g protein. **Diabetic Exchanges:** 3 lean meat, 1-1/2 starch, 1 fat.

Greasing a Grill

Seasoned with oregano and Parmesan cheese, these plump turkey burgers served on crusty Italian bread with warmed spaghetti sauce are a delicious change-of-pace entree.

Spray the food grate with nonstick cooking spray before starting the grill. Never spray directly over the fire (gas or coal) as you can cause a fire.

To grease an already hot grate, fold a paper towel into a small pad. Holding the pad with long-handled tongs, dip in vegetable oil and rub over the grate. Clean the grate with a stiff wire brush after cooking.

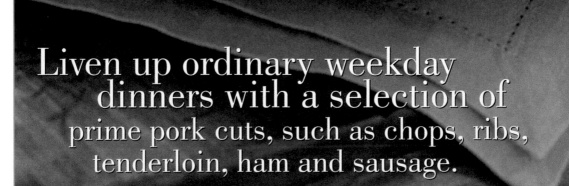

Sweet 'n' Sour Ribs (p. 188)

Liven up ordinary weekday
dinners with a selection of
prime pork cuts, such as chops, ribs,
tenderloin, ham and sausage.

Pleasing Pork

Pasta Sausage Supper (p. 176)

Weeknight Pork Chops

Prep/Total Time: 20 min.

4   bone-in pork loin chops
    (8 ounces *each*)
1   tablespoon vegetable oil
1/4   cup seedless strawberry
    jam
2   tablespoons cider vinegar
1   tablespoon prepared
    mustard

In a large skillet, cook pork chops in oil over medium-high heat for 2-3 minutes on each side. Reduce heat; cook, uncovered, for 10-15 minutes or until meat juices run clear.

In a small microwave-safe bowl, combine the jam, vinegar and mustard. Cover and microwave on high for 20-25 seconds or until heated through. Serve over pork chops.

Yield: 4 servings.

Shopping for Pork

For a speedy but simply scrumptious meal, make Weeknight Pork Chops. While the chops sizzle on the stovetop, you can quickly mix together the mustard, vinegar and strawberry jam and heat it in the microwave. This colorful sauce is delicious served over the pan-cooked pork chops.

Purchase pork before the "sell by" date on the packaging for the best quality. Make sure the package is cold and has no holes or tears.

Tortilla Burgers

Prep/Total Time: 25 min.

1   teaspoon ground cumin
1/2   teaspoon dried oregano
1/2   teaspoon crushed red pepper flakes
1/4   teaspoon seasoned salt
1   pound ground pork
4   flour *or* corn tortillas (6 inches), warmed
Salsa, sour cream and shredded cheddar cheese, optional

In a small bowl, combine the first four ingredients. Crumble pork over seasonings and mix well. Shape into four patties.

Grill, covered, over medium heat for 6-7 minutes on each side or until meat is no longer pink. Serve on tortillas with salsa, sour cream and cheese if desired.

Yield: 4 servings.

Tasty Toppings For Burgers

With pork instead of ground beef and tortillas in place of buns, these grilled Southwestern-style burgers stand out from all others.

Set out a platter of condiments so family members can pile on their own favorite toppings. Traditional additions include lettuce and tomato and onion slices. But don't forget about the salsa, pickled jalapeno slices, guacamole, sour cream and shredded cheddar cheese!

Super Supper Hero

Prep/Total Time: 20 min.

2-1/2 cups cubed eggplant
    1 cup thinly sliced red onion
    1 cup *each* julienned green, sweet yellow and red peppers
  1/4 cup olive oil
  1/2 cup chopped tomato
    1 teaspoon dried oregano
  1/2 teaspoon salt
  1/4 teaspoon pepper
    1 unsliced loaf (1 pound) Italian bread
Lettuce leaves
  1/2 pound sliced fully cooked ham
  1/2 pound sliced cooked turkey breast
  1/4 pound sliced hard salami
    8 slices part-skim mozzarella cheese (8 ounces)

In a large skillet, saute the eggplant, onion and peppers in oil for 5 minutes or until vegetables are crisp-tender. Add the tomato, oregano, salt and pepper. Remove from the heat and set aside.

Cut bread in half lengthwise; hollow out the bottom, leaving a 3/4-in. shell (discard removed bread or save for another use). Layer with lettuce, ham, turkey, salami and cheese. Top with sauteed vegetables. Replace bread top. Secure with toothpicks; cut into slices.

Yield: 4-6 servings.

Super Sandwich For Supper

Super Supper Hero is so versatile. You can serve it with the works or just your family's favorite meats, vegetables and cheeses. It's a hearty, in-hand meal.

Dress up a package of shoestring potatoes to serve with the sandwich. Just combine 1/2 cup grated Parmesan cheese, 2 teaspoons Italian seasoning and 1/2 teaspoon salt. Sprinkle over the baked fries and mix gently.

Kielbasa Biscuit Pizza

Prep: 15 min. **Bake:** 35 min.

- 2 tubes (12 ounces *each*) refrigerated buttermilk biscuits
- 2-1/2 cups garden-style spaghetti sauce
- 1/2 pound smoked kielbasa *or* Polish sausage, cubed
- 1 can (8 ounces) mushroom stems and pieces, drained
- 1/2 cup chopped green pepper
- 1/2 cup chopped sweet red pepper
- 1 cup (4 ounces) shredded part-skim mozzarella cheese
- 1 cup (4 ounces) shredded cheddar cheese

Separate biscuits; cut each biscuit into fourths. Arrange in a greased 13-in. x 9-in. x 2-in. baking dish (do not flatten). Bake at 375° for 12-15 minutes or until biscuits begin to brown.

Spread spaghetti sauce over biscuit crust. Sprinkle with the sausage, mushrooms, peppers and cheeses. Bake for 20-25 minutes or until bubbly and cheese is melted. Let stand for 5 minutes before cutting.

Yield: 8 servings.

Deliciously Different Pizza

This is a quick and tasty pizza that your family will love. It's a bit different than most because it's made with refrigerated buttermilk biscuits instead of pizza dough and in a 9 x 13 pan. Kielbasa, mushrooms, peppers and cheese are the pleasing toppings. Since it serves eight, it's great for a large family or when having company.

The recipe calls for 1 cup each of shredded mozzarella and cheddar cheese. Many grocery stores carry shredded pizza cheese, which conveniently combines the two.

Jamaican Pork Tenderloin

Prep: 10 min. + marinating **Grill:** 20 min.

- 1/3 cup orange juice
- 1/3 cup reduced-sodium soy sauce
- 3 tablespoons lemon juice
- 2 tablespoons olive oil
- 1 large onion, chopped
- 1 cup chopped green onions
- 1 jalapeno pepper
- 3 tablespoons minced fresh thyme *or* 2 teaspoons dried thyme
- 3/4 teaspoon salt
- 3/4 teaspoon *each* ground allspice, cinnamon and nutmeg
- 1/4 teaspoon ground ginger
- 1/4 teaspoon pepper
- 2 pork tenderloins (1 pound *each*)

In a food processor, combine the orange juice, soy sauce, lemon juice, oil, onions, jalapeno, thyme, salt, allspice, cinnamon, nutmeg, ginger and pepper. Cover and process until smooth. Pour into a large resealable plastic bag; add the pork. Seal bag and turn to coat; refrigerate overnight.

Drain and discard marinade. Coat grill rack with nonstick cooking spray before starting grill. Prepare grill for indirect heat. Grill, covered, over indirect medium-hot heat for 20-25 minutes or until a meat thermometer reads 160°. Let stand 5 minutes.

Yield: 6 servings.

Editor's Note: When cutting or seeding hot peppers, use rubber or plastic gloves to protect your hands. Avoid touching your face.

Pork Tenderloin Particulars

A spicy citrus marinade adds plenty of flavor to this tenderloin overnight. Then you can grill the meat in just minutes the next day.

When buying pork tenderloin, look for meat that's firm and grayish pink in color. For the best flavor and tenderness, the meat should have a small amount of marbling. Don't overcook lean, fresh pork; it cooks quickly and becomes dry and tough. Pork is done at 160°.

Sweet-Sour Franks

Prep/Total Time: 25 min.

1 can (20 ounces) pineapple tidbits
1 teaspoon beef bouillon granules
1/3 cup boiling water
1 tablespoon cornstarch
1 tablespoon brown sugar
2 tablespoons cider vinegar
1 tablespoon soy sauce
1 medium onion, chopped
1 medium green pepper, julienned
2 tablespoons butter
5 hot dogs, halved lengthwise and cut into 1/2-inch slices
3 cups hot cooked rice

Drain pineapple, reserving juice. Set aside 1 cup pineapple and 6 tablespoons juice; refrigerate remaining pineapple and juice for another use. Dissolve bouillon in water. In a small bowl, combine the cornstarch, brown sugar, vinegar, soy sauce, bouillon and reserved juice until smooth; set aside.

In a large skillet, saute the onion and green pepper in butter. Stir cornstarch mixture; stir into skillet. Bring to a boil; cook and stir for 2 minutes or until thickened. Add the hot dogs and reserved pineapple; cook until heated through. Serve over rice.

Yield: 3 servings.

A Word on Sweet-Sour

While many are familiar with sweet-and-sour pork, sweet-and-sour sauce is used to flavor a number of stir-fried meats, such as beef and chicken. Here, hot dogs are used, with family-pleasing results. It also makes an excellent dipping sauce.

The "sweet" in sweet-and-sour sauce comes from either white or brown sugar. As for the "sour," this is achieved by adding vinegar. You can vary the quantities of sugar and/or vinegar in this recipe to either increase or reduce the sweetness of the sauce.

Curly Noodle Pork Supper

Prep/Total Time: 25 min.

1 pound pork tenderloin, cut into 1/4-inch strips
1 medium sweet red pepper, cut into 1-inch pieces
1 cup fresh broccoli florets
4 green onions, cut into 1-inch pieces
1 tablespoon vegetable oil
1-1/2 cups water
2 packages (3 ounces *each*) pork ramen noodles
1 tablespoon minced fresh parsley
1 tablespoon soy sauce

In a large skillet, cook the pork, red pepper, broccoli and onions in oil until meat is no longer pink; drain. Add the water, noodles with contents of seasoning packets, parsley and soy sauce. Bring to a boil. Reduce heat; cook for 3-4 minutes or until the noodles are tender.

Yield: 3-4 servings.

Slicing Pork Tenderloin

This hearty meal-in-one is loaded with tender pork strips and ramen noodles. Broccoli and red pepper add a bounty of fresh-from-the-garden flavor that will bring 'em back for seconds.

Cut the pork tenderloin while it's still partially frozen into thin, even slices, then cut the slices into strips. You can even use pork tenderloin strips in place of beef or chicken in your favorite fajitas.

Au Gratin Ham Potpie

Prep: 15 min. **Bake:** 40 min.

- 1 package (4.9 ounces) au gratin potatoes
- 1-1/2 cups boiling water
- 2 cups frozen peas and carrots
- 1-1/2 cups cubed fully cooked ham
- 1 can (10-3/4 ounces) condensed cream of chicken soup, undiluted
- 1 can (4 ounces) mushroom stems and pieces, drained
- 1/2 cup milk
- 1/2 cup sour cream
- 1 jar (2 ounces) diced pimientos, drained
- 1 sheet refrigerated pie pastry

In a large bowl, combine the potatoes, contents of sauce mix, boiling water, peas and carrots, ham, soup, mushrooms, milk, sour cream and pimientos. Pour into an ungreased 2-qt. round baking dish.

Roll out pastry to fit top of dish; place over potato mixture. Flute edges; cut slits in pastry. Bake at 400° for 40-45 minutes or until golden brown. Let stand for 5 minutes before serving.

Yield: 4-6 servings.

Dig into Comfort Food!

Potpies are down-home comfort food at its very finest…and this recipe is no exception! Ham, au gratin potatoes, peas, carrots and mushrooms in a sour cream sauce all under a flaky pastry crust—who wouldn't want to dig in?

To flute the potpie's edges, position your thumb and index finger about 1 inch apart on the edge of the crust, pointed out. Position the index finger on your other hand between the two fingers and gently push the pastry toward the center in an upward direction. Continue around the edge.

Scalloped Potatoes with Ham

Prep/Total Time: 30 min.

4 medium potatoes, peeled
and thinly sliced
2 tablespoons butter
1/3 cup water
1/2 cup milk
2 to 3 tablespoons dry
onion soup mix
3 tablespoons minced fresh
parsley
1 cup cubed process cheese
(Velveeta)
1 cup cubed fully cooked
ham

In a large skillet, cook potatoes in butter until potatoes are evenly coated. Add water; bring to a boil. Reduce heat; cover and simmer for 14-15 minutes or until potatoes are tender.

Meanwhile, in a small bowl, combine the milk, soup mix and parsley; stir in cheese. Pour over potatoes. Add ham; cook and stir gently over medium heat until cheese is melted and sauce is smooth.

Yield: 4 servings.

Make Ham on Weekend for Weekday Meals

This saucy skillet dish is great for when you're running late because it takes so little time to prepare.

Bake a large ham on the weekend, and you'll likely have leftovers. Leftover ham can be refrigerated for 3 to 5 days or frozen for 2 months. Cubed, it's perfect to use in fuss-free recipes like this one, or in soups, casseroles, stir-fries and more.

Breaded Pork Roll-Ups

Prep/Total Time: 20 min.

        1   egg
      1/3   cup milk
    1-1/4   cups dry bread crumbs
        1   teaspoon seasoned salt
        4   boneless pork loin chops (1/4 inch thick
            and 4 ounces *each*)
        4   thin slices deli ham
        2   tablespoons vegetable oil

In a shallow bowl, lightly beat egg and milk. In another shallow bowl, combine bread crumbs and seasoned salt. Flatten pork chops to 1/8-in. thickness; place a ham slice on each. Fold sides and ends over ham and roll up; secure each with a toothpick. Dip roll-ups in egg mixture, then roll in crumbs.

In a large skillet, cook the pork chops in oil over medium heat for 2-3 minutes on each side or until chops are lightly browned. Cook, uncovered, 10-12 minutes longer or until meat is no longer pink, turning occasionally. Discard toothpicks.

Yield: 4 servings.

Fare Looks Like You Fussed

Pretty swirls of ham and a golden coating make this delightful main course perfect for company. Add a few tablespoons Parmesan cheese to the bread crumbs for even more flavor.

Toss together raisin coleslaw to serve with the roll-ups. In a small bowl, combine 1/2 cup mayonnaise, 1-1/2 teaspoons honey, 3/4 teaspoon sugar, 3/4 teaspoon prepared mustard and 1/8 teaspoon celery salt. In a serving bowl, toss 2 cups shredded cabbage, 1 cup grated carrots and 1/2 cup golden raisins. Add mayonnaise mixture and stir to coat. Cover and refrigerate until serving. Serves four.

Lime-Glazed Pork Chops

Prep/Total Time: 25 min.

☑ Uses less fat, sugar or salt. Includes Nutrition Facts and Diabetic Exchanges.

- 1/3 cup orange marmalade
- 1 jalapeno pepper, seeded and finely chopped
- 2 tablespoons lime juice
- 1 teaspoon grated fresh gingerroot
- 4 bone-in pork loin chops (8 ounces *each*)
- 4 teaspoons minced fresh cilantro

Lime wedges

For glaze, in a small saucepan, combine the marmalade, jalapeno, lime juice and ginger. Cook and stir over medium heat for 5 minutes or until marmalade is melted. Remove from heat; set aside.

Coat grill rack with nonstick cooking spray before starting the grill. Grill pork chops, covered, over medium heat for 6-7 minutes on each side or until juices run clear, brushing with glaze during the last 5 minutes of grilling. Sprinkle with cilantro and serve with lime wedges.

Yield: 4 servings.

Editor's Note: When cutting or seeding hot peppers, use rubber or plastic gloves to protect your hands. Avoid touching your face.

Nutrition Facts: One pork chop equals 286 calories, 8 g fat (3 g saturated fat), 86 mg cholesterol, 85 mg sodium, 18 g carbohydrate, 1 g fiber, 34 g protein. **Diabetic Exchanges:** 4 lean meat, 1 fruit.

Citrus Glaze Is Great!

A wonderful sweet-sour citrus glaze makes these tender pork chops tangy and tasty.

When buying bone-in pork chops, try to find cuts at least 3/4 inch or thicker. The meat closest to the bone takes longer to cook, so thinner chops tend to overcook and dry out before the area by the bone is cooked.

Brush on thick or sweet glazes during the last 5 to 10 minutes of grilling, basting and turning every few minutes to prevent burning.

Cheesy Ham Tortellini

Prep/Total Time: 30 min.

1   package (19 ounces)
    frozen cheese tortellini
1   jar (17 ounces) Alfredo
    sauce
1   package (16 ounces)
    frozen California-blend
    vegetables, thawed
2   cups cubed fully cooked
    ham
1/3 cup grated Parmesan
    cheese
1   tablespoon minced fresh
    parsley

Cook tortellini according to package directions. Meanwhile, in a large saucepan, combine the Alfredo sauce, vegetables and ham. Bring to a boil over medium heat. Reduce heat; cover and simmer for 15-20 minutes or until vegetables are crisp-tender.

Drain tortellini; add to sauce. Stir in Parmesan cheese; cook until heated through. Sprinkle with parsley.

Yield: 6 servings.

Make the Most Of Leftovers

Trying to finish up leftover ham? This creamy skillet supper is colorful as well as quick to make.

Using up leftover food helps save money because your family can enjoy two meals from one main dish. Creating a meal from leftovers saves precious minutes because it takes advantage of items that are already cooked. Best of all, time-saving dishes like the one here can be so taste-tempting, no one will realize they're eating leftovers!

Kielbasa with Baked Beans

Prep/Total Time: 20 min.

1/2 cup chopped onion
1 tablespoon butter
2 teaspoons vegetable oil
1 pound smoked kielbasa *or* Polish sausage, cut into 1/8-inch slices
1 can (28 ounces) pork and beans
1 cup ketchup
2 tablespoons Worcestershire sauce
1 tablespoon steak sauce

In a large skillet, saute the onion in butter and oil until tender. Add sausage; cook for 2-3 minutes or until browned, stirring occasionally. Drain. Stir in the remaining ingredients. Bring to a boil. Reduce heat; cover and simmer for 10 minutes or until heated through.

Yield: 4 servings.

Not Just a Side Dish

If you like pork and beans alongside sandwiches and more, you'll love these kielbasa and beans as a hearty main dish! The saucy, one-skillet supper can be on the table in just 20 minutes and would be delicious served with warm slices of corn bread.

Kielbasa is a generic term for Polish sausage. It comes in dozens of flavors and can be smoked or fresh. Kielbasa is usually sold in medium rings about 18 inches long and 1-1/2 inches thick.

Chili Verde

Prep/Total Time: 15 min.

2 cups cubed cooked pork (about 1 pound)
1 can (16 ounces) kidney beans, rinsed and drained
1 can (15 ounces) pinto beans, rinsed and drained
1 can (15 ounces) chili with beans, undrained
1 can (14-1/2 ounces) stewed tomatoes
1-1/2 to 2 cups green salsa
1 large onion, chopped
2 cans (4 ounces *each*) chopped green chilies
2 garlic cloves, minced
1 tablespoon minced fresh cilantro
2 teaspoons ground cumin

In a large saucepan, combine all of the ingredients. Bring to a boil. Reduce heat; simmer, uncovered, for 10 minutes or until heated through.

Yield: 8 servings.

The Goods on Green Salsa

Leftover pork adds heartiness to this zippy chili that's great on a cool night with a stack of tortillas.

This recipe calls for green salsa, which is made from tomatillos—a green, tomato-like fruit with a papery outer husk. They have a lemon-herb flavor and are used in Mexican cooking. Look for green salsa in the ethnic aisle of most grocery stores.

Pork Soft-Shell Tacos

Prep/Total Time: 20 min.

☑ Uses less fat, sugar or salt. Includes Nutrition Facts and Diabetic Exchanges.

- 1 pork tenderloin (1 pound), cut into 1-inch strips
- 1 small onion, chopped
- 1 teaspoon canola oil

MOLE SAUCE:

- 2/3 cup enchilada sauce
- 1 tablespoon dry roasted peanuts
- 1 tablespoon semisweet chocolate chips
- 1 tablespoon raisins
- 1 garlic clove, minced
- 1 teaspoon ground cumin
- 1/4 teaspoon crushed red pepper flakes
- 1/2 cup frozen corn, thawed
- 8 corn tortillas (6 inches), warmed
- 1 cup shredded lettuce
- 1/4 cup reduced-fat sour cream
- 1/4 cup sliced green onions

What Is Mole Sauce?

Mole is a dark-brown Mexican sauce generally made from dry chilies, nuts, spices, vegetables, chocolate and seasonings. The chocolate contributes richness to the sauce without adding overt sweetness to it.

If you're short on time, don't make the sauce from scratch. It's available in jars in the ethnic section of most grocery stores.

In a large nonstick skillet or wok, stir-fry pork and onion in oil for 3-4 minutes or until pork is no longer pink; drain and keep warm.

In the same skillet, combine the enchilada sauce, peanuts, chocolate chips, raisins, garlic, cumin and red pepper flakes. Cook and stir over medium heat for 2-3 minutes or until chocolate is melted. Pour into a blender; cover and process until smooth. Return to skillet. Stir in corn and pork mixture; cook until heated through. Spoon pork mixture down one half of each tortilla; fold remaining side over filling. Serve with lettuce, sour cream and green onions.

Yield: 4 servings.

Nutrition Facts: 2 tacos equals 370 calories, 10 g fat (3 g saturated fat), 67 mg cholesterol, 263 mg sodium, 41 g carbohydrate, 5 g fiber, 30 g protein. **Diabetic Exchanges:** 3 lean meat, 2-1/2 starch.

Confetti Sausage 'n' Rice

Prep/Total Time: 30 min.

1 pound smoked sausage, cut into 1/2-inch slices
1 tablespoon butter
2 tablespoons chopped onion
1/4 cup chopped green pepper
1/4 cup chopped sweet red pepper
1/4 cup chopped celery
2 cups hot water
1 cup uncooked long grain rice
2/3 cup frozen peas and carrots
1 can (4 ounces) mushroom stems and pieces, drained
1/4 cup frozen corn
2 teaspoons chicken bouillon granules

In a large skillet, brown sausage in butter; remove with a slotted spoon and keep warm. In the drippings, saute the onion, peppers and celery until tender. Stir in the remaining ingredients.

Bring to a boil. Reduce heat; cover and simmer for 15 minutes or until rice is tender. Return the sausage to the pan; cook and stir until heated through.

Yield: 4 servings.

The Makings Of Sausage

Smoked sausage, green and red pepper, peas, carrots, mushrooms and rice make this dish a hearty and colorful meal-in-one.

Originally, sausage-making was a way to preserve meat trimmings left over on the butcher's table. Salt and other spices were added to help extend the shelf life. Sausage is cured either by drying, smoking or salting and is generally made from pork, but also from beef, veal, lamb, chicken, turkey and game.

Pasta Sausage Supper

Prep/Total Time: 25 min.

  1 package (16 ounces) uncooked penne pasta
  1 pound smoked kielbasa *or* Polish sausage,
     cut into 1/4-inch slices
  1 medium green pepper, julienned
  1 medium sweet red pepper, julienned
  1 medium onion, halved and sliced
  1 tablespoon vegetable oil
  1 jar (26 ounces) meatless spaghetti sauce, warmed

Cook pasta according to package directions. Meanwhile, in a large skillet, saute the sausage, peppers and onion in oil until vegetables are crisp-tender.

Drain pasta; divide among six serving plates. Top with spaghetti sauce. Using a slotted spoon, top with sausage mixture.

Yield: 6 servings.

Swift Stovetop Meal

Slices of creamy onion-garlic bread are a nice accompaniment to this saute. In a small mixing bowl, beat two 3-ounce packages of softened cream cheese, 1/4 cup softened butter, 1/4 cup grated Parmesan cheese and 1/2 teaspoon garlic powder until smooth. Beat in 8 chopped green onions. Spread over cut sides of Italian bread that has been halved lengthwise. Broil 4 inches from the heat for 3 to 4 minutes or until lightly browned.

Fajita Tortilla Bowls

Prep/Total Time: 30 min.

6   spinach tortillas
2   tablespoons butter,
      melted
1   tablespoon vegetable oil
1   pound boneless pork loin
      chops, cut into thin strips
1   envelope fajita seasoning
      mix
1   medium onion, thinly
      sliced
1   sweet red pepper, thinly
      sliced
1   green pepper, thinly sliced
4-1/2   cups shredded lettuce
1   medium tomato, chopped

Place six 10-oz. custard cups upside down in a shallow baking pan; set aside. Brush both sides of tortillas with butter; place in a single layer on ungreased baking sheets.

Bake, uncovered, at 425° for 1 minute. Place a tortilla over each custard cup, pinching sides to form a bowl shape. Bake 7-8 minutes longer or until crisp. Remove tortillas from cups to cool on wire racks.

Heat oil in a large skillet over medium-high heat. Add pork and seasoning mix; cook and stir until meat juices run clear. Remove pork with a slotted spoon. In the drippings, saute onion and peppers until crisp-tender. Place lettuce in tortilla bowls; top with pork, pepper mixture and tomato.

Yield: 6 servings.

Picking Out Peppers

When brushed with butter and baked over custard cups, spinach tortillas make crunchy "bowls" for lettuce salad topped with pork, tomatoes and peppers. If you don't own custard cups, shape aluminum foil into 4-inch-diameter balls and use them instead.

Sweet peppers are available year-round. Select firm peppers with smooth, shiny skin and bright colors. Avoid those that are shriveled or have soft spots. Rinse peppers under cold water. Remove stem, seeds and membranes (ribs). Slice according to recipe directions.

In-a-Hurry Hot Dog Dinner

Prep/Total Time: 30 min.

1 package (1 pound) hot dogs, halved lengthwise and sliced
2 tablespoons butter, *divided*
2 medium onions, halved and sliced
3 celery ribs, coarsely chopped
1 medium green pepper, julienned
1 garlic clove, minced
1 can (14-1/2 ounces) stewed tomatoes, undrained
1 teaspoon dried oregano
1/2 teaspoon paprika
1/4 teaspoon pepper
Hot cooked noodles *or* rice

In a large skillet, cook and stir hot dogs in 1 tablespoon butter over medium-high heat until lightly browned; remove hot dogs and keep warm.

In the same skillet, saute the onions, celery, green pepper and garlic in remaining butter until tender. Add the tomatoes, oregano, paprika, pepper and hot dogs. Cook and stir until heated through. Serve over noodles or rice.

Yield: 4-6 servings.

Swift Supper Stars Hot Dogs

It's so simple to combine sliced hot dogs with green pepper, onions and tomatoes for this well-seasoned entree that can be served plain or over cooked noodles or rice.

Prefer hot dogs whole in a bun? Try this trick for extra flavor without lots of effort. Pierce the franks a few times with a fork. Then marinate them in Worcestershire sauce for 30 minutes before grilling. You can even stir a little garlic and onion powder into the marinade.

Ham and Bean Soup

Prep/Total Time: 30 min.

2 medium carrots, sliced
2 celery ribs, chopped
1/2 cup chopped onion
2 tablespoons butter
4 cans (15-1/2 ounces *each*) great northern beans, rinsed and drained
4 cups chicken broth
2 cups cubed fully cooked ham
1 teaspoon chili powder
1/2 teaspoon minced garlic
1/4 teaspoon pepper
1 bay leaf

In a large saucepan, saute the carrots, celery and onion in butter until tender. Stir in the remaining ingredients; cook for 15 minutes or until heated through. Discard bay leaf before serving.

Yield: 7 servings.

Bean Soup in Brief

If you like ham and bean soup but don't want to spend hours in the kitchen cooking a batch, this tasty and timely version will leave you and your family with satisfied smiles.

You can find packages of cubed cooked ham near the processed meats in your grocery store. Fully cooked ham can be eaten without heating, such as when tossed in salads, but should generally be heated for the best flavor.

Great northern beans are grown in the Midwest and have a delicate, distinctive flavor. They can be substituted for any white beans in most recipes.

Pork Schnitzel

Prep/Total Time: 20 min.

6 boneless pork cutlets (1/2 inch thick and 4 ounces *each*)
1/2 cup all-purpose flour
2 teaspoons seasoned salt
1/2 teaspoon pepper
2 eggs
1/4 cup milk
1-1/2 cups dry bread crumbs
2 teaspoons paprika
6 tablespoons vegetable oil

DILL SAUCE:

1-1/2 cups chicken broth, *divided*
2 tablespoons all-purpose flour
1/2 teaspoon dill weed
1 cup (8 ounces) sour cream

Flatten pork cutlets to 1/4-in. thickness. In a shallow bowl, combine the flour, seasoned salt and pepper. In another bowl, beat eggs and milk. In another bowl, combine bread crumbs and paprika. Dip cutlets into flour mixture, then into egg mixture, then into crumb mixture.

In a large skillet, cook pork in oil, a few pieces at a time, for 3-4 minutes per side or until meat is no longer pink. Remove to a serving platter; keep warm.

For sauce, pour 1 cup broth into skillet, scraping bottom of pan to loosen browned bits. Combine flour and remaining broth until smooth; stir into skillet. Bring to a boil; cook and stir for 2 minutes or until thickened. Reduce heat. Stir in dill and sour cream; heat through (do not boil). Pour over pork.

Yield: 6 servings.

All Will Enjoy Ethnic Fare

German for "cutlet," schnitzel is a cut of meat—usually veal, pork or turkey—that has been flattened, dipped in egg, breaded and fried.

You don't have to be German, though, to enjoy this great-tasting dish! A creamy dill sauce dresses it up nicely, making it delicious fare for company, too. Serve it with mashed potatoes...cinnamon applesauce...or even some sauerkraut!

Creamy Bratwurst Stew

Prep: 20 min. **Cook:** 7-1/2 hours

    4   medium potatoes, cubed
    2   medium carrots, coarsely chopped
    2   celery ribs, chopped
    1   cup chopped onion
  3/4   cup chopped green pepper
    2   pounds fresh bratwurst links, cut into 1-inch slices
  1/2   cup chicken broth
    1   teaspoon salt
    1   teaspoon dried basil
  1/2   teaspoon pepper
    2   cups half-and-half cream
    3   tablespoons cornstarch
    3   teaspoons cold water

In a 5-qt. slow cooker, combine the potatoes, carrots, celery, onion and green pepper. Top with bratwurst slices. Combine the broth, salt, basil and pepper; pour over top. Cover and cook on low for 6-7 hours or until the vegetables are tender and the sausage is no longer pink.

Stir in cream. Combine cornstarch and water until smooth; stir into stew. Cover and cook on high for 30 minutes or until gravy is thickened.

Yield: 8 servings.

The Basics of Bratwurst

A rich sauce coats this hearty combination of potatoes, carrots and bratwurst chunks that conveniently cooks in a slow cooker. This stew would be so comforting on a cold winter evening along with a crusty loaf of bread.

Bratwurst is a German sausage made of pork and veal and seasoned with a variety of spices, including ginger, nutmeg and coriander or caraway. Bratwurst is sometimes available precooked but is generally sold fresh and must be fully cooked before eating.

Apple-Ham Grilled Cheese

Prep/Total Time: 20 min.

1 cup chopped tart apples
1/3 cup mayonnaise
1/4 cup finely chopped walnuts
8 slices process American cheese
8 slices sourdough bread
4 slices fully cooked ham
1/4 cup butter, softened

Combine apples, mayonnaise and walnuts. Place a slice of cheese on four slices of bread. Layer each with 1/3 cup of the apple mixture, a slice of ham and another slice of cheese; cover with remaining bread.

Butter the outsides of the sandwiches. Cook in a large skillet over medium heat on each side until bread is golden brown and cheese is melted.

Yield: 4 servings.

A New Kind of Grilled Cheese

Is your gang tired of the same-old grilled cheese? Give this deliciously different recipe a try! The addition of an apple-mayo-walnut filling makes these stand out from the rest.

Or try raspberry grilled cheese. On four slices of bread, spread 1/4 cup preserves, then top with 1/4 cup pecans, 2 to 4 tablespoons sliced green onions and 8 slices Muenster or baby Swiss cheese. Top each with another slice of bread; butter outsides of bread. Cook in a skillet for 3 to 4 minutes on each side or until golden brown.

Garden Ham 'n' Noodles

Prep/Total Time: 30 min.

4 cups water

6 cups uncooked wide egg
noodles

2 medium carrots, diced

1 medium zucchini, halved
and thinly sliced

1 cup heavy whipping
cream

1 cup milk

1/2 to 1 teaspoon salt

1/2 pound fully cooked ham,
cubed

1 can (15-1/4 ounces) whole kernel corn, drained

1 cup shredded Parmesan cheese

In a Dutch oven, bring water to a boil. Add the noodles, carrots
and zucchini. Cook for 7-8 minutes or until the noodles and vegetables are tender.

Meanwhile, in a large skillet, combine the cream, milk and salt;
bring to a boil. Reduce heat; simmer, uncovered, for 5 minutes
or until thickened. Stir in ham and corn; cook until mixture is
heated through.

Drain noodle mixture; stir into ham mixture. Sprinkle with
Parmesan cheese and toss to coat.

Yield: 6-8 servings.

The Dirt on Carrots

This blend of ingredients
makes a very filling and
comforting dish. It would
be especially good in the
summer when there's an
abundance of fresh zucchini and carrots.

Select only crisp, firm,
smooth, well-shaped car-
rots with deep orange col-
or. Trim the tops and roots
when present. Young car-
rots may be used unpeeled
if they are well scrubbed;
larger carrots should be
thinly peeled with a veg-
etable peeler. Two medi-
um carrots equals 1 cup
sliced or shredded.

Spaghetti Squash Supper

Prep/Total Time: 30 min.

1 medium spaghetti squash
   (3 to 3-1/2 pounds)
1/2 cup water
1 pound bulk Italian
   sausage
1 medium onion, chopped
1 medium green pepper,
   chopped
1 small zucchini, chopped
1 garlic clove, minced
1 can (15-1/2 ounces) great
   northern beans, rinsed
   and drained
1 can (14-1/2 ounces) Italian stewed tomatoes
1 teaspoon Italian seasoning
1/4 teaspoon seasoned salt
Shredded Parmesan cheese

Halve squash lengthwise and discard seeds. Pierce skin with a fork or knife; place cut side down in a microwave-safe dish. Add the water; cover and microwave on high for 10-15 minutes or until squash is tender. Let stand for 5 minutes.

Meanwhile, in a large skillet, cook sausage until no longer pink; drain. Add the onion, green pepper, zucchini and garlic. Cook, uncovered, for 8-10 minutes or until the vegetables are crisp-tender, stirring occasionally; drain. Add the beans, tomatoes, Italian seasoning and salt. Cover and simmer for 10 minutes or until heated through.

Using a fork, scoop out the spaghetti squash strands; place in a serving dish. Top with sausage mixture. Sprinkle with Parmesan cheese.

Yield: 6 servings.

New Twist on Spaghetti

Here is a deliciously different way to serve "spaghetti." This meal is loaded with vegetables and flavor. For a change of pace, you can substitute ground beef or turkey for the Italian sausage. For chili lovers, season it with cumin and chili powder.

Drain, rinse and pat cooked pork sausage dry with paper towels before using in a recipe to cut calories and fat.

Hearty Baked Potatoes

Prep/Total Time: 15 min.

    4 large baking potatoes (about 3 pounds)
2-1/2 cups California-blend vegetables
    2 cups cubed fully cooked ham
    1 can (10-3/4 ounces) condensed cream of broccoli
      soup, undiluted
 1/2 cup shredded cheddar cheese
 1/4 teaspoon garlic powder
 1/4 teaspoon pepper

Scrub and pierce potatoes; place on a microwave-safe plate. Microwave, uncovered, on high for 12-14 minutes or until tender, turning once. Meanwhile, in a small saucepan, combine the remaining ingredients. Cook and stir over medium-low heat until cheese is melted.

Cut an X in the top of each potato; fluff pulp with a fork. Top with vegetable mixture.

Yield: 4 servings.

Editor's Note: This recipe was tested in a 1,100-watt microwave.

Preparing Potatoes For Baking

Adding ham to these veggie-topped potatoes makes them a complete meal-in-one. With plenty of cheese and a tasty sauce, too, they're sure to satisfy even the biggest appetites.

Russets and Idahos are good baking potatoes. They have a high starch content that produces a fluffy, dry texture when baked. Before baking potatoes, scrub them with a vegetable brush under cold water. Pierce with a fork.

Canadian Bacon Pizza Loaf

Prep/Total Time: 20 min.

     1   unsliced loaf (1 pound) French bread
1-1/2 cups pizza sauce
     4   ounces Canadian bacon, chopped
     1   can (20 ounces) pineapple tidbits, drained
     1   small green pepper, sliced
     2   cups (8 ounces) shredded part-skim mozzarella cheese

Cut loaf in half lengthwise; place on an ungreased baking sheet. Spread cut sides of bread with pizza sauce. Top with Canadian bacon, pineapple, green pepper and cheese. Broil 4-6 in. from the heat for 5-8 minutes or until cheese is melted.

Yield: 8-10 slices.

All About Canadian Bacon

This unique, sweet-and-sour pizza is as much fun to assemble as it is to eat. Topped with Canadian bacon, pineapple tidbits, green pepper, and mozzarella cheese, the loaf will be a welcome change from more traditional pizzas.

Canadian bacon (known as back bacon in Canada) is not really bacon because it is much leaner and has the flavor and consistency of ham. Use Canadian bacon as you would ham rather than bacon.

Maple-Glazed Kabobs

Prep/Total Time: 30 min.

- 8 small new potatoes *or* 1 large potato, cut into 8 chunks
- 3 carrots, cut into 8 pieces (2 inches *each*)
- 1 pork tenderloin (1 pound)
- 1 large green *or* sweet red pepper
- 8 large mushrooms
- 1/4 cup butter, cubed
- 1/4 cup maple syrup
- 1-1/2 teaspoons grated orange peel

Place potatoes and carrots in a large saucepan and cover with water. Bring to a boil. Reduce heat; cover and cook for 10-15 minutes or until crisp-tender. Drain.

Cut pork into 12 equal pieces and pepper into eight chunks. Onto four metal or soaked wooden skewers, alternately thread meat and vegetables; set aside.

In a small saucepan, combine the butter, maple syrup and orange peel; cook and stir over low heat until butter is melted.

Grill kabobs, uncovered, over medium heat for 5 minutes; turn and baste with butter mixture. Cook 12-14 minutes longer or until the meat juices run clear, turning and basting frequently.

Yield: 4 servings.

Give Them Some Space

In this easy grilled recipe, cubes of potato, carrot, pork, pepper and mushrooms are threaded onto skewers, while a simple glaze made with maple syrup is used for basting. Your family will love the slightly sweet kabobs!

Leave a little space between pieces of food as you thread them onto skewers to promote thorough cooking. Always place cooked food on a clean plate—never place on a plate that held raw food.

Sweet 'n' Sour Ribs

Prep: 10 min. **Cook:** 8 hours

3 to 4 pounds boneless
    country-style pork ribs
1 can (20 ounces) pineapple
    tidbits, undrained
2 cans (8 ounces *each*)
    tomato sauce
1/2 cup thinly sliced onion
1/2 cup thinly sliced green
    pepper
1/2 cup packed brown sugar
1/4 cup cider vinegar
1/4 cup tomato paste
2 tablespoons
    Worcestershire sauce
1 garlic clove, minced
Salt and pepper to taste

Place ribs in an ungreased 5-qt. slow cooker. In a large bowl, combine the remaining ingredients; pour over the ribs. Cover and cook on low for 8-10 hours or until meat is tender. Thicken the sauce if desired.

Yield: 8 servings.

Rely on Slow Cooker For Tender Ribs

If you're looking for a change from typical barbecued ribs, you'll enjoy this recipe. Serve them with garlic mashed potatoes and a salad or coleslaw.

Country-style ribs are meaty sections from the rib end of the pork loin. They are sold both in slabs and individually with and without bones.

Ribs usually need quite a bit of time to tenderize. This recipe is handy because they can cook all day in the slow cooker and you don't have to tend to them.

Orange Pork Stir-Fry

Prep/Total Time: 30 min.

> 2 teaspoons cornstarch
> 1/3 cup orange juice
> 1/3 cup teriyaki sauce
> 1 tablespoon Dijon mustard
> 2 teaspoons minced fresh gingerroot
> 1 teaspoon minced garlic
> 1/2 to 1 teaspoon grated orange peel
> 1 pound pork tenderloin, cut into 2-inch strips
> 1 tablespoon vegetable oil
> 1 package (16 ounces) frozen Japanese-style stir-fry vegetables
> Hot cooked rice

In a small bowl, combine cornstarch and orange juice until smooth. Stir in the teriyaki sauce, mustard, ginger, garlic and orange peel; set aside.

In a large skillet or wok, stir-fry pork in oil until no longer pink; remove and keep warm. Add vegetables to the skillet; cook and stir for 2-3 minutes or until tender. Stir orange juice mixture; add to skillet. Bring to a boil; cook and stir for 1-2 minutes or until thickened. Stir in pork. Serve with rice.

Yield: 4 servings.

Grating Citrus Fruit

Orange juice and grated orange peel lend a citrusy touch to this colorful pork-and-vegetable medley.

Also called zest, citrus peel can be grated into fine shreds with a microplane grater. For slightly thicker and longer shreds, use a zester; for long, continuous strips, use a stripper.

Remove only the colored portion of the peel, not the bitter white pith.

Stuffed Ham Rolls

Prep/Total Time: 30 min.

  2 **cups seasoned stuffing cubes**
1/2 **cup boiling water**
  2 **teaspoons plus 2 tablespoons butter,** *divided*
  8 **fully cooked ham slices (1/8 inch thick)**
  8 **slices Swiss cheese**
  1 **egg, lightly beaten**
  1 **tablespoon water**
1/2 **cup dry bread crumbs**

In a large bowl, combine the stuffing, boiling water and 2 teaspoons butter. Cover and let stand for 5 minutes. Fluff with a fork. Top each ham slice with a cheese slice. Place 1/4 cup stuffing off-center over cheese. Roll up and secure with a toothpick.

In a shallow bowl, combine egg and water. In another shallow bowl, add bread crumbs. Dip ham rolls in egg mixture, then roll in crumbs.

In a large skillet, saute ham rolls in remaining butter for 4-5 minutes or until golden brown, turning once. Discard toothpicks.

Yield: 4 servings.

A Pleasing Pairing

Pasta with brussels sprouts pair well with this entree.

In a large saucepan, bring 6 cups water and 1/2 teaspoon salt to a boil. Add a 10-ounce package of frozen brussels sprouts and 1 cup of uncooked spiral pasta. Return to a boil. Reduce heat; simmer, uncovered, for 6 to 8 minutes or until tender. Drain.

Combine 1/4 cup melted butter, 2 tablespoons heavy whipping cream, 2 tablespoons grated onion, 1/2 teaspoon salt, 1/4 teaspoon ground nutmeg and 1/4 teaspoon pepper; pour over pasta and brussels sprouts and toss to coat. Serves four.

Raisin Sauce for Ham

Prep/Total Time: 15 min.

☑ Uses less fat, sugar or salt. Includes
Nutrition Facts and Diabetic Exchanges.

> 1/4 **cup raisins**
>   5 **tablespoons water,** *divided*
> 1/2 **cup orange juice**
>   2 **tablespoons unsweetened crushed**
>   **pineapple, undrained**
>   1 **tablespoon cornstarch**
> 1/2 **teaspoon rum extract, optional**
>   1 **boneless fully cooked ham steak (1 pound)**

In a large saucepan, combine the raisins, 4 tablespoons water, orange juice and pineapple. Bring to a boil. Combine cornstarch and remaining water until smooth; gradually stir into raisin mixture. Cook and stir for 2 minutes or until thickened. Remove from the heat; stir in extract if desired.

Cut the ham steak into four pieces. In a large skillet coated with nonstick cooking spray, cook ham over medium heat for 1-2 minutes on each side or until browned. Serve with the raisin sauce.

Yield: 4 servings.

Nutrition Facts: 3 ounces cooked ham with 1/4 cup raisin sauce equals 237 calories, 10 g fat (3 g saturated fat), 60 mg cholesterol, 1,451 mg sodium, 16 g carbohydrate, trace fiber, 21 g protein. **Diabetic Exchanges:** 3 lean meat, 1 fruit.

Dress Up Ham Steak

Here's a tart, fruity, rum raisin sauce that can make an ordinary ham steak something to celebrate!

Here are two more ways to dress up ham steak. Rub both sides of the meat with a blend of 2 teaspoons Cajun seasoning and 1/2 teaspoon sugar, then fry or grill until heated through.

Or cover a browned ham steak with thinly sliced apples, pour some maple syrup over the apples and simmer until the fruit is cooked through.

Pork Salad Croissants

Prep/Total Time: 15 min.

  1   medium tart apple, diced
1/2   cup halved seedless red grapes
1/2   cup mayonnaise
  2   tablespoons chopped walnuts
  2   tablespoons chutney
1/2   teaspoon salt
1/4   teaspoon ground ginger
  2   cups cubed cooked pork tenderloin
  4   croissants, split
Lettuce leaves

In a large bowl, combine the first seven ingredients. Add pork; toss to coat. Line each croissant with a lettuce leaf. Top with about 3/4 cup pork salad.

Yield: 4 servings.

Stock Up on Pork Tenderloin

Looking for a change of pace from more traditional chicken and tuna salad sandwiches? Try this rapid recipe that combines apple chunks, grapes, chopped walnuts and cubed pork with ginger, chutney and mayonnaise.

Look for sales on pork tenderloin and stock up. Use it in 3 to 5 days or freeze for up to 1 year. It's handy to keep tenderloin in the freezer for last-minute meals since it thaws and cooks quickly.

Spicy Pepper Penne

Prep/Total Time: 30 min.

  1 package uncooked penne
     pasta
1/2 teaspoon minced fresh
     rosemary *or* 1/8 teaspoon
     dried rosemary, crushed
  2 packages (3-1/2 ounces
     each) sliced pepperoni,
     halved
1/2 cup sliced pepperoncinis
  1 jar (7 ounces) roasted
     sweet red peppers,
     drained and chopped
3-1/2 cups boiling water
1/2 cup heavy whipping
     cream
1/2 cup grated Parmesan cheese

In a large skillet, layer the pasta, rosemary, pepperoni, pepperoncinis and red peppers. Add water; bring to a boil. Reduce heat; cover and simmer for 12 minutes or until pasta is tender. Add cream and Parmesan cheese; toss to coat.

Yield: 8 servings.

All About Pepperoncinis

This zesty combination of pepperoni, pasta and peppers will add a little kick to your dinner lineup.

Pepperoncinis are thin, 2- to 3-inch-long chilies that have a bright red, wrinkled skin. They have a slightly sweet flavor that can range from medium to medium-hot.

Pepperoncinis are most often sold pickled and can be found in the pickle and olive section of your grocery store.

Straw and Hay

Prep/Total Time: 20 min.

1 cup milk
1/2 cup cottage cheese
1 tablespoon cornstarch
1/4 teaspoon salt
1/4 teaspoon pepper
1/8 teaspoon ground nutmeg
1/2 cup shredded Parmesan
   cheese, *divided*
8 ounces uncooked
   fettuccine
1/2 cup cubed fully cooked ham
   (4 ounces)
1 garlic clove, minced
1/2 cup frozen peas, thawed

In a blender, combine the milk, cottage cheese and cornstarch; cover and process until smooth. Transfer to a small saucepan; add the salt, pepper and nutmeg. Cook and stir over medium heat until mixture comes to a boil. Cook and stir for 2 minutes or until thickened. Remove from the heat; stir in 1/4 cup Parmesan cheese until melted.

Cook fettuccine according to package directions. Meanwhile, in a large nonstick skillet coated with nonstick cooking spray, cook ham and garlic for 2 minutes. Add peas; cook until heated through. Remove from the heat; stir in cheese sauce. Drain fettuccine. Add to the sauce and toss to coat. Sprinkle with remaining Parmesan cheese.

Yield: 6 servings.

Strange Name, Delicious Supper

Straw and Hay is not only quick and easy to prepare, it's pretty, too. This colorful pasta dish combines cubed ham, Parmesan cheese, peas and fettuccine.

The trick is to have all the ingredients ready at the same time, so you can toss it all together without having to reheat. If your family likes seafood, substitute shrimp or scallops for the ham. You could also use linguine in place of the fettuccine. A simple tossed green salad would round out the meal.

Pork Chops Italiano

Prep/Total Time: 25 min.

4   bone-in pork loin chops (3/4 inch thick
    and 8 ounces *each*)
1/4 teaspoon pepper
2   tablespoons butter
1   can (8 ounces) tomato sauce
1/4 cup water
1   teaspoon Italian seasoning
1/2 teaspoon dried basil
4   slices part-skim mozzarella cheese
1   medium green pepper, cut into rings

Sprinkle pork chops with pepper. In a large skillet, brown chops in butter on both sides; drain. Combine the tomato sauce, water, Italian seasoning and basil; pour over chops. Bring to a boil. Reduce heat; cover and simmer for 6-8 minutes or until meat juices run clear. Top each pork chop with cheese and green pepper. Cover and cook 3-5 minutes longer or until cheese is melted.

Yield: 4 servings.

Swift Skillet Fare Satisfies

Juicy pork chops are covered with a basil-seasoned tomato sauce and melted mozzarella cheese in this Italian-style entree. You'll be surprised how great they taste! They're so easy and fast, too. Any cut of chop can be used. We used bone-in but you could also use boneless. Just make sure the cuts are at least 3/4 inch thick.

For a speedy side dish, toss together cooked spiral pasta and broccoli florets. And warm up slices of store-bought pie for a comforting finish to this delicious dinner.

O'Brien Sausage Skillet

Prep/Total Time: 20 min.

- 1 package (28 ounces) frozen O'Brien hash brown potatoes
- 1 pound smoked kielbasa *or* Polish sausage, cut into 1/4-inch slices
- 2 medium tart apples, peeled and chopped
- 1 medium onion, chopped
- 1 tablespoon vegetable oil
- 1 cup (4 ounces) shredded cheddar cheese

Prepare potatoes according to package directions. Meanwhile, in a large skillet, saute the sausage, apples and onion in oil for 10 minutes or until apples and onion are tender; drain.

Spoon the sausage mixture over potatoes; sprinkle with cheese. Cover and cook for 3-5 minutes or until the cheese is melted.

Yield: 6-8 servings.

Meat-and-Potato Skillet Meal

Perfect for busy nights when you have little time to cook, this skillet dish is so quick and satisfying. Featuring O'Brien hash browns, sausage and apples, it would also be welcomed for breakfast or brunch. Granny Smith, Jonathan, Rome Beauty and Empire apples are good picks for this recipe.

When you're in a hurry, O'Brien hash browns also make speedy mashed potatoes. There's no need to peel or cut them, and because the pieces are small, they cook very quickly.

Pizza Patties

Prep/Total Time: 25 min.

1/3 cup finely chopped green
     pepper
  1 small onion, finely
     chopped
1/4 cup grated Parmesan
     cheese
  1 pound bulk Italian
     sausage
  1 cup spaghetti sauce
  4 sandwich buns, split
1/2 cup shredded part-skim
     mozzarella cheese

In a large bowl, combine the green pepper, onion and Parmesan cheese. Crumble sausage over mixture and mix just until combined. Shape into four patties. In a large skillet, cook patties over medium heat for 7-8 minutes on each side or until meat is no longer pink; drain.

Add the spaghetti sauce; bring to a boil. Reduce heat; cover and simmer for 7-8 minutes or until heated through. Place a patty on the bottom of each bun; drizzle with spaghetti sauce. Sprinkle with mozzarella cheese; replace tops.

Yield: 4 servings.

Italian-Style Hamburgers

Is your family tired of ho-hum hamburgers? With Italian sausage, green pepper, spaghetti sauce and mozzarella cheese, Pizza Patties will become a new-found favorite.

To cut preparation at mealtime, mix and shape these patties the night before and then refrigerate. Handle the mixture as little as possible when shaping to keep the final product light in texture. If you like lots of sauce, you may want to serve some extra spaghetti sauce on the side for dipping.

Pork and Corn Casserole

Prep: 15 min. **Bake:** 30 min.

7 cups uncooked egg noodles
1 pound ground pork
1 small green pepper, chopped
1 can (14-3/4 ounces) cream-style corn
1 can (11-1/2 ounces) condensed chicken with rice soup, undiluted
1 jar (2 ounces) diced pimientos, drained
8 ounces process cheese (Velveeta), cubed
1/2 cup dry bread crumbs
2 tablespoons butter, melted

Cook noodles according to package directions; drain. Meanwhile, in a large skillet, cook pork and green pepper over medium heat until meat is no longer pink; drain.

In a large bowl, combine the noodles, corn, soup, pimientos, cheese and pork mixture. Transfer to a greased shallow 2-1/2-qt. baking dish. Combine bread crumbs and butter; sprinkle over noodle mixture. Bake, uncovered, at 350° for 30-35 minutes or until bubbly and top is golden brown.

Yield: 6-8 servings.

Which Bakeware Is the Best?

A satisfying supper includes Pork and Corn Casserole fresh from the oven, a garden salad and buttermilk biscuits. It's a winner every time!

Casseroles are best baked in baking dishes made of oven-safe glass or ceramic. Metal pans may discolor, if the ingredients are acidic, or may give off a metallic flavor. For even cooking, try to bake the casserole in the dish size called for in the recipe.

Jiffy Ground Pork Skillet

Prep/Total Time: 30 min.

1-1/2 cups uncooked penne pasta
    1 pound ground pork
  1/2 cup chopped onion
    1 can (14-1/2 ounces) stewed tomatoes
    1 can (8 ounces) tomato sauce
    1 teaspoon Italian seasoning
    1 medium zucchini, cut into 1/4-inch slices

Cook pasta according to package directions. Meanwhile, in a large skillet, cook pork and onion over medium heat until meat is no longer pink; drain. Add the tomatoes, tomato sauce and Italian seasoning. Bring to a boil. Reduce heat; cover and cook for 5 minutes or until heated through.

Drain pasta; add to skillet. Stir in zucchini. Cover and cook for 3-5 minutes or until zucchini is crisp-tender.

Yield: 6 servings.

Ground Pork Great For Busy Cooks

Some people call it dinner hour, but others may call it rush hour! With this super-quick, mouth-watering meal, you'll have plenty of time to slow down and share with your family around the table.

Ground pork, just like ground beef, is a quick-cooking meat that can be used by itself or in an endless variety of casseroles, meat loaves and other dishes. Uncooked ground pork should be stored in its original wrapping in the refrigerator for no more than 2 to 3 days.

Pear-Topped Ham Steak

Prep/Total Time: 20 min.

1   can (15-1/4 ounces) sliced pears
1   fully cooked ham steak (1/2 inch thick and about 1 pound)
1   tablespoon olive oil
2   teaspoons cornstarch
1   teaspoon ground ginger
1   tablespoon cold water
1   to 3 teaspoons minced fresh mint

Drain pears, reserving the juice; set pears and juice aside. In a large skillet, brown ham steak in oil on both sides; drain. Remove ham from pan and keep warm.

Combine cornstarch, ginger and water until smooth; stir in reserved pear juice. Gradually add to the skillet. Bring to a boil. Reduce heat; simmer, uncovered, for 1-2 minutes or until thickened. Add ham and reserved pears; cook until heated through. Sprinkle with mint.

Yield: 4 servings.

Fruit Sauce Spruces Up Ham Steak

Mint and ginger flavor the fruity sauce served over Pear-Topped Ham Steak. The sweetness of the pears contrasts nicely with the saltiness of the ham.

Lemon mint beans are a delightful side dish. In a saucepan, cook a 16-ounce package of fresh or frozen cut green beans in a small amount of water until tender; drain. Add 1 tablespoon lemon juice, 1 tablespoon snipped fresh mint, 1/4 teaspoon grated lemon peel and 1/2 teaspoon salt; toss to coat. Serves four.

Pepperoni Pizza Bake

Prep/Total Time: 30 min.

- 1 package (16 ounces) wide egg noodles
- 2-1/4 cups pizza sauce, *divided*
- 1 cup sliced fresh mushrooms
- 1 can (2-1/4 ounces) sliced ripe olives, drained
- 1 package (3-1/2 ounces) sliced pepperoni
- 2 cups (8 ounces) shredded part-skim mozzarella cheese

Cook noodles according to package directions; drain. In a large bowl, combine noodles and 3/4 cup pizza sauce. Transfer to a greased 13-in. x 9-in. x 2-in. baking dish. Top with remaining pizza sauce.

Layer with the mushrooms, olives and pepperoni. Sprinkle with cheese. Bake, uncovered, at 375° for 15-18 minutes or until heated through and cheese is melted.

Yield: 8 servings.

Try Other Toppings

Egg noodles make a great "crust" for this comforting pizza bake and don't require the time it takes dough to rise. To save even more time, use a food processor to quickly chop up the ingredients or buy presliced and shredded veggies and cheese.

If your family likes "kitchen sink" pizza with every topping imaginable, you can add sausage, herbs, peppers and unique sauces to this casserole.

Or put different toppings on certain sections of the dish so you each have a portion with your favorite trimmings.

Spicy Zucchini
Quesadillas (p. 210)

Your family won't miss the meat
when they dig into these mouth-watering
main courses showcasing vegetables,
cheese, beans, potatoes, pasta and rice!

Make It **Meatless**

Make It Meatless

Zesty Garlic-Avocado Sandwiches (p. 212)

Vegetarian Penne (p. 209)

Garden Squash Ravioli

Prep/Total Time: 10 min.

1 package (24 ounces) frozen miniature cheese ravioli
1 medium yellow summer squash, cut into 1/2-inch pieces
1 medium zucchini, cut into 1/2-inch pieces
2 cans (one 15 ounces, one 8 ounces) tomato sauce
1 teaspoon garlic salt
1 teaspoon dried minced onion
1 teaspoon dried oregano
1 teaspoon dried basil
1/2 teaspoon sugar
1/2 teaspoon chili powder
1/4 teaspoon pepper

In a large saucepan, cook ravioli according to package directions. Meanwhile, in a 1-1/2-qt. microwave-safe dish, combine the squash, zucchini, tomato sauce and seasonings. Cover and cook on high for 6-7 minutes or until vegetables are tender. Drain ravioli; top with sauce.

Yield: 6 servings.

Editor's Note: This recipe was tested with an 850-watt microwave.

Only 10 Minutes To Supper!

When time is tight at the end of an especially hectic day, turn to this main dish that can be prepared in only 10 minutes from start to finish! While the frozen ravioli is cooking on the stovetop, use the microwave to prepare the garden-fresh sauce. Then just ladle the sauce over the pasta for a satisfying supper! Scoop up your family's favorite flavor of ice cream for a super, simple dessert.

Chili Bread

Prep/Total Time: 20 min.

> 1 loaf (1 pound) French bread
> 1 can (16 ounces) kidney beans, rinsed and drained
> 1 can (15 ounces) chili without beans
> 3/4 to 1 cup spaghetti sauce
> 1 garlic clove, minced
> 1 medium tomato, chopped
> 2 green onions, thinly sliced
> 1 cup (4 ounces) shredded part-skim mozzarella cheese
> 2 tablespoons grated Parmesan cheese

Cut bread in half lengthwise; place with cut side up on a foil-lined baking sheet. In a large bowl, combine the beans, chili, spaghetti sauce and garlic; spread over cut side of bread. Top with tomato and onions. Sprinkle with cheeses. Bake at 350° for 10-12 minutes or until the cheese is melted.

Yield: 8 servings.

Chili Eaten Out of Hand

Cans of kidney beans and chili, sprinkled with colorful red tomatoes, green onions and mozzarella cheese, make a tasty topping for a loaf of crusty French bread. Not only does this open-faced sandwich taste terrific, it can be made in minutes.

A side salad or bowl of soup are simple ways to complete the meal. Or serve Chili Bread as an appetizer at your next gathering with friends. Just cut it into smaller slices.

Picante Biscuit Bake

Prep: 5 min. **Bake:** 30 min.

> 2 tubes (12 ounces *each*) refrigerated buttermilk biscuits
> 1 jar (16 ounces) picante sauce *or* salsa
> 1 medium green pepper, chopped
> 1 medium onion, chopped
> 1 can (2-1/4 ounces) sliced ripe olives, drained
> 2 cups (8 ounces) shredded Monterey Jack cheese

Quarter the biscuits; place in a greased 13-in. x 9-in. x 2-in. baking dish. Top with picante sauce, green pepper, onion and olives. Bake, uncovered, at 350° for 20 minutes. Sprinkle with cheese. Bake 10 minutes longer or until the cheese is melted.

Yield: 6 servings.

Casserole Is Quick to Fix

This tasty Mexican-flavored casserole calls for just six convenient ingredients, so it's a breeze to put together on a weeknight.

To make it even heartier, you can add a pound of cooked ground beef or turkey. Or try a pizza variation using pizza sauce, pepperoni and mozzarella cheese. Whichever way you choose to make it, it will be a hit with all ages!

Make It **Meatless**

Pasta-Filled Peppers

Prep: 30 min. **Cook:** 5 min.

6 medium sweet red, green *or* yellow peppers
6 ounces uncooked spaghetti
3/4 cup diced onion
2 garlic cloves, minced
2 teaspoons canola oil
1-3/4 cups diced fresh tomatoes
1 tablespoon all-purpose flour
3/4 teaspoon salt
1-1/4 cups vegetable broth
3/4 cup shredded part-skim mozzarella cheese
1/4 cup minced fresh basil
3 tablespoons grated Parmesan cheese

Place whole peppers on a broiler pan; broil 6 in. from the heat for 10-15 minutes or until skins are blistered and blackened, turning often. Immediately place peppers in a bowl; cover and let stand for 10 minutes. Peel off and discard charred skins. Carefully cut tops off peppers and discard; remove seeds. Set peppers aside.

Cook spaghetti according to package directions. Meanwhile, in a large nonstick skillet, saute onion and garlic in oil until tender. Add tomatoes; cook for 1 minute. In a small bowl, combine the flour, salt and broth until smooth. Gradually stir into tomato mixture.

Bring to a boil; cook and stir for 1 minute or until slightly thickened. Drain spaghetti; add to tomato mixture and toss to coat. Sprinkle with mozzarella cheese, basil and Parmesan; toss. Spoon into peppers. Place in a 3-qt. microwave-safe baking dish. Cover and microwave on high for 2-4 minutes or until heated through.

Yield: 6 servings.

Pick These Pretty Peppers for Supper

Bell peppers provide a rainbow of colorful "cups" for serving up this fresh-tasting, tomato-herb pasta dish. Spaghetti noodles replace the more common ground beef and rice usually used to stuff peppers.

It's important to immediately place the blackened peppers in a bowl and cover with plastic wrap. This gives the peppers time to cool before handling and softens them. If they are still a little hard to peel after 10 minutes, let the peppers stand 5 to 10 minutes longer.

Four-Cheese Spinach Pizza

Prep/Total Time: 30 min.

✓ Uses less fat, sugar or salt. Includes Nutrition Facts and Diabetic Exchanges.

2 packages (10 ounces *each*) fresh spinach
3/4 cup shredded part-skim mozzarella cheese, *divided*
1/2 cup fat-free cottage cheese
1/3 cup grated Parmesan cheese
1/4 teaspoon salt
1/8 teaspoon pepper
1 prebaked Italian bread shell crust (10 ounces)
1 medium tomato, chopped
1/4 cup chopped green onions
1/4 cup sliced ripe olives
1 teaspoon minced fresh basil
1 teaspoon olive oil
1 teaspoon balsamic vinegar
1 garlic clove, minced
1/2 cup crumbled feta cheese

In a large nonstick skillet coated with nonstick cooking spray, saute spinach for 2-3 minutes or until wilted; remove from the skillet. Cool slightly; chop.

In a large bowl, combine 1/4 cup mozzarella cheese, cottage cheese and Parmesan cheese. Stir in the spinach, salt and pepper. Spread over crust to within 1/2 in. of edge. In a large bowl, combine the tomato, onions, olives, basil, oil, vinegar and garlic; sprinkle over spinach mixture. Top with the feta cheese and remaining mozzarella cheese. Bake at 400° for 12-14 minutes or until cheese softens and is lightly browned.

Yield: 6 servings.

Nutrition Facts: 1 slice equals 270 calories, 11 g fat (4 g saturated fat), 24 mg cholesterol, 823 mg sodium, 28 g carbohydrate, 1 g fiber, 17 g protein. **Diabetic Exchanges:** 1-1/2 starch, 1-1/2 fat, 1 lean meat, 1 vegetable.

Picking Out Fresh Spinach

You'll especially want to make this pizza in summer when fresh spinach and basil are plentiful—they are key to its wonderful taste!

You can buy spinach loose at farmers markets or bagged at the grocery store. When buying it loose, look for small, crisp, dark-green leaves. And when buying bagged spinach, gently squeeze it to make sure leaves are springy. The thicker the spinach stems, the more likely it is to be overgrown and bitter.

Make It **Meatless**

Vegetarian Penne

Prep/Total Time: 30 min.

  2   cups uncooked penne pasta
1/3   cup finely chopped onion
  1   small yellow summer squash, sliced
  1   small zucchini, sliced
1/2   cup sliced fresh mushrooms
  1   teaspoon minced garlic
  3   tablespoons butter
  1   tablespoon all-purpose flour
1/2   teaspoon salt
1/4   teaspoon dried parsley flakes
1/4   teaspoon dried thyme
1/4   teaspoon pepper
1/4   cup heavy whipping cream

Cook pasta according to package directions. Meanwhile, in a large skillet, saute the onion, summer squash, zucchini, mushrooms and garlic in butter until tender.

In a small bowl, whisk the remaining ingredients until smooth; add to the skillet. Cook for 2-3 minutes or until thickened. Drain pasta and add to vegetable mixture. Cook for 2-3 minutes or until heated through.

Yield: 6-8 servings.

Toss Together This Pleasing Pairing

Pasta and fresh vegetables are a pleasing pairing. Here, penne combines with onion, yellow summer squash, zucchini and mushrooms in a creamy sauce. It makes a hearty meal by itself but could also be served as an impressive side dish alongside any meaty entree.

To cook pasta evenly and prevent it from sticking together, always cook pasta in plenty of boiling water. To prevent a boil-over, cook pasta in a large kettle or Dutch oven.

Spicy Zucchini Quesadillas

Prep/Total Time: 15 min.

1 large onion, chopped
1/2 cup chopped sweet red pepper
1 teaspoon plus 2 tablespoons butter, softened, *divided*
2 cups shredded zucchini
2 tablespoons taco seasoning
8 flour tortillas (7 inches)
8 ounces pepper Jack cheese, shredded
Salsa, sour cream and pickled jalapeno pepper slices

In a large skillet, saute onion and red pepper in 1 teaspoon butter for 3 minutes. Stir in zucchini and taco seasoning; saute 3-4 minutes longer or until vegetables are tender. Remove vegetables from the heat.

Spread remaining butter over one side of each tortilla. Place tortillas butter side down on a griddle. Sprinkle about 1/4 cup cheese and 1/4 cup zucchini mixture over half of each tortilla; fold over.

Cook over low heat for 1-2 minutes on each side or until cheese is melted. Serve with salsa, sour cream and jalapenos.

Yield: 4 servings.

Zesty Use for Zucchini

Garden bursting with zucchini? Put it to delicious use in these zesty quesadillas! Save time by shredding the zucchini in a food processor fitted with a shredding disc.

For milder quesadillas, use Monterey Jack instead of pepper Jack cheese. If you want them even spicier, add some red pepper flakes or even some chopped jalapenos.

Budget Macaroni & Cheese

Prep/Total Time: 20 min.

1   package (7 ounces) elbow
    macaroni
3   tablespoons butter
3   tablespoons all-purpose
    flour
1/4 teaspoon salt
Dash pepper
1   cup milk
1   cup (4 ounces) shredded
    cheddar cheese

Cook the macaroni according to package directions. Meanwhile, in a large saucepan, melt butter over medium-low heat. Add the flour, salt and pepper; stir until smooth. Gradually add milk.

Bring to a boil; cook and stir for 2 minutes or until thickened. Remove from the heat; stir in cheese until melted. Drain pasta. Add to the cheese mixture; toss to coat.

Yield: 4 servings.

Presidential Beginnings?

Packaged macaroni and cheese mixes just can't compare to this creamy and comforting homemade version that's easy on the budget. It's a hearty meal in itself, but could also be served as a side dish alongside any meaty entree. The recipe calls for regular cheddar cheese, but you can use the sharp variety if you prefer.

It's believed that macaroni and cheese was created by founding father Thomas Jefferson, who was known for his great interest in food, and that he served the dish in the White House in 1802.

Zesty Garlic-Avocado Sandwiches

Prep/Total Time: 30 min.

1   package (8 ounces) cream
    cheese, softened
2   medium ripe avocados,
    peeled
1   garlic clove, minced
1/8 teaspoon salt
6   whole grain bagels, split
    and toasted
6   slices tomato
1/2 cup sliced cucumber
6   slices red onion
6   sweet red pepper rings
6   lettuce leaves

In a small mixing bowl, beat the cream cheese, avocados, garlic and salt until smooth. Spread on bagels; top with tomato, cucumber, onion, pepper rings and lettuce.

Yield: 6 servings.

Avocado Advice

Here's a flavorful bagel sandwich filled with an avocado, garlic and cream cheese spread that's topped with tomato, cucumber, onion, pepper rings and lettuce. For variation, add fresh chives or minced sun-dried tomato to the cream cheese. Leftover spread makes an excellent veggie dip.

Perfectly ripe avocados are the easiest to peel. When buying avocados, choose those that yield slightly to gentle palm pressure. They should be heavy for their size and unblemished. Avoid any that have dark, sunken spots.

Creamy Garden Spaghetti

Prep/Total Time: 30 min.

1/2	pound fresh broccoli, broken into florets
1-1/2	cups sliced zucchini
1-1/2	cups sliced fresh mushrooms
1	large carrot, sliced
1	tablespoon olive oil
8	ounces uncooked spaghetti
1/4	cup chopped onion
3	garlic cloves, minced
2	tablespoons butter
2	tablespoons all-purpose flour
1	vegetable bouillon cube
1	teaspoon dried thyme
2	cups milk
1/2	cup shredded Swiss cheese
1/2	cup shredded part-skim mozzarella cheese

In a large skillet, saute the broccoli, zucchini, mushrooms and carrot in oil until crisp-tender. Remove from the heat and set aside. Cook spaghetti according to package directions. Meanwhile, in a large saucepan, saute onion and garlic in butter until tender. Stir in the flour, bouillon and thyme until blended; gradually add milk. Bring to a boil; cook and stir for 2 minutes or until thickened.

Reduce heat to low; stir in cheeses until melted. Add the vegetables; cook until heated through. Drain spaghetti; add to vegetable mixture and toss to coat.

Yield: 4 servings.

Editor's Note: This recipe was prepared with Knorr vegetable bouillon.

Pasta Primer

Cooking with pasta gives you so many choices! Here, spaghetti is combined with broccoli, zucchini, mushrooms and carrots and tossed in a cheese sauce.

In general, you want to select the right pasta for the sauce. A light, thin sauce should have a thin pasta such as angel hair or vermicelli. Heavier sauces need thicker pastas like fettuccine. For chunky or meaty sauces, choose a tubular-shaped pasta such as rigatoni.

Angel Hair Pasta with Garden Vegetables

Prep/Total Time: 30 min.

✓ Uses less fat, sugar or salt.
Includes Nutrition Facts.

- 8 ounces uncooked angel hair pasta
- 1 cup fresh snow peas
- 1 cup sliced fresh mushrooms
- 1 cup thinly sliced fresh carrots
- 1 cup chopped sweet yellow, red *or* green pepper
- 1/3 cup chopped fresh basil
- 2 garlic cloves, minced
- 2 tablespoons olive oil
- 2 teaspoons cornstarch
- 1 cup vegetable broth
- 1/4 teaspoon salt
- 3 medium tomatoes, peeled and chopped
- 1/4 cup grated Parmesan cheese

Cook pasta according to package directions. Meanwhile, in non-stick skillet, saute the snow peas, mushrooms, carrots, yellow pepper, basil and garlic in oil for 2-3 minutes or until crisp-tender.

In a small bowl, combine the cornstarch, broth and salt until smooth; gradually stir into the vegetable mixture. Bring to a boil. Reduce heat; cook and stir for 3-5 minutes or until vegetables are crisp-tender and sauce is thickened. Remove from the heat; stir in tomatoes. Drain pasta; divide between four plates. Top with vegetable mixture; sprinkle with Parmesan cheese.

Yield: 4 servings.

Nutrition Facts: 2 cups equals 333 calories, 11 g fat (2 g saturated fat), 5 mg cholesterol, 714 mg sodium, 49 g carbohydrate, 5 g fiber, 14 g protein.

Working with Fresh Vegetables

This family-pleasing pasta dish is especially fun to make when your garden is full of fresh vegetables. It's quick to fix, delicious and can always be different— just choose the vegetables that have ripened that day!

Handle vegetables gently—they bruise easily, and a bruised spot will lead to decay. Before preparing, make sure your countertops, cutting boards and utensils are clean. Wash your hands in hot, soapy water. Rinse vegetables under cool running water.

Cheesy Walnut Burgers

Prep/Total Time: 30 min.

1-1/2 cups (6 ounces) shredded sharp cheddar cheese
   1 cup finely chopped walnuts
   1 cup soft bread crumbs
 1/2 cup finely chopped onion
   1 egg, lightly beaten
   1 tablespoon ketchup
   2 teaspoons minced fresh basil *or* thyme
 1/4 teaspoon salt
 1/8 teaspoon lemon-pepper seasoning
   2 tablespoons vegetable oil
   6 hamburger buns, split
Ketchup *or* plain yogurt, optional

In a large bowl, combine the first nine ingredients; shape into six 3/4-in.-thick patties. In a large skillet, cook patties in oil over medium heat until golden brown on both sides.

To bake, place patties on a greased baking sheet. Bake at 350° for 12-13 minutes on each side, turning once, or until browned. Serve on buns with ketchup or yogurt if desired.

Yield: 6 servings.

You'll Go Nuts For These Burgers

You won't miss the meat in these patties! Sharp cheddar cheese, finely chopped walnuts, bread crumbs, onion and seasonings combine as a delicious substitute. They brown quickly cooked in a little oil on the stovetop but will turn out just as nicely baked in the oven instead.

Serve these golden-brown, crispy burgers with lettuce, tomatoes and ketchup or plain yogurt on either regular or whole wheat buns.

Broccoli Fettuccine Alfredo

Prep/Total Time: 30 min.

1 package (12 ounces) fettuccine
1 cup chopped fresh *or* frozen broccoli
3 tablespoons butter
1 tablespoon all-purpose flour
2/3 cup milk
1/4 cup grated Parmesan cheese

Cook fettuccine according to package directions. Meanwhile, in a large saucepan, bring 1 in. of water and broccoli to a boil. Reduce heat; cover and simmer for 4-6 minutes or until crisp-tender. Drain.

In a large saucepan, melt butter over medium heat. Stir in flour until smooth. Gradually whisk in milk. Bring to a boil; cook and stir for 2 minutes or until thickened. Remove from the heat; stir in Parmesan cheese and broccoli. Drain fettuccine; top with the broccoli mixture.

Yield: 4 servings.

Don't Overcook Broccoli

Broccoli Fettuccine Alfredo is a versatile pasta dish sure to appeal to your whole family. Instead of broccoli, you can use green beans, carrots or any other of your favorite vegetables. You can even add cubed cooked chicken.

Overcooking broccoli will cause it to break apart, lose its color, diminish its taste, and will cause the loss of many nutrients. Throwing a few chunks of bread into the water when cooking broccoli will help remove the aroma.

Tomato Basil Fettuccine

Prep/Total Time: 25 min.

✓ Uses less fat, sugar or salt. Includes Nutrition Facts and Diabetic Exchanges.

- 8 ounces uncooked fettuccine
- 1/4 cup chopped onion
- 1/8 teaspoon crushed red pepper flakes
- 1 tablespoon butter
- 1 can (14-1/2 ounces) diced tomatoes, undrained
- 1/4 teaspoon salt
- 1/3 cup fat-free evaporated milk
- 1/4 cup chopped fresh basil
- 2 tablespoons grated Parmesan cheese

Cook fettuccine according to package directions. Meanwhile, in a large nonstick skillet, saute onion and red pepper flakes in butter until onion is tender. Add tomatoes and salt; cook and stir over medium-high heat until most of the liquid is evaporated.

Remove from the heat; let stand for 1 minute. Gradually whisk in milk. Drain fettuccine and place in a large bowl. Add the basil, Parmesan cheese and tomato mixture; toss to coat.

Yield: 4 servings.

Nutrition Facts: One serving equals 236 calories, 5 g fat (2 g saturated fat), 11 mg cholesterol, 507 mg sodium, 40 g carbohydrate, 3 g fiber, 10 g protein. **Diabetic Exchanges:** 2 starch, 1 lean meat, 1/2 fat.

Reach for the Wheat

This creamy pasta dish tastes terrific as is, but you could also toss in some chopped cooked chicken.

Pasta made from nutritionally superior whole wheat flour is now available in a variety of shapes and sizes with a texture that is almost identical to white flour pasta. That means your kids won't know the difference!

Sweet Pepper Burritos

Prep/Total Time: 30 min.

☑ Uses less fat, sugar or salt.
Includes Nutrition Facts.

 1 medium onion, chopped
 1 tablespoon canola oil
 2 medium sweet red peppers, diced
 1 medium sweet yellow pepper, diced
 1 medium green pepper, diced
 2 teaspoons ground cumin
 2 cups cooked brown rice
1-1/2 cups (6 ounces) shredded reduced-fat cheddar cheese
 3 ounces fat-free cream cheese, cubed
 1/2 teaspoon salt
 1/2 teaspoon pepper
 6 flour tortillas (10 inches), warmed
Salsa, optional

In a large nonstick skillet, saute onion in oil for 2 minutes. Add peppers; saute for 5 minutes or until crisp-tender. Sprinkle with cumin; saute 1 minute longer. Stir in the rice, cheeses, salt and pepper.

Spoon about 2/3 cup of filling off-center on each tortilla; fold sides and ends over filling and roll up. Place seam side down in a 13-in. x 9-in. x 2-in. baking dish coated with nonstick cooking spray.

Cover and bake at 425° for 10-15 minutes or until heated through. Let stand for 5 minutes. Serve with salsa if desired.

Yield: 6 servings.

Nutrition Facts: 1 burrito (calculated without salsa) equals 429 calories, 13 g fat (5 g saturated fat), 21 mg cholesterol, 671 mg sodium, 54 g carbohydrate, 9 g fiber, 18 g protein.

Brown Rice in Brief

Diners meet up with plenty of flavor when they dig into these meatless burritos that are bursting with sweet peppers, cheese, onion and brown rice.

Brown rice is the least processed form of rice. It has the outer hull removed, but still retains the bran layers that give it its characteristic tan color and nut-like flavor. The outer layer of the bran gives this rice a chewier texture than white rice.

Uncooked brown rice should be used within 6 months or it will go rancid.

Three-Cheese Spaghetti Bake

Prep: 20 min. **Bake:** 30 min.

1   package (16 ounces) spaghetti
2   cups (8 ounces) shredded part-skim mozzarella
    cheese, *divided*
3/4 cup grated Parmesan cheese
1/2 cup grated Romano cheese
3   eggs, lightly beaten
1   tablespoon olive oil
2   teaspoons garlic powder
Salt and pepper to taste
1   jar (28 ounces) spaghetti sauce

Cook spaghetti according to package directions; drain. Transfer to a large bowl. Add 1 cup mozzarella cheese, Parmesan, Romano, eggs, oil, garlic powder, salt and pepper.

Press into a greased 13-in. x 9-in. x 2-in. baking dish. Top with spaghetti sauce. Cover and bake at 350° for 20 minutes. Uncover; sprinkle with the remaining mozzarella. Bake 10 minutes longer or until heated through and cheese is melted.

Yield: 6-8 servings.

Quick and Easy Casserole

This casserole makes great use of convenience products like boxed pasta, jarred spaghetti sauce and packaged shredded cheese.

Experiment with any variety of spaghetti sauce you like. For an even heartier casserole, add a pound of cooked ground beef or turkey.

Serve the pleasing pasta bake with a tomato salad and toasted garlic bread. Spumoni or neapolitan ice cream would make a nice no-fuss dessert.

Vegetable Noodle Bake

Prep: 15 min. **Bake:** 20 min.

    1   can (14-1/2 ounces) diced tomatoes, drained
3/4   cup canned tomato puree
1/3   cup chopped onion
1-1/4   teaspoons dried oregano
1/4   teaspoon garlic powder
1/4   teaspoon salt
1/8   teaspoon pepper
2-1/2   cups uncooked medium egg noodles
1/2   cup small-curd cottage cheese
    1   package (10 ounces) frozen chopped spinach, thawed and squeezed dry
1/3   cup shredded American cheese

In a large saucepan, combine the tomatoes, tomato puree, onion, oregano, garlic powder, salt and pepper. Bring to a boil. Reduce heat; simmer, uncovered, for 15 minutes. Meanwhile, cook noodles according to package directions; drain.

Spread 1/3 cup tomato mixture in a greased shallow 2-qt. baking dish. Top with half of the noodles. Spread with cottage cheese; top with spinach. Drizzle with 1/2 cup tomato mixture; top with remaining noodles and tomato mixture. Sprinkle with American cheese. Cover and bake at 350° for 20-25 minutes or until cheese is melted.

Yield: 4 servings.

Traditional Taste In Less Time

Lasagna fixings, minus the meat, make Vegetable Noodle Bake a satisfying casserole that's quicker to make than the traditional entree, but retains all the wonderful flavor.

If you have ground beef, you can cook it and add it, but no one will miss the meat because the dish is so tasty. Italian Salad (p. 266) and Pull-Apart Herb Bread (p. 268) would make great accompaniments.

Make It **Meatless**

Taco Twist Soup

Prep/Total Time: 20 min.

✓ Uses less fat, sugar or salt. Includes Nutrition Facts and Diabetic Exchanges.

- 1 medium onion, chopped
- 2 garlic cloves, minced
- 2 teaspoons olive oil
- 3 cups vegetable broth
- 1 can (15 ounces) black beans, rinsed and drained
- 1 can (14-1/2 ounces) diced tomatoes
- 1-1/2 cups picante sauce
- 1 cup uncooked spiral pasta
- 1 small green pepper, chopped
- 2 teaspoons chili powder
- 1 teaspoon ground cumin
- 1/2 cup shredded reduced-fat cheddar cheese
- 3 tablespoons reduced-fat sour cream

In a large saucepan, saute onion and garlic in oil until tender. Add the broth, beans, tomatoes, picante sauce, pasta, green pepper, chili powder and cumin. Bring to a boil, stirring frequently. Reduce heat; cover and simmer for 10-12 minutes or until pasta is tender, stirring occasionally. Serve with cheese and sour cream.

Yield: 6 servings.

Nutrition Facts: 1 cup equals 216 calories, 5 g fat (2 g saturated fat), 12 mg cholesterol, 1,052 mg sodium, 33 g carbohydrate, 6 g fiber, 10 g protein. **Diabetic Exchanges:** 2 vegetable, 1-1/2 starch, 1 lean meat, 1/2 fat.

Count on Black Beans

Spiral pasta is what puts the "twist" in Taco Twist Soup. It's also loaded with black beans, tomatoes, onion and green pepper ...and gets zip from garlic, cumin and chili powder. Try personalizing the soup with spicy or mild picante sauce. And top off bowlfuls with sour cream and cheddar cheese.

Canned black beans can be a real time-saver for busy cooks. Unopened cans stay fresh in the pantry for up to 1 year. Drain and rinse thoroughly before using.

Individual Grilled Pizzas

Prep/Total Time: 30 min.

1-1/2 cups all-purpose flour

1/2 cup whole wheat flour

1 package (1/4 ounce) quick-rise yeast

1/2 teaspoon salt

1/2 teaspoon sugar

3/4 cup warm water (120° to 130°)

1 tablespoon olive oil

PESTO:

1 cup chopped fresh basil

1/4 cup plain yogurt

2 tablespoons unsalted sunflower kernels

1 tablespoon olive oil

1 garlic clove, minced

1/8 teaspoon *each* salt and pepper

TOPPINGS:

1 cup (4 ounces) shredded part-skim mozzarella cheese, *divided*

2 medium tomatoes, thinly sliced

2 green onions, finely chopped

Coarsely ground pepper

2 tablespoons grated Parmesan cheese

Pizza...Special Delivery!

Featuring garden-fresh vegetables and a light pesto sauce, these small pizzas will be popular with your gang because they can add whatever toppings they prefer.

While the grill is still warm, use it to make another crowd-pleaser for dessert—s'mores!

In a large bowl, combine flours, yeast, salt and sugar. Add water and oil; mix until a soft dough forms. Turn onto a floured surface; knead until smooth and elastic, about 5-7 minutes. Cover; let stand 10-15 minutes. Meanwhile, in a blender, combine pesto ingredients. Cover; process until smooth, scraping sides often. Set aside.

Divide dough into fourths. Roll each portion into a 6-in. circle. Coat grill rack with nonstick cooking spray before starting grill. Prepare grill for indirect medium heat. Grill dough over direct heat area. Cover; cook for 1 minute or until puffed and golden. Turn; place over indirect heat. Spread pesto over crusts. Top with 2/3 cup mozzarella cheese, tomatoes, onions, pepper, Parmesan and remaining mozzarella. Grill, covered, for 3-5 minutes or until cheese is melted and crust is lightly browned.

Yield: 4 servings.

Make It **Meatless**

Veggie Brown Rice Wraps

Prep/Total Time: 20 min.

☑ Uses less fat, sugar or salt.
Includes Nutrition Facts.

> 1 medium sweet red *or* green pepper, diced
> 1 cup sliced fresh mushrooms
> 2 garlic cloves, minced
> 1 tablespoon olive oil
> 2 cups cooked brown rice
> 1 can (16 ounces) kidney beans, rinsed and drained
> 1 cup frozen corn, thawed
> 1/4 cup chopped green onions
> 1/2 teaspoon ground cumin
> 1/2 teaspoon pepper
> 1/4 teaspoon salt
> 6 flour tortillas (8 inches), warmed
> 1/2 cup shredded reduced-fat cheddar cheese
> 3/4 cup salsa

Brown Rice Is Better

Salsa gives a bit of zip to the brown rice and bean filling in these meatless tortilla wraps.

Brown rice contains four times the amount of insoluble fiber found in white rice—a great reason for eating brown rice instead of white. Brown rice is also filled with protein, calcium, phosphorus, iron, vitamin E, and most of the B vitamins.

To get 2 cups cooked brown rice, start with 1/2 cup uncooked rice.

In a large nonstick skillet, saute the red pepper, mushrooms and garlic in oil until tender. Add the rice, beans, corn, green onions, cumin, pepper and salt. Cook and stir for 4-6 minutes or until heated through.

Spoon 3/4 cup onto each tortilla. Sprinkle with cheese; drizzle with salsa. Fold sides of tortilla over filling; serve immediately.

Yield: 6 servings.

Nutrition Facts: 1 wrap equals 377 calories, 8 g fat (2 g saturated fat), 7 mg cholesterol, 675 mg sodium, 62 g carbohydrate, 7 g fiber, 15 g protein.

Cast aside everyday dinners and net some compliments with an assortment of from-the-sea favorites!

Primavera Fish Fillets (p. 228)

Fast **Fish & Seafood**

Clam Chowder (p. 231)

Taste of Home's Weeknight Cooking Made Easy

Catfish with Shrimp Salsa

Prep/Total Time: 30 min.

  2   tablespoons Cajun *or*
      blackened seasoning
1/2   teaspoon ground cumin
1/2   teaspoon ground coriander
  4   catfish fillets (6 ounces *each*)
  2   to 3 tablespoons
      vegetable oil

SALSA:
  1   medium green pepper, diced
3/4   cup diced onion
  1   celery rib, diced
  1   jalapeno pepper, seeded and chopped
  2   garlic cloves, minced
  1   tablespoon butter
1-1/2 cups fresh *or* frozen corn
  3   plum tomatoes, seeded and chopped
  2   packages (5 ounces *each*) frozen cooked salad
      shrimp, thawed
1/2   teaspoon Cajun *or* blackened seasoning

Dash hot pepper sauce

In a small bowl, combine the Cajun seasoning, cumin and coriander; rub over catfish fillets. In a large skillet, fry fillets in oil over medium-high heat for 4-5 minutes on each side or until fish flakes easily with a fork. Remove and keep warm.

Spice Up Suppertime

Cajun seasoning, cumin and coriander spice up these catfish fillets nicely. The colorful corn and shrimp salsa makes an excellent accompaniment.

Although frozen cooked salad shrimp can be thawed quickly in cold water, they'll have better flavor if defrosted in the refrigerator. So plan ahead when preparing this dish.

In the same skillet, saute the green pepper, onion, celery, jalapeno and garlic in butter until tender. Add the corn, tomatoes and shrimp; cook and stir for 4-5 minutes or until corn is tender. Stir in Cajun seasoning and hot pepper sauce. Serve with catfish.

Yield: 4 servings.

Editor's Note: When cutting or seeding hot peppers, use rubber or plastic gloves to protect your hands. Avoid touching your face.

Fish Stick Sandwiches

Prep/Total Time: 25 min.

   1/4   cup butter, melted
    2   tablespoons lemon juice
    1   package (11.4 ounces) frozen breaded fish sticks
    2   tablespoons mayonnaise
    6   hot dog buns, split

Shredded lettuce, chopped onion and chopped tomatoes, optional

In a shallow bowl, combine butter and lemon juice. Dip fish sticks in butter mixture. Place in a single layer in an ungreased baking pan. Bake at 400° for 15-18 minutes or until crispy.

Spread mayonnaise on bottom of buns; add fish sticks. Top with lettuce, onion and tomato if desired. Replace bun tops.

Yield: 6 servings.

Meal Appeals to Kids of All Ages

Make the most of convenient frozen fish sticks with these fun, family-pleasing sandwiches. And use a package of mac and cheese to make soup to serve alongside.

Set aside the cheese sauce packet from a 14-ounce package of deluxe macaroni and cheese. In a large saucepan, bring 8 cups water to a boil; add macaroni and cook for 8 to 10 minutes or until tender.

Meanwhile, in another large saucepan, bring 1 cup water to a boil. Add 1 cup fresh broccoli florets and 2 tablespoons finely chopped onion; cook for 3 minutes. Stir in a 10-3/4-ounce can of condensed cheddar cheese soup, 2-1/2 cups milk, 1 cup chopped fully cooked ham and contents of cheese sauce packet, then heat through. Drain macaroni; stir into soup. Serves eight.

Primavera Fish Fillets

Prep/Total Time: 25 min.

✓ Uses less fat, sugar or salt. Includes Nutrition Facts and Diabetic Exchanges.

- 2 **celery ribs, sliced**
- 1 **large carrot, cut into 2-inch julienne strips**
- 1 **small onion, chopped**
- 1/4 **cup water**
- 2 **tablespoons white wine** *or* **chicken broth**
- 1/2 **teaspoon dried thyme**
- 1 **can (10-3/4 ounces) condensed cream of mushroom soup, undiluted**
- 1 **pound frozen cod** *or* **haddock fillets, thawed**

In a large skillet, combine the first six ingredients. Bring to a boil. Reduce heat; cover and simmer for 5-7 minutes or until vegetables are crisp-tender. Stir in soup until blended; bring to a boil. Add fillets. Reduce heat; cover and simmer for 5-7 minutes or until fish flakes easily with a fork.

Yield: 4 servings.

Nutrition Facts: 1 serving (prepared with reduced-fat reduced-sodium soup) equals 151 calories, 4 g fat (1 g saturated fat), 51 mg cholesterol, 415 mg sodium, 7 g carbohydrate, 1 g fiber, 21 g protein. **Diabetic Exchanges:** 2-1/2 lean meat, 1/2 starch.

Frozen Fish Facts

Fishing for a fast supper? Cook tender cod fillets and vegetables in a flavorful sauce that's easy to make with convenient cream of mushroom soup.

Buy frozen fish in packages that are solidly frozen, tightly sealed and free of freezer burn and odor. The thicker the package, the longer it will take to defrost. When defrosting fish in the refrigerator, place a tray under the package to catch any liquid or juices. Allow 12 or more hours to thaw a 1-pound package.

Zesty Salmon Burgers

Prep/Total Time: 20 min.

1 can (14-3/4 ounces)
   salmon, drained, skin
   and bones removed
2 eggs
1/2 cup dry bread crumbs
1/4 cup finely chopped onion
1/4 cup mayonnaise
1 to 2 tablespoons prepared
   horseradish
1 tablespoon pimientos
1/4 teaspoon salt
1/8 teaspoon pepper
2 tablespoons butter
4 kaiser rolls, split

Lettuce leaves

In a large bowl, combine the first nine ingredients. Shape into four patties. In a large skillet, cook patties in butter over medium heat for 5-6 minutes on each side or until browned. Serve on rolls with lettuce.

Yield: 4 servings.

Serve Salad with Savory Burgers

For a refreshing side dish, serve crunchy pea salad alongside Zesty Salmon Burgers.

   In a bowl, combine a 10-ounce package of thawed frozen peas, an 8-ounce can of drained sliced water chestnuts, 1 cup thinly sliced celery and 1/2 cup sliced green onions. In a small bowl, combine 1/4 cup mayonnaise, 1/4 cup sour cream and 1/2 teaspoon seasoned salt. Add to pea mixture; toss to coat. Chill until serving. Serves eight.

Tuna Cheese Melts

Prep/Total Time: 25 min.

1/2 cup sour cream
1/2 teaspoon garlic salt
8 slices light rye bread
1 can (6 ounces) tuna,
   drained and flaked
2 tablespoons mayonnaise
4 slices process American
   cheese
4 tablespoons butter,
   divided

In a small bowl, combine sour cream and garlic salt; spread on one side of each slice of bread. In another small bowl, combine tuna and mayonnaise; spread on four slices of bread. Top with cheese and remaining bread; gently press together.

Melt 2 tablespoons butter in a large skillet over medium heat. Add two sandwiches; toast sandwiches until bread is lightly browned on both sides and cheese is melted. Repeat with remaining butter and sandwiches.

Yield: 4 servings.

New Ways to Try Tuna

It's easy to dress up a typical tuna sandwich with American cheese and rye bread, spread with a mixture of sour cream and garlic salt. It makes a filling supper served with potato salad purchased from your supermarket's deli.

Tuna salad is both thrifty to make and fun to eat. You can serve it on a bed of lettuce, stuffed in a tomato or spread on a tortilla rolled up with lettuce and tomato.

Clam Chowder

Prep/Total Time: 30 min.

6   bacon strips, diced
1/2   cup finely chopped onion
2   cans (10-3/4 ounces *each*) condensed cream
      of potato soup, undiluted
1-1/2   cups milk
3   cans (6-1/2 ounces *each*) minced clams,
      undrained
1   tablespoon lemon juice
1/4   teaspoon dried thyme
1/4   teaspoon pepper
Minced fresh parsley

In a large skillet, cook bacon over medium heat until crisp. Using a slotted spoon, remove to paper towels; drain, reserving 1 tablespoon drippings.

In the same skillet, saute onion in reserved drippings until tender. Stir in soup and milk. Add the clams, lemon juice, thyme, pepper and bacon; cook until heated through. Garnish with parsley.

Yield: 5 servings.

All About Chowder

Here's a quick chowder that will have you in and out of the kitchen in no time. Served with crusty bread and a salad, it's the perfect meal to warm up a chilly evening.

Chowder comes from the French word chaudiére, a caldron in which fisherman made their stews fresh from the sea.

New England-style chowder is made with milk or cream; Manhattan-style with tomatoes. Versatile chowder can contain any of several varieties of seafood and vegetables.

Crab Mornay

Prep/Total Time: 30 min.

1 package (10 ounces) frozen pastry shells
1/2 cup butter, cubed
1 jar (6 ounces) sliced mushrooms, drained
6 green onions, sliced
1 jar (4 ounces) diced pimientos, drained
2 tablespoons all-purpose flour
1 can (12 ounces) evaporated milk
2 cups (8 ounces) shredded Swiss cheese
3 cans (6 ounces *each*) crabmeat, drained, flaked and cartilage removed
1 teaspoon salt
1/8 teaspoon cayenne pepper
1/3 cup minced fresh parsley

Bake pastry shells according to package directions. Meanwhile, place butter in a 2-qt. microwave-safe dish. Cover and microwave on high for 20-30 seconds or until melted. Add the mushrooms, onions and pimientos. Cover and cook on high for 2-3 minutes or until vegetables are crisp-tender.

Combine the flour and milk until smooth; gradually stir into the vegetable mixture. Microwave, uncovered, on high for 2-3 minutes or until thickened, stirring often. Add the cheese, crab, salt and cayenne. Cook, covered, on high for 30-60 seconds or until the cheese is melted. Spoon into the pastry shells and sprinkle with parsley.

Yield: 6 servings.

Editor's Note: This recipe was tested in a 1,100-watt microwave.

Eye-Appealing Meal Is Easy

Prepared pastry shells overflow with a creamy combination of canned crab and mushrooms in this microwave entree.

Prepare green peas supreme as a pretty side. In a large skillet, cook 4 ounces diced Canadian bacon in 1 tablespoon butter until lightly browned. Add 3 cups frozen peas, 12 peeled pearl onions, 1/2 cup water, 1/2 teaspoon sugar, 1/2 teaspoon salt and 1/4 teaspoon pepper. Cover and cook over medium heat until vegetables are tender, about 10 to 15 minutes; drain. Serves six.

Glazed Salmon

Prep/Total Time: 20 min.

1/2	cup olive oil
1/3	cup molasses
2	teaspoons minced garlic
1-1/2	teaspoons grated lemon peel
4	salmon fillets (6 ounces *each*)

In a small bowl, combine the oil, molasses, garlic and lemon peel; reserve half of the mixture for serving.

Coat grill rack with nonstick cooking spray before starting the grill. Grill salmon, uncovered, over medium heat for 6-8 minutes on each side or until fish flakes easily with a fork, basting frequently with the molasses mixture. Serve with the reserved molasses mixture.

Yield: 4 servings.

Be Savvy When Buying Salmon

After just one bite, your family will agree they never tasted such delicious salmon…and it takes only minutes to prepare!

Look for fresh salmon steaks and fillets that are firm with a deep "salmon pink" color. The meat should have a slight sheen and appear somewhat translucent. Choose steaks and fillets with smooth cuts. Cuts of salmon that have gaps are indicative of old fish. Use or freeze fresh salmon within 2 days of purchase.

Instead of Frying Fish

Prep/Total Time: 25 min.

1 pound walleye, perch *or* pike fillets
1/4 cup milk
1 cup crushed potato chips
1/4 cup grated Parmesan cheese
1/4 teaspoon dried thyme
1 tablespoon dry bread crumbs
2 tablespoons butter, melted

Cut fish into serving-size pieces. Place milk in a shallow bowl. In another shallow bowl, combine the potato chips, Parmesan cheese and thyme. Dip the fish in the milk, then roll in the potato chip mixture.

Sprinkle a greased 8-in. square baking dish with bread crumbs. Place fish over crumbs; drizzle with butter. Bake, uncovered, at 500° for 12-14 minutes or until fish flakes easily with a fork.

Yield: 4 servings.

Fish and Food Safety

With this recipe for walleye, the crispy potato chip coating bakes up toasty brown, while the fillets stay nice and moist.

Prepare fish within 1 to 2 days after it is caught or purchased because it is highly perishable. Refrigerate it in the coldest area of your refrigerator.

For longer-term storage, wrap fish in freezer paper, heavy-duty foil or heavy-duty plastic bags. Freeze oily fish for up to 3 months and lean fish for as long as 6 months.

Classic Crab Cakes

Prep/Total Time: 20 min.

1 pound canned crabmeat, drained, flaked and cartilage removed
2 to 2-1/2 cups soft bread crumbs
1 egg, beaten
3/4 cup mayonnaise
1/3 cup *each* chopped celery, green pepper and onion
1 tablespoon seafood seasoning
1 tablespoon minced fresh parsley
2 teaspoons lemon juice
1 teaspoon Worcestershire sauce
1 teaspoon prepared mustard
1/4 teaspoon pepper
1/8 teaspoon hot pepper sauce
2 to 4 tablespoons vegetable oil
Lemon slices, optional

In a large bowl, combine the crab, bread crumbs, egg, mayonnaise, vegetables and seasonings. Shape into eight patties. Broil patties or cook in a skillet in oil for 4 minutes on each side or until golden brown. Serve with lemon if desired.

Yield: 8 servings.

Crab Cake Clues

Golden brown and flecked with green pepper, celery and onion, these tender crab cakes are very easy to prepare.

You can shape the patties ahead of time, wrap them individually in plastic wrap and pack them into freezer bags. Later, defrost and cook as many as needed.

You can also place cooked crab cakes on English muffin halves, top with shredded cheddar cheese and broil for 2 to 3 minutes for sandwiches.

Crumb-Topped Salmon

Prep/Total Time: 30 min.

1-1/2   **cups soft bread crumbs**
  2   **tablespoons minced fresh parsley**
  1   **tablespoon minced fresh thyme *or* 1 teaspoon dried thyme**
  2   **garlic cloves, minced**
  1   **teaspoon grated lemon peel**
1/2   **teaspoon salt**
1/4   **teaspoon lemon-pepper seasoning**
1/4   **teaspoon paprika**
  4   **salmon fillets (6 ounces *each*)**
Refrigerated butter-flavored spray

In a large bowl, combine the first eight ingredients; set aside. Pat salmon dry. Place skin side down in a 13-in. x 9-in. x 2-in. baking dish coated with nonstick cooking spray. Spritz salmon with butter-flavored spray; cover with crumb mixture. Spritz crumbs with butter-flavored spray. Bake, uncovered, at 350° for 15-20 minutes or until fish flakes easily with a fork.

Yield: 4 servings.

Editor's Note: This recipe was tested with I Can't Believe It's Not Butter Spray.

Making Soft Bread Crumbs

These delicious salmon fillets are great for weeknight meals but also wonderful for company since they take only a few minutes to prepare, yet taste like you fussed. The bread crumb topping is a nice complement to the fish.

To make the bread crumbs, tear several slices of fresh white, French or whole wheat bread into 1-inch pieces. Place in a food processor or blender; cover and push pulse button several times to make coarse crumbs. One slice of bread yields about 1/2 cup crumbs.

Hot 'n' Sour Shrimp

Prep/Total Time: 30 min.

1	tablespoon brown sugar
2	teaspoons cornstarch
2	tablespoons water
2	tablespoons cider vinegar
2	tablespoons soy sauce
1	tablespoon vegetable oil
1	large sweet red pepper, julienned
3/4	cup sliced fresh mushrooms
1	pound uncooked medium shrimp, peeled and deveined
2	garlic cloves, minced
1/4	teaspoon crushed red pepper flakes
1/2	small cucumber, seeded and sliced

Hot cooked spaghetti, optional

In a small bowl, combine the first five ingredients until smooth; set aside. In a skillet or wok, heat oil; stir-fry red pepper and mushrooms for 4 minutes. Add the shrimp, garlic and pepper flakes; stir-fry 3-4 minutes longer or until shrimp turn pink and vegetables are crisp-tender.

Stir cornstarch mixture and add to pan. Bring to a boil; cook and stir for 1 minute or until thickened. Add cucumber; cook and stir 1 minute longer or until heated through. Serve with spaghetti if desired.

Yield: 4 servings.

Selecting the Best Shrimp

Looking for something quick, colorful and chock-full of healthy ingredients to set before your family and friends? Try spooning this hearty shrimp stir-fry over spaghetti.

Fresh shrimp should have a firm texture. Avoid shrimp that have a yellow color to their meat or black spots or rings on the shells (unless they are Tiger shrimp) or meat. Shrimp in the shell (fresh or frozen) are available in different sizes (medium, large, extra large, jumbo).

Asparagus Crab Casserole

Prep/Total Time: 20 min.

2 packages (8 ounces *each*) imitation crabmeat, flaked
2 cups cooked rice
1 package (12 ounces) frozen cut asparagus
1 can (10-3/4 ounces) condensed broccoli cheese soup, undiluted
1 cup milk
1/3 cup chopped onion
1 tablespoon lemon juice
1 tablespoon butter, melted
1 teaspoon dill weed
1/2 teaspoon lemon-pepper seasoning
1/4 cup sliced almonds, toasted, optional

In a large bowl, combine the first 10 ingredients. Transfer to a greased 2-qt. microwave-safe dish. Cover loosely and microwave on high for 3-5 minutes or until heated through, stirring twice. Sprinkle with almonds if desired.

Yield: 8 servings.

Editor's Note: This recipe was tested in a 1,100-watt microwave.

Comfort Food Cooks Up Quick

On very busy weeknights, you're sure to appreciate this comfort food that seems special but can be put on the table fast.

Crabmeat, cooked rice and asparagus combine with convenient canned broccoli cheese soup and seasonings in the creamy microwave casserole.

Add a green salad, bread and a fruit dessert, such as Rhubarb Cobbler (p. 310) or Strawberry Broil (p. 314), for a complete, satisfying meal.

Broiled Halibut Kabobs

Prep/Total Time: 30 min.

1-1/4   pounds halibut fillets
    1   medium green pepper, cut into 1-inch pieces
    1   medium onion, cut into 1-inch wedges
    1   can (20 ounces) pineapple chunks, drained
    8   to 10 cherry tomatoes

BARBECUE SAUCE:

  1/2   cup ketchup
  1/4   cup vegetable oil
    3   tablespoons orange juice
    2   to 3 green onions, finely chopped
    2   garlic cloves, minced
    1   teaspoon grated orange peel
  1/4   teaspoon salt

Cut fish into 1-in. pieces. On metal or soaked wooden skewers, alternately thread the fish, green pepper, onion, pineapple and tomatoes. Place on a greased broiler pan.

In a small bowl, whisk the sauce ingredients until blended. Spoon some sauce over the kabobs. Broil 5-6 in. from the heat for 5-7 minutes on each side or until fish flakes easily with a fork, basting occasionally with sauce.

Yield: 4 servings.

A New Way to Serve Fish "Sticks"

The orange-flavored barbecue sauce complements these halibut kabobs nicely. A tossed salad and tall glasses of fresh lemonade would be refreshing accompaniments.

For dessert, serve slices of angel food cake topped with lemon sauce. In a small mixing bowl, beat a 3-ounce package of softened cream cheese until smooth. Add 1-3/4 cups cold milk and a 3.4-ounce package of instant lemon pudding mix; beat 2 minutes or until thickened. Serve over cake.

Halibut with Kiwi Salsa

Prep/Total Time: 20 min.

✓ Uses less fat, sugar or salt. Includes Nutrition Facts and Diabetic Exchanges.

- 2 medium mangoes, peeled and cubed (about 1-1/3 cups)
- 4 kiwifruit, peeled and cubed
- 1/2 cup diced sweet red pepper
- 1/2 cup diced onion
- 1 jalapeno pepper, seeded and minced
- 2 tablespoons lemon juice, *divided*
- 1 tablespoon lime juice
- 2 teaspoons minced fresh mint *or* 3/4 teaspoon dried mint
- 1 teaspoon honey
- 1/2 teaspoon salt, *divided*
- 1 tablespoon olive oil
- 4 halibut fillets (4 ounces *each*)
- 1/4 teaspoon chili powder

In a large bowl, combine mangoes, kiwi, red pepper, onion, jalapeno, 1 tablespoon lemon juice, lime juice, mint, honey and 1/4 teaspoon salt. Cover; refrigerate until serving. In a bowl, combine oil and remaining lemon juice; drizzle over both sides of fish. Sprinkle with chili powder and remaining salt. If grilling fish, coat grill rack with nonstick cooking spray before starting grill. Grill fillets, covered, over medium heat or broil 6 in. from heat for 5-7 minutes on each side or until fish flakes easily with a fork. Serve with salsa.

Yield: 4 servings.

Editor's Note: When cutting or seeding hot peppers, use rubber or plastic gloves to protect your hands. Avoid touching your face.

Nutrition Facts: 1 fillet with 1/2 cup salsa equals 301 calories, 8 g fat (1 g saturated fat), 54 mg cholesterol, 391 mg sodium, 21 g carbohydrate, 3 g fiber, 37 g protein. **Diabetic Exchanges:** 5 very lean meat, 1 fruit, 1 vegetable, 1 fat.

Picking Out Kiwifruit

These halibut fillets are topped with a fruity salsa of kiwifruit, golden mango and red peppers for an eye-catching presentation.

Green kiwifruit is available year-round. Select plump fruit that yields to gentle pressure. Avoid fruit with soft spots or shriveled skin. Firm fruit will still need to ripen. Store un-ripened kiwi at room temperature. Once ripened, store in the refrigerator for 2 to 3 days.

Coconut Fried Shrimp

Prep/Total Time: 20 min.

- 1-1/4 cups all-purpose flour
- 1-1/4 cups cornstarch
- 6-1/2 teaspoons baking powder
- 1/2 teaspoon salt
- 1/4 teaspoon Cajun seasoning
- 1-1/2 cups cold water
- 1/2 teaspoon vegetable oil
- 2-1/2 cups flaked coconut
- 1 pound uncooked large shrimp, peeled and deveined
- Additional oil for deep-fat frying
- 1 cup orange marmalade
- 1/4 cup honey

Peeling and Deveining Shrimp

Remove the shell from raw shrimp by opening the shell at the underside or leg area and peeling it back. A gentle pull may be necessary to release the shell from tail area.

To remove the black vein running down the back of the shrimp, make a slit with a paring knife along the back from the head area to tail. Rinse shrimp under cold water to remove exposed vein.

In a small bowl, combine the first five ingredients. Stir in water and oil until smooth. Place coconut in another bowl. Dip shrimp into batter, then coat with coconut. In an electric skillet or deep-fat fryer, heat oil to 375°. Fry shrimp, a few at a time, for 3 minutes or until golden brown. Drain on paper towels.

In a saucepan, heat marmalade and honey; stir until blended. Serve as a dipping sauce for the shrimp.

Yield: 4 servings.

Catch-of-the-Day Casserole

Prep: 15 min. **Bake:** 30 min.

4 ounces small shell pasta
1 can (10-3/4 ounces) condensed cream of celery soup, undiluted
1/2 cup mayonnaise
1/4 cup milk
1/4 cup shredded cheddar cheese
1 package (10 ounces) frozen peas, thawed
1 can (7-1/2 ounces) salmon, drained, bones and skin removed
1 tablespoon finely chopped onion

Cook pasta according to package directions. Meanwhile, in a large bowl, combine the soup, mayonnaise, milk and cheese until blended. Stir in peas, salmon and onion. Drain pasta; add to salmon mixture. Transfer to a greased 2-qt. baking dish. Bake, uncovered, at 350° for 30-35 minutes or until bubbly.

Yield: 4 servings.

Editor's Note: Reduced-fat or fat-free mayonnaise is not recommended for this recipe.

Cooking with Canned Salmon

This cheesy salmon, pasta and pea blend will win over any doubters who say they aren't fond of fish! If your family is a fan of tuna, you can use that instead with equally good results.

Salmon in 12-ounce cans has already been boned and skinned. If using a 14-3/4-ounce or 7-1/2-ounce can, remove the bones and skin after draining. Although it's not harmful to store food in an open can in the refrigerator for a day or so, it's better to store leftover canned goods in a glass or plastic covered container.

Almond Sole Fillets

Prep/Total Time: 10 min.

1/3 cup butter, cubed
1/4 cup slivered almonds
  1 pound sole fillets
  2 tablespoons lemon juice
1/2 teaspoon dill weed
1/4 teaspoon salt
1/4 teaspoon pepper
1/4 teaspoon paprika

In a microwave-safe bowl, combine butter and almonds. Microwave, uncovered, on high for 2 minutes or until almonds are golden brown. Place the fillets in a greased microwave-safe 11-in. x 7-in. x 2-in. dish. Top with the almond mixture.

In a small bowl, combine the lemon juice, dill, salt and pepper; drizzle over fish. Sprinkle with paprika. Cover and microwave on high for 4-5 minutes or until fish flakes easily with a fork.

Yield: 4 servings.

Editor's Note: This recipe was tested with an 850-watt microwave.

Fish Supper Is Fast to Fix

This buttery treatment is a great way to prepare sole, perch or halibut. It cooks quickly in the microwave, so it's perfect for a busy weeknight. In fact, it can be on the table in only 10 minutes!

Pick up cobs of corn in the frozen vegetable section of your grocery store to serve alongside the fish. Combine 1/2 cup softened butter, 2 tablespoons minced fresh basil, 2 tablespoons minced fresh parsley and 1/2 teaspoon salt. Serve with the corn.

Lime Fish Tacos

Prep/Total Time: 20 min.

✓ Uses less fat, sugar or salt. Includes Nutrition Facts and Diabetic Exchanges.

- **1 pound red snapper *or* orange roughy fillets**
- **1 garlic clove, minced**
- **2 tablespoons butter**
- **7 teaspoons lime juice, *divided***
- **1/4 teaspoon white pepper**
- **2 tablespoons reduced-fat sour cream**
- **2 tablespoons fat-free mayonnaise**

Dash hot pepper sauce

- **7 flour tortillas (8 inches), warmed**
- **1 cup shredded lettuce**
- **1 cup chopped fresh tomato**

Remove skin from fish and cut fish into 1-in. cubes. In a nonstick skillet, saute garlic in butter and 5 teaspoons lime juice for 30 seconds. Add fish and pepper. Cook for 6-8 minutes over medium heat until fish flakes easily with a fork, gently stirring occasionally.

Meanwhile, combine the sour cream, mayonnaise, hot pepper sauce and remaining lime juice. Place a spoonful of fish on each tortilla. Top each with lettuce, tomato and sour cream sauce; fold over.

Yield: 7 servings.

Nutrition Facts: 1 taco equals 238 calories, 7 g fat (3 g saturated fat), 24 mg cholesterol, 366 mg sodium, 28 g carbohydrate, 1 g fiber, 15 g protein. **Diabetic Exchanges:** 2 starch, 1-1/2 lean meat.

No Bones About It

The secret to getting your family to eat fish just may be tucked inside these tempting tacos! The tastes and textures blend in a surprisingly pleasing way. Lime adds a zippy twist to the flaky fillets and the creamy sauce.

Before cooking fish, gently run your fingers over the fish to find any bones. Easily pull them out with clean kitchen pliers or tweezers.

Crab Melt Loaf

Prep/Total Time: 30 min.

 1 pound imitation crabmeat, chopped
1/2 cup mayonnaise
1/4 cup thinly sliced green onions
1/4 cup diced celery
 2 cups (8 ounces) shredded part-skim mozzarella cheese
1/8 teaspoon salt
1/8 teaspoon pepper
 1 loaf (1 pound) unsliced French bread, halved lengthwise

In a large bowl, combine the crab, mayonnaise, green onions and celery. Stir in the cheese, salt and pepper. Spread over bottom of bread; replace top. Wrap in a large piece of heavy-duty aluminum foil. Place on an ungreased baking sheet. Bake at 400° for 20 minutes or until heated through. Cut into slices.

Yield: 8 servings.

Sandwich and Salad Satisfy

Instead of crab, you can use canned tuna or salmon to make this sandwich loaf. Cheddar cheese can replace the mozzarella, and you can substitute a croissant for the French bread.

Serve romaine with oranges and almonds as a refreshing side. In a bowl, toss 8 cups torn romaine, an 11-ounce drained can of mandarin oranges, 2 thinly sliced green onions and 1/4 cup toasted slivered almonds. In a jar with a tight-fitting lid, combine 1/4 cup each sugar, vegetable oil and white vinegar; shake well. Drizzle over salad and toss to coat. Serves eight.

Snapper with Spicy Pineapple Glaze

Prep/Total Time: 30 min.

✓ Uses less fat, sugar or salt. Includes Nutrition Facts and Diabetic Exchanges.

- **1/2 cup pineapple preserves**
- **2 tablespoons rice wine vinegar**
- **2 teaspoons minced fresh gingerroot**
- **2 garlic cloves, minced**
- **3/4 teaspoon salt, *divided***
- **1/4 teaspoon cayenne pepper**
- **4 fresh *or* frozen red snapper fillets (6 ounces *each*), thawed**
- **3 teaspoons olive oil**

In a small bowl, combine the preserves, vinegar, ginger, garlic, 1/2 teaspoon salt and cayenne; set aside. Place fillets on a broiler pan coated with nonstick cooking spray. Spoon oil over both sides of fillets; sprinkle with remaining salt.

Broil 4-6 in. from the heat for 5 minutes. Baste with half of the glaze. Broil 5-7 minutes longer or until fish flakes easily with a fork. Baste with remaining glaze.

Yield: 4 servings.

Nutrition Facts: 1 fillet equals 304 calories, 6 g fat (1 g saturated fat), 63 mg cholesterol, 552 mg sodium, 27 g carbohydrate, trace fiber, 35 g protein. **Diabetic Exchanges:** 5 very lean meat, 2 fruit.

Testing Fish For Doneness

Ginger and cayenne bring spice to this tangy treatment for red snapper fillets. Sweet pineapple preserves round out the delectable combination of tropical flavors.

To test fish for doneness, gently insert the tines of a fork at an angle into the thickest part of the fish and gently part the meat. When it is opaque and flakes into sections, it is completely cooked.

Broccoli Shrimp Alfredo

Prep/Total Time: 30 min.

1 package (16 ounces) fettuccine
1 pound uncooked medium shrimp, peeled and deveined
3 garlic cloves, minced
1/2 cup butter, cubed
1 package (8 ounces) cream cheese, cubed
1 cup milk
1/2 cup shredded Parmesan cheese
1 package (10 ounces) frozen broccoli florets
1/2 teaspoon salt
Dash pepper

Cook fettuccine according to package directions. Meanwhile, in a large skillet, saute shrimp and garlic in butter until shrimp turn pink. Remove and keep warm. In the same skillet, combine the cream cheese, milk and Parmesan cheese; cook and stir until cheeses are melted and mixture is smooth.

Place 1 in. of water in a saucepan; add broccoli. Bring to a boil. Reduce heat; cover and simmer for 6-8 minutes or until tender. Drain. Stir the broccoli, shrimp, salt and pepper into cheese sauce; cook until heated through. Drain fettuccine; top with the shrimp mixture.

Yield: 4 servings.

Appetizing Alfredo

Why buy store-bought when you can combine cream cheese, milk and shredded Parmesan cheese to produce a homemade Alfredo sauce that's as swift as it is superb? Toss it with fresh shrimp and convenient frozen broccoli, then serve the mixture over pasta for an effortless entree that's sure to be popular in your home.

Try the recipe with sea scallops, lobster or your family's favorite seafood, too. It's great with a pitcher of iced tea and buttery soft breadsticks.

Poached Perch with Broccoli

Prep/Total Time: 30 min.

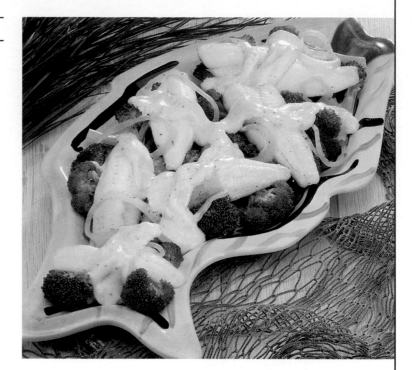

1 pound fresh broccoli, cut
　　into spears
3/4 cup water
1 small onion, sliced
1 bay leaf
1 teaspoon salt
1/2 teaspoon dried tarragon
2 pounds perch fillets

GARLIC SAUCE:

1 cup mayonnaise
1 tablespoon lemon juice
1 garlic clove, minced
1/2 teaspoon ground mustard
1/4 teaspoon salt
1/4 teaspoon pepper

Place broccoli in a steamer basket. Place in a saucepan over 1 in. of water; bring to a boil. Cover and steam until crisp-tender; set aside and keep warm.

In a large skillet, combine the water, onion, bay leaf, salt and tarragon; bring to a boil. Reduce heat; add perch fillets in batches. Cover and cook until fish is firm and flakes easily with a fork. Remove fish and onions with a slotted spoon; keep warm. Discard bay leaf.

In a large bowl, combine the sauce ingredients. Stir in 2-4 tablespoons cooking liquid until sauce reaches desired consistency. Arrange broccoli on a serving platter; top with fish, onions and garlic sauce.

Yield: 4-6 servings.

What Is Poaching?

Everyone who tastes them will love these tender fillets served with broccoli in a creamy garlic sauce. The recipe is quick and easy to prepare and so delicious tasting.

Poaching involves gently cooking food in liquid that's just below the boiling point. It produces a delicate flavor in foods, while imparting some of the liquid's flavor to the ingredient being poached.

Basil Tuna Steaks

Prep/Total Time: 20 min.

✓ Uses less fat, sugar or salt. Includes Nutrition Facts and Diabetic Exchanges.

6	tuna steaks (6 ounces *each*)
4-1/2	teaspoons olive oil
3	tablespoons minced fresh basil
3/4	teaspoon salt
1/4	teaspoon pepper

Drizzle both sides of tuna steaks with oil. Sprinkle with the basil, salt and pepper.

Coat grill rack with nonstick cooking spray before starting the grill. Grill tuna, covered, over medium heat for 6-8 minutes on each side or until fish flakes easily with a fork.

Yield: 6 servings.

Nutrition Facts: 1 tuna steak equals 214 calories, 5 g fat (1 g saturated fat), 77 mg cholesterol, 358 mg sodium, trace carbohydrate, trace fiber, 40 g protein. **Diabetic Exchanges:** 5 very lean meat, 1 fat.

The Basics of Basil

Five-ingredient Basil Tuna Steaks are simply delicious and can be grilled in such a short time. Fresh basil is what gives the tuna its fabulous flavor.

Called the "royal herb" by ancient Greeks, basil is a member of the mint family. It has a sweet flavor with hints of mint, pepper and cloves. Refrigerate basil, wrapped in slightly damp paper towel and then in a resealable plastic bag, for up to 4 days.

Spanish Corn with Fish Sticks

Prep: 20 min. **Bake:** 40 min.

1/4 **cup chopped onion**
1/4 **cup chopped green pepper**
1/4 **cup butter, cubed**
1/4 **cup all-purpose flour**
1-1/2 **teaspoons salt**
1/4 **teaspoon pepper**
2 **teaspoons sugar**
2 **cans (14-1/2 ounces *each*) stewed tomatoes**
2 **packages (10 ounces *each*) frozen corn, partially thawed**
2 **packages (12 ounces *each*) frozen fish sticks**

In a large skillet, saute onion and green pepper in butter until tender. Stir in the flour, salt, pepper and sugar until blended. Add tomatoes; bring to a boil. Cook and stir for 2 minutes or until thickened. Reduce heat; simmer, uncovered, for 3-5 minutes or until heated through, stirring occasionally. Stir in corn.

Transfer to two greased 11-in. x 7-in. x 2-in. baking dishes. Cover and bake at 350° for 25 minutes. Uncover; arrange fish sticks over the top. Bake 15 minutes longer or until fish sticks are heated through.

Yield: 8-10 servings.

Fish Stick Supper Sure to Please

Simple to assemble and economical, too, this tasty casserole is bound to become a family favorite. The recipe makes two large casseroles, which serve eight to 10 people. If you have a smaller family, it can easily be cut in half to feed four or five. And if you don't have frozen fish sticks on hand, you could use any breaded boneless fish fillets instead.

Grilled Spiced Fish

Prep: 5 min. + marinating **Grill:** 10 min.

✓ Uses less fat, sugar or salt. Includes Nutrition Facts and Diabetic Exchanges.

- 1 **tablespoon olive oil**
- 4 **red snapper** *or* **orange roughy fillets (6 ounces *each*)**
- 2 **teaspoons paprika**
- 1 **teaspoon salt**
- 1 **teaspoon onion powder**
- 1 **teaspoon garlic powder**
- 1/2 **teaspoon cayenne pepper**
- 1/4 **teaspoon white pepper**
- 1/4 **teaspoon *each* dried oregano, basil and thyme**

Spoon oil over fish. In a small bowl, combine the seasonings; sprinkle over fish and press into both sides. Cover and refrigerate for 30 minutes.

Coat grill rack with nonstick cooking spray before starting the grill. Grill fillets, covered, over medium heat for 3-5 minutes on each side or until fish flakes easily with a fork.

Yield: 4 servings.

Nutrition Facts: 1 fillet equals 154 calories, 5 g fat (1 g saturated fat), 34 mg cholesterol, 694 mg sodium, 1 g carbohydrate, trace fiber, 25 g protein. **Diabetic Exchanges:** 4 very lean meat, 1/2 fat.

Rev Up the Flavor With Rubs

These moist, flaky fillets provide a welcome change of pace at summer cookouts. Even steak lovers will be smacking their lips!

Paprika, salt, onion powder, garlic powder, cayenne pepper, oregano, basil and thyme form the savory rub that's worked into the fish. A rub should sit for at least 30 minutes on delicate entrees like fish or boneless chicken breasts, and from 3 hours to overnight for roasts and other larger cuts of meat.

Breaded Flounder Fillets

Prep/Total Time: 20 min.

✓ Uses less fat, sugar or salt. Includes Nutrition Facts and Diabetic Exchanges.

- 1/4 **cup all-purpose flour**
- 1/4 **cup cornmeal**
- 1 **teaspoon salt**
- 1/2 **teaspoon paprika**
- 1/2 **teaspoon pepper**
- 2 **egg whites**
- 1/4 **cup fat-free milk**
- 4 **flounder fillets (6 ounces** *each***)**
- 1 **tablespoon grated Parmesan cheese**

In a shallow bowl, combine the flour, cornmeal, salt, paprika and pepper. In another shallow bowl, beat egg whites and milk. Coat fish with cornmeal mixture, then dip into egg white mixture. Coat fish again in cornmeal mixture.

In a 15-in. x 10-in. x 1-in. baking pan coated with nonstick cooking spray, arrange fish in a single layer. Sprinkle with Parmesan cheese. Bake, uncovered, at 425° for 8-10 minutes or until fish flakes easily with a fork.

Yield: 4 servings.

Nutrition Facts: 1 fillet equals 236 calories, 3 g fat (1 g saturated fat), 83 mg cholesterol, 789 mg sodium, 14 g carbohydrate, 1 g fiber, 37 g protein. **Diabetic Exchanges:** 5 very lean meat, 1 starch.

Many Ways to Cook Fillets

It doesn't take long to bake Breaded Flounder Fillets in the oven. A light coating, which has a mild cornmeal flavor, helps the delicate fish stay moist. The breading also would be good on other types of fish, such as orange roughy, grouper or sole.

Boneless fish fillets are very versatile. They can be baked, broiled, grilled, poached, sauteed, steamed, deep-fried or pan-fried.

Microwave Tuna 'n' Chips

Prep/Total Time: 15 min.

1   **can (10-3/4 ounces) condensed cream of celery soup, undiluted**
1/4   **cup milk**
1   **can (12 ounces) tuna, drained and flaked**
3/4   **cup frozen peas, thawed**
1/3   **cup chopped celery**
1   **tablespoon chopped onion**
1   **teaspoon Worcestershire sauce**
1-1/2   **cups crushed potato chips, *divided***
1   **tablespoon shredded cheddar cheese**

In a large bowl, combine soup and milk. Stir in the tuna, peas, celery, onion and Worcestershire sauce. Place half in a greased shallow 1-qt. microwave-safe dish. Sprinkle with 1/2 cup potato chips. Top with remaining tuna mixture.

Microwave, uncovered, on high for 4-5 minutes or until bubbly. Top with remaining potato chips; sprinkle with cheese. Microwave 1 minute longer or until cheese is melted. Let stand for 5 minutes before serving.

Yield: 3 servings.

Editor's Note: This recipe was tested with an 850-watt microwave.

Casserole Cooks Quick in Microwave

Your kids are going to like this made-quickly-in-the-microwave casserole so much, they'll request it frequently! Cooking meals in the microwave works best for foods that have a high moisture content, like fish, poultry and vegetables.

For a change of pace, you can use canned chicken and cream of chicken soup in place of the tuna and cream of celery.

Minty Peach Halibut

Prep/Total Time: 20 min.

>   1 jar (10 ounces) peach preserves
>   2 teaspoons minced fresh mint
>   4 halibut steaks (6 ounces *each*)
> 1/2 teaspoon salt
> 1/4 teaspoon pepper

In a small saucepan, combine preserves and mint. Bring to a boil; cook and stir for 2 minutes. Remove from the heat; set aside. Sprinkle fish with salt and pepper.

Broil 4 in. from the heat for 5 minutes. Spoon half of peach mixture over fish. Broil 1 minute longer; turn. Broil 3-4 minutes longer or until fish flakes easily with a fork, basting once with remaining peach mixture.

Yield: 4 servings.

A Head's Up On Halibut

Here, halibut steaks get fabulous flavor from a deliciously different sauce that combines minced fresh mint and peach preserves.

Halibut is a firm, fine-textured fish with a delicate flavor. Look for halibut steaks with pure white flesh and a slightly sweet smell. Steer clear of halibut that is brown in color or looks dry.

Halibut poaches, grills, broils, braises and steams particulary well. It is also good roasted or sauteed.

Orange Roughy Bundles

Prep/Total Time: 25 min.

☑ Uses less fat, sugar or salt. Includes
Nutrition Facts and Diabetic Exchanges.

- 4 fresh *or* frozen orange
  roughy fillets (6 ounces
  each), thawed
- 1/4 cup grated Parmesan
  cheese
- 1/8 to 1/4 teaspoon cayenne
  pepper
- 2 medium zucchini, cut into
  1/4-inch slices
- 1 small sweet red pepper, julienned
- 1/2 teaspoon salt

Place each fillet on a piece of heavy-duty foil (about 12-in. square).
Sprinkle with Parmesan cheese and cayenne. Top with the zucchini, red pepper and salt. Fold foil over vegetables and seal tightly.

Prepare grill for indirect heat. Grill, covered, over indirect heat for
8-10 minutes or until fish flakes easily with a fork.

Yield: 4 servings.

Nutrition Facts: 1 packet equals 159 calories, 3 g fat (1 g saturated fat),
38 mg cholesterol, 499 mg sodium, 4 g carbohydrate, 2 g fiber, 28 g protein. **Diabetic Exchanges:** 4 very lean meat, 1 vegetable.

Cooking in Foil Packets

Cleanup is a breeze when
it comes to this simple
seafood supper. Each
meal-in-one packet con-
tains zucchini, red pepper
and a flaky full-flavored
fish fillet. It cooks in no
time and is just as deli-
cious with flounder or sole.

When making the pack-
ets, fold the foil around the
ingredients and double-
fold all of the seams, leaving enough room in the
packet for the steam to cir-
culate. Place the packets
on the grill with the seam
side up to prevent leaks
and to avoid possible flare-
ups. Open the cooked
packets carefully to allow
the steam to escape.

Orzo Shrimp Stew

Prep/Total Time: 15 min.

2-1/2 cups reduced-sodium
      chicken broth
   5 cups fresh broccoli florets
   1 can (14-1/2 ounces) diced
      tomatoes, undrained
   1 cup uncooked orzo
   1 pound uncooked medium
      shrimp, peeled and
      deveined
  3/4 teaspoon salt
  1/4 teaspoon pepper
   2 teaspoons dried basil
   2 tablespoons butter

In a large nonstick skillet or saucepan, bring broth to a boil. Add the broccoli, tomatoes and orzo. Reduce heat; simmer, uncovered, for 5 minutes, stirring occasionally. Add the shrimp, salt and pepper. Cover and cook for 4-5 minutes or until shrimp turn pink and orzo is tender. Stir in basil and butter.

Yield: 4 servings.

The Secrets of Fresh Shrimp

Since this recipe doesn't skimp on shrimp, it's great for those who really enjoy seafood! The mildly seasoned stew has other satisfying ingredients, too, like broccoli, tomatoes and orzo pasta.

Before storing fresh, uncooked shrimp, rinse them under cold running water and drain thoroughly. Tightly cover and refrigerate for up to 2 days.

As with all shellfish, shrimp should be cooked briefly or it will become tough and rubbery. Cook only until the shrimp turn pink and opaque.

Mom's Fried Fish

Prep/Total Time: 30 min.

    2 **eggs, beaten**
1-1/2 **cups crushed saltines (about 45 crackers)**
    2 **pounds whitefish fillets, cut in half lengthwise**
Oil for frying
TARTAR SAUCE:
    1 **cup mayonnaise**
    2 **tablespoons sweet pickle relish**
    1 **tablespoon finely chopped onion**

Place eggs and cracker crumbs in separate shallow bowls. Dip fillets into eggs, then coat with crumbs. Let stand for 5 minutes.

In an electric skillet or deep-fat fryer, heat oil to 375°. Fry fillets, a few at a time, for 2 minutes on each side or until fish is golden brown and flakes easily with a fork. Drain on paper towels. In a small bowl, combine all of the tartar sauce ingredients. Serve with fish.

Yield: 6 servings.

Pointers on Frying Fish

This fried fish just like Mom used to make is flaky and flavorful with a golden cracker-crumb coating. The recipe calls for 2 pounds of whitefish fillets. Any type of whitefish would work well, including orange roughy, ocean perch, cod, haddock, pollock and red snapper.

Make sure the temperature of the oil you're frying the fish in is 375°. If it's not, the fish could end up soggy and greasy. Blot fish on paper towels after frying to absorb excess grease.

Potato Fish Skillet

Prep/Total Time: 25 min.

 4 **medium red potatoes, cubed**
 6 **tablespoons butter, cubed**
 2 **tablespoons olive oil**
 1 **pound grouper** *or* **other lean fish, cut into 3/4-inch pieces**
 1/2 **cup all-purpose flour**
 2 **cups sliced fresh mushrooms**
 1/2 **cup chopped celery**
 1/4 **cup chopped onion**
 3 **garlic cloves, minced**
 4-1/2 **teaspoons lemon juice**
Salt and pepper to taste

In a large skillet, stir-fry potatoes in butter and oil for 8-10 minutes or until lightly browned.

Meanwhile, place flour in a large resealable plastic bag. Add fish, a few pieces at a time, and shake to coat. Add to the skillet. Cover and cook for 4 minutes, stirring occasionally.

Add the mushrooms, celery, onion and garlic. Cover and cook 4-6 minutes longer or until fish flakes easily with a fork. Sprinkle with lemon juice, salt and pepper.

Yield: 4 servings.

Is a Last-Minute Lifesaver

Red potatoes, fish, mushrooms, celery and onion combine to make this filling one-dish skillet meal. Serve some cooked carrots on the side, and your supper is complete.

Grouper is a lean fish with a firm texture. Due to its low fat content, it dries out easily during cooking and is best cooked with some liquid or fat.

Remove the fishy smell from your hands, knife and cutting board by rubbing them all thoroughly with lemon wedges.

258

Tilapia with Corn Salsa

Prep/Total Time: 10 min.

- 4 tilapia fillets (6 ounces *each*)
- 1 tablespoon olive oil
- 1/4 teaspoon salt
- 1/4 teaspoon pepper
- 1 can (15 ounces) black beans, rinsed and drained
- 1 can (11 ounces) whole kernel corn, drained
- 3/4 cup Italian salad dressing
- 2 tablespoons chopped green onion
- 2 tablespoons chopped sweet red pepper

Drizzle both sides of fillets with oil; sprinkle with salt and pepper. Broil 4-6 in. from the heat for 5-7 minutes or until fish flakes easily with a fork. Meanwhile, in a small bowl, combine the remaining ingredients. Serve with fish.

Yield: 4 servings.

All About Tilapia

If your family loves fish, this super-fast and delicious dish will be popular at your house. Though it tastes like it takes a long time, it cooks in minutes under the broiler.

The low-fat flesh of tilapia is white, sometimes tinged with pink, sweet and fine textured. It's suitable for baking, broiling, grilling and steaming.

Leftover fish makes a delicious salad the next day. If desired, cut the fish into chunks and marinate overnight in salad dressing; serve over greens.

Black Beans and Rice (p. 271)

Round out your weeknight meals with an assortment of garden-fresh veggies, satisfying grains, hearty breads and cool salads.

Swift Sides & Salads

Blueberry-Orange Onion Salad (p. 286)

Guacamole Tossed Salad

Prep/Total Time: 15 min.

2 medium tomatoes, seeded
    and chopped
1/2 small red onion, sliced and
    separated into rings
6 bacon strips, cooked and
    crumbled
1/3 cup vegetable oil
2 tablespoons cider vinegar
1 teaspoon salt
1/4 teaspoon pepper
1/4 teaspoon hot pepper
    sauce
2 large ripe avocados,
    peeled and cubed
4 cups torn salad greens

In a large salad bowl, combine the tomatoes, onion and bacon. In a small bowl, whisk the oil, vinegar, salt, pepper and hot pepper sauce. Pour over tomato mixture; toss gently. Add avocados.

Place the greens in a large salad bowl; add avocado mixture and toss to coat. Serve immediately.

Yield: 4 servings.

Removing an Avocado Pit

This fresh-tasting blend of tomatoes, red onion, greens and avocados gets added pizzazz from crumbled bacon and a slightly spicy vinaigrette.

To easily pit an avocado, halve it lengthwise, cutting around the pit. Twist halves in opposite directions. Use a tablespoon to slip under the pit to loosen it.

To remove half an avocado from its skin, loosen from skin with a large spoon and scoop out. Slice or cut as desired.

Five-Fruit Salad

Prep/Total Time: 5 min.

1-1/3 cups frozen unsweetened strawberries,
   thawed and halved
  1 cup fresh blueberries
  1 medium banana, sliced
  3/4 cup green grapes
  1 can (21 ounces) peach pie filling

In a large bowl, combine all ingredients. Refrigerate until serving.

Yield: 6 servings.

Fruit Salad Is So Pleasing

Five-Fruit Salad looks so impressive when served in a clear glass bowl...everyone will want to dig right in! It's a wonderful side dish served with any meal, but is also fun for breakfast or dessert.

Peach pie filling is an unexpected ingredient in the yummy medley of packaged and fresh fruits. Feel free to replace any of the fruits called for with your family's favorites.

Noodles with Broccoli

Prep/Total Time: 20 min.

> 5 cups chicken broth
> 4 cups uncooked spiral pasta *or* egg noodles
> 1 package (10 ounces) frozen broccoli florets
> 1/2 cup shredded Asiago cheese, *divided*
> 1/4 teaspoon salt
> 1/4 teaspoon garlic powder
> 1/2 cup butter, cubed
> 2 tablespoons vegetable oil

In a large saucepan, bring broth to a boil; add pasta and broccoli. Cook, uncovered, for 5-6 minutes or until tender; drain.

In a large skillet, saute the pasta, broccoli, 1/4 cup cheese, salt and garlic powder in butter and oil; toss to coat. Sprinkle with remaining cheese.

Yield: 4 servings.

Chicken Broth Adds Extra Flavor

For a speedy side dish that cooks in no time on the stovetop, try Noodles with Broccoli. Your family will be amazed that something that looks so simple tastes so good!

Simmering in water can drain some of the flavor from food. That's why, for added flavor, we cooked the noodles and broccoli in chicken broth instead. Try cooking other foods in broth as well, like rice and potatoes.

Dilled Corn and Peas

Prep/Total Time: 20 min.

✓ Uses less fat, sugar or salt. Includes Nutrition Facts and Diabetic Exchanges.

- 2-1/2 cups fresh *or* frozen sugar snap peas
- 2 cups fresh *or* frozen corn
- 1 small sweet red pepper, julienned
- 1/4 cup water
- 1 tablespoon butter
- 1 teaspoon minced fresh dill *or* 1/4 teaspoon dill weed
- 1/8 teaspoon salt, optional
- 1/8 teaspoon pepper

Place the peas, corn, red pepper and water in a large saucepan; cover and cook over high heat for 2-4 minutes or until vegetables are crisp-tender; drain. Add the butter, dill, salt if desired and pepper; toss to coat.

Yield: 8 servings.

Nutrition Facts: 1/2 cup (calculated without salt) equals 84 calories, 2 g fat (0 saturated fat), 0 cholesterol, 20 mg sodium, 16 g carbohydrate, 0 fiber, 4 g protein. **Diabetic Exchanges:** 1 vegetable, 1/2 starch, 1/2 fat.

Cooking with Fresh Herbs

Seasoned with fresh dill, this striking combination of crisp colorful vegetables is an easy but impressive addition to any meal.

Kitchen shears are great for snipping fresh herbs into small pieces. Many fresh herbs lose much of their flavor when heated, so try to add them during the final minutes of cooking time. Or add the herbs when the dish begins cooking, then stir in a little more just before serving.

Italian Salad

Prep/Total Time: 30 min.

✓ Uses less fat, sugar or salt. Includes Nutrition Facts and Diabetic Exchanges.

   3 slices Italian bread, cubed
Butter-flavored nonstick cooking
    spray
   1 teaspoon Italian seasoning
1/2 teaspoon garlic powder
   2 bunches romaine, torn
   2 cups grape tomatoes,
    halved
   1 can (2-1/4 ounces) sliced ripe olives, drained
1/4 cup grated Parmesan cheese
   1 small red onion, thinly sliced and separated
    into rings
   6 pepperoncinis
1/2 cup fat-free Italian salad dressing

For croutons, spritz bread cubes with butter-flavored spray; place in a bowl. Sprinkle with Italian seasoning and garlic powder; toss to evenly coat. Transfer to a 15-in. x 10-in. x 1-in. baking pan coated with nonstick cooking spray. Bake at 450° for 8-10 minutes or until golden brown, stirring once or twice. Cool.

Meanwhile, in a large bowl, combine the romaine, tomatoes, olives, Parmesan cheese, onion and pepperoncinis. Drizzle with salad dressing and toss to coat. Top with croutons.

Yield: 6 servings.

Editor's Note: Look for pepperoncinis (pickled peppers) in the pickle and olive section of your grocery store.

Nutrition Facts: 1-1/2 cups equals 120 calories, 3 g fat (1 g saturated fat), 3 mg cholesterol, 943 mg sodium, 18 g carbohydrate, 4 g fiber, 6 g protein. **Diabetic Exchanges:** 2 vegetable, 1/2 starch, 1/2 fat.

Why Go Out? You Can Make It at Home

You'll find this tossed salad to be just like one served at a popular Italian restaurant chain, only lighter! It features romaine, grape tomatoes, sliced ripe olives, red onion rings and pepperoncinis topped off with homemade croutons.

Home-baked croutons are fresher and better tasting than store-bought, plus, they're easy to make as you'll see in this recipe.

Cool the croutons completely before using. They can be made ahead and stored in a resealable plastic bag at room temperature for up to 1 week.

Zucchini 'n' Carrot Coins

Prep/Total Time: 15 min.

> 1 pound carrots, thinly sliced
> 2 tablespoons butter
> 1 small onion, sliced and separated into rings
> 2 small zucchini, cut into 1/4-inch slices
> 2 teaspoons dried basil
> 1/2 teaspoon salt
> 1/4 teaspoon pepper

In a large skillet, saute carrots in butter for 4-5 minutes or until crisp-tender. Add the onion; cook for 1 minute. Stir in the remaining ingredients. Cover and cook for 4-5 minutes or until vegetables are crisp-tender.

Yield: 4 servings.

Get Clued in On Carrots

You'll especially enjoy preparing this recipe during the warm summer months when fresh zucchini and carrots are plentiful. The easy, colorful side dish is attractive served with any type of meat.

Store carrots in a plastic bag in the refrigerator for up to 2 weeks. As they age, they'll lose flavor and firmness. Limp carrots will regain much of their crispness if soaked for 30 minutes in ice water.

Some of a carrot's flavor and nutrients are lost when peeled. Unless carrots are very old or the peel is discolored, simply scrub them well and leave the peel on.

Pull-Apart Herb Bread

Prep/Total Time: 30 min.

1	garlic clove, minced
1/4	cup butter, melted
2	tubes (10.2 ounces *each*) refrigerated biscuits
1	cup (4 ounces) shredded cheddar cheese
1/4	teaspoon dried basil
1/4	teaspoon fennel seed
1/4	teaspoon dried oregano

In a large skillet, saute garlic in butter; set aside. Separate biscuits; place half in an even layer in a greased 9-in. springform pan. Brush with butter mixture; sprinkle with half of the cheese and herbs. Repeat.

Place the pan on a baking sheet. Bake at 375° for 20-25 minutes or until golden brown. Remove to wire rack; serve warm.

Yield: 8 servings.

Hurry-Up Herbed Bread

The ingredients for this recipe are simple, but the results are delicious. So complete your next dinner with this eye-catching bread. Your family will have fun pulling off each herbed, cheesy piece!

Crumbled cooked bacon and chopped green pepper would be tasty additions to the bread.

Garden Pasta Salad

Prep/Total Time: 30 min.

✓ Uses less fat, sugar or salt.
Includes Nutrition Facts.

   2 **cups uncooked spiral pasta**
   1 **cup fresh broccoli florets**
1/4 **cup sliced carrots**
1/4 **cup chopped green pepper**
1/4 **cup chopped sweet red pepper**
1/4 **cup sliced zucchini**
1/2 **cup ranch salad dressing**
   1 **tablespoon Dijon mustard**

Cook pasta according to package directions. Meanwhile, in a large bowl, combine the broccoli, carrots, peppers and zucchini. Drain and rinse pasta in cold water; add to vegetables. Combine salad dressing and mustard; pour over pasta mixture and toss to coat. Refrigerate until serving.

Yield: 4 servings.

Nutrition Facts: 1 cup (prepared with fat-free ranch dressing) equals 239 calories, 1 g fat (0 saturated fat), 0 cholesterol, 414 mg sodium, 49 g carbohydrate, 0 fiber, 7 g protein.

A Bowlful of Fresh Flavor

Fresh produce is put to delicious use in this pleasing pasta salad. Convenient bottled dressing, with added spark from Dijon mustard, gives fast flavor to the cool combination that's the perfect side dish for most any meal.

Elbow macaroni, shell, rotini, bow ties, tortellini and radiatore are good pasta choices for salads such as this one because they hold up well.

Mixed Green Salad

Prep/Total Time: 20 min.

✓ Uses less fat, sugar or salt. Includes Nutrition Facts and Diabetic Exchanges.

3-1/2 cups baby spinach
    2 cups torn leaf lettuce
  1/2 cup chopped sweet red pepper
  1/2 cup sliced red onion
  1/4 cup mandarin oranges
  1/4 cup sliced fresh mushrooms

DRESSING:
    2 tablespoons olive oil
    1 tablespoon raspberry vinegar
    1 teaspoon sugar
  1/4 teaspoon minced fresh parsley
  1/4 teaspoon minced fresh basil

Pepper to taste

In a large salad bowl, combine spinach, lettuce, red pepper, onion, oranges and mushrooms. In a jar with a tight-fitting lid, combine the dressing ingredients; shake well. Drizzle over salad and toss to coat.

Yield: 4 servings.

Nutrition Facts: 1 serving equals 96 calories, 7 g fat (1 g saturated fat), 0 cholesterol, 25 mg sodium, 8 g carbohydrate, 2 g fiber, 2 g protein. **Diabetic Exchanges:** 1 vegetable, 1 fat.

Clean Those Greens!

You can toss together this pretty medley of greens, mushrooms, red pepper, onion and oranges in no time. The recipe calls for raspberry vinegar in the homemade dressing, but cider vinegar works nicely in a pinch.

Some greens, such as arugula or escarole, may be sandy or dirty and should be swished in a sink or bowl of cold water. Lift greens out, allowing the sand and grit to sink to the bottom. Repeat in clean water if necessary. Rinse the other greens gently in cool water. Pat dry with paper towel.

Black Beans and Rice

Prep/Total Time: 20 min.

    1   medium onion, chopped
    1   medium green pepper, chopped
    1   medium sweet red pepper, chopped
    1   garlic clove, minced
  1/2   teaspoon dried basil
  1/4   teaspoon pepper
    1   tablespoon tomato sauce
    1   can (15 ounces) black beans, rinsed
        and drained
    1   cup cooked long grain rice
    1   tablespoon red wine vinegar
  1/4   cup shredded cheddar cheese

In a nonstick skillet coated with nonstick cooking spray, saute the onion, green and red peppers, garlic, basil and pepper until tender. Stir in tomato sauce. Add the beans, rice and vinegar; heat through. Transfer to a serving dish; sprinkle with cheese.

Yield: 4 servings.

Full of Nutrition And Flavor

Chock-full of beans, rice, bell peppers and cheddar cheese, this skillet side dish is hearty enough to serve as a meatless main course, too.

Black beans are a member of the legume family and add a tasty source of protein and fiber to the diet. Include them with your other favorite toppings next time you make baked potatoes. Or make a dip by layering black beans, guacamole, chopped tomatoes and diced onions in a bowl.

Brussels Sprouts Supreme

Prep/Total Time: 15 min.

1 **pound fresh brussels sprouts, trimmed**
1 **cup chopped celery**
2 **tablespoons butter**
2 **tablespoons all-purpose flour**
1 **cup milk**
1/2 **cup cubed process cheese (Velveeta)**
1/4 **teaspoon salt**
Pinch cayenne pepper, optional

Cut an X in the core of each brussels sprout. Place brussels sprouts, celery and a small amount of water in a large saucepan; cover and cook for 8-9 minutes or until crisp-tender.

Meanwhile, in another large saucepan, melt butter. Stir in flour until smooth. Gradually add milk; bring to a boil. Reduce heat; cook and stir for 2 minutes or until thickened. Add cheese, salt and cayenne if desired; stir until cheese is melted. Drain brussels sprouts and celery; top with cheese sauce.

Yield: 4-6 servings.

The Origin of Brussels Sprouts

A member of the cabbage family, this small green veggie averages 1 inch in diameter. The name originates from Brussels, Belgium, where brussels sprouts were first grown centuries ago.

A creamy cheese sauce is the perfect accompaniment for the bold flavor of brussels sprouts. Even those who say they don't normally care for the vegetable should enjoy it served this way.

Lemony Tossed Salad

Prep/Total Time: 10 min.

4 cups ready-to-serve salad
  greens
2 medium tomatoes, cut
  into wedges
3/4 cup sliced cucumber
1/2 cup olive oil
1/4 cup lemon juice
1 garlic clove, minced
1 teaspoon sugar
1 teaspoon dried oregano
  or mint
Salt and pepper to taste

In a salad bowl, combine salad greens, tomatoes and cucumber. In a jar with a tight-fitting lid, combine the remaining ingredients; shake well. Drizzle over salad and toss to coat.

Yield: 4 servings.

Time-Saving Tossed Salad

Lemony Tossed Salad is quick and simple to toss together with ready-to-serve salad greens and garden-fresh tomatoes and cucumbers. It's a refreshing start to any meal. The from-scratch vinaigrette dressing is light and lemony.

Packaged salad mixes are available in the produce section. These are already washed and torn. Store in their plastic bag in the refrigerator crisper drawer. Once opened, tightly close the bag. Follow the use-by date stamped on the package.

Santa Fe Rice Salad

Prep/Total Time: 20 min.

☑ Uses less fat, sugar or salt.
Includes Nutrition Facts.

- 1 **medium green pepper, julienned**
- 1 **medium sweet red pepper, julienned**
- 1 **small onion, thinly sliced**
- 2 **teaspoons canola oil**
- 2 **cups cooked rice**
- 1 **can (16 ounces) kidney beans, rinsed and drained**
- 1 **can (11 ounces) Mexicorn, drained**
- 1 **jar (8 ounces) picante sauce**
- 6 **cups shredded lettuce**
- 3/4 **cup shredded reduced-fat cheddar cheese**
- 6 **tablespoons reduced-fat sour cream**

Tortilla chips

In a nonstick skillet, saute peppers and onion in oil for 6-7 minutes or until tender. Stir in the rice, beans, corn and picante sauce until heated through. Place 1 cup of lettuce on each of six salad plates. Top with 1 cup rice mixture, 2 tablespoons cheese and 1 tablespoon sour cream. Serve with tortilla chips.

Yield: 6 servings.

Nutrition Facts: 1 cup salad with 10 tortilla chip equals 353 calories, 7 g fat (3 g saturated fat), 15 mg cholesterol, 800 mg sodium, 59 g carbohydrate, 9 g fiber, 15 g protein.

Keep Cooked Rice On Hand

This warm rice and bean salad served with crunchy tortilla chips is sure to turn any mealtime into a fast fiesta! Your whole family will enjoy the snappy salad.

On a weekend when you have more time, cook a good-sized pot of rice. Having the cooked rice in the refrigerator will be quite a time-saver during the week. You can quickly make fried rice, rice pilaf, rice pudding and even add it to soups.

Flavorful Herb Bread

Prep: 15 min. **Bake:** 3-4 hours

  1   cup warm milk (70° to 80°)
  1   egg
  2   tablespoons butter, softened
 1/4 cup dried minced onion
  2   tablespoons sugar
1-1/2 teaspoons salt
  2   tablespoons dried parsley flakes
  1   teaspoon dried oregano
3-1/2 cups bread flour
  2   teaspoons active dry yeast

In a bread machine pan, place all ingredients in order suggested by manufacturer. Select basic bread setting. Choose crust color and loaf size if available. Bake according to bread machine directions (check dough after 5 minutes of mixing; add 1 to 2 tablespoons water or flour if needed).

Yield: 1 loaf (2 pounds).

Editor's Note: If your bread machine has a time-delay feature, we recommend you do not use it for this recipe.

Bread Bakes by Itself

Conveniently made in a bread machine, this herbed loaf has a wonderful texture and slices beautifully. Serve thick slices with soup, chili or stew for dunking or alongside any meaty entree in place of dinner rolls. The slices are also scrumptious for making sandwiches.

Bread recipes containing eggs, milk, sour cream, cottage cheese and other dairy or perishable products should be baked immediately and not placed on a "timed-bake" cycle.

Herbed Potatoes and Veggies

Prep/Total Time: 25 min.

> 4 medium baking potatoes
> 1-1/2 cups diced zucchini
> 3 tablespoons olive oil
> 2 tablespoons plus 1 teaspoon savory herb with garlic soup mix
> 1/4 teaspoon pepper
> 10 cherry tomatoes, halved

Scrub and pierce potatoes; place on a microwave-safe plate. Cover and microwave on high for 5-6 minutes on each side or until tender. When potatoes are cool enough to handle, cut into cubes.

In a large skillet, saute potatoes and zucchini in oil for 5 minutes or until vegetables are tender. Sprinkle with soup mix and pepper. Cook until heated through, stirring occasionally. Add tomatoes; cook 1 minute longer.

Yield: 6 servings.

Editor's Note: This recipe was tested in a 1,100-watt microwave.

Soup Mix Makes Potatoes Savory

After just one taste, your family is sure to request this great-tasting side dish time and again. A package of savory herb with garlic soup mix is what gives the potato, zucchini and tomato combination its fabulous flavor—no extra seasoning is needed!

If you have leftover baked potatoes on hand, skip the first step of the recipe and just cut them into cubes; finish as directed.

Colorful Vegetable Saute

Prep/Total Time: 15 min.

>   2   medium sweet red
>   peppers, julienned
>   2   medium green peppers,
>   julienned
>   2   medium zucchini,
>   julienned
>   4   medium carrots, julienned
>   1   tablespoon olive oil
>   4   cups thinly sliced red
>   cabbage
>   1/4   teaspoon salt
>   1/4   teaspoon pepper
>   4   teaspoons white wine
>   vinegar
>   1/4   cup water
>   1   tablespoon sesame seeds, toasted

In a large skillet, saute peppers, zucchini and carrots in oil for 5 minutes. Add cabbage, salt and pepper; saute 1 minute longer. Combine vinegar and water; pour over the vegetables. Saute 3 minutes more. Sprinkle with sesame seeds; cook and stir for 1 minute.

Yield: 8-10 servings.

How to Toast Sesame Seeds

This fresh-tasting mixture is so pretty and tasty—and a delightful way to enjoy your garden's bounty. A sprinkling of toasted sesame seeds adds a pleasant crunch to the colorful saute without much work.

Toasting sesame seeds brings out their nutty flavor. Toast them in a skillet over medium heat, or in a 350° oven, stirring occasionaly, just until they are golden brown. Or pick up a bottle of toasted sesame seeds in the Oriental food aisle of the grocery store.

Summer Vegetable Medley

Prep/Total Time: 15 min.

1/2 cup butter, melted

1-1/4 teaspoons *each* minced fresh parsley, basil and chives

3/4 teaspoon salt

1/4 teaspoon pepper

3 medium ears sweet corn, husks removed, cut into 2-inch pieces

1 medium sweet red pepper, cut into 1-inch pieces

1 medium sweet yellow pepper, cut into 1-inch pieces

1 medium zucchini, cut into 1/4-inch slices

10 large fresh mushrooms

In a large bowl, combine the butter, parsley, basil, chives, salt and pepper. Add the vegetables; toss to coat.

Place vegetables in a disposable foil pan. Grill, covered, over medium-high heat for 5 minutes; stir. Grill 5 minutes longer or until the vegetables are tender.

Yield: 6-8 servings.

A Kernel on Fresh Corn

This swift side dish is as beautiful as it is delicious. Red and yellow peppers, zucchini, corn and mushrooms are seasoned with garden-fresh herbs. Grilled in a foil pan, it's no fuss.

Fresh corn is available May through August; peak season is July through August. Select corn that has fresh green, tightly closed husks with dark brown, dry (but not brittle) silk. Ears should have plump, tender, small kernels in tight rows up to the tip. Kernels should be firm enough to resist slight pressure. A fresh kernel with spurt "milk" if punctured.

Zesty Corn and Beans

Prep/Total Time: 25 min.

  1 **can (14-1/2 ounces) Cajun *or* Mexican
      diced tomatoes, undrained**
  2 **cups frozen corn**
  1 **cup canned black beans, rinsed and drained**
1/4 **teaspoon dried oregano**
1/4 **teaspoon chili powder**
Hot cooked rice

In a large saucepan, combine the tomatoes, corn, beans, oregano and chili powder. Cook over medium heat for 6-8 minutes or until the corn is tender, stirring occasionally. Serve over rice.

Yield: 6 servings.

Makes a Simple Side or Relish

When you're in the mood for Mexican food, reach for this zesty side dish. It pairs well with any of the Southwestern entrees in this book, such as Steak Tortillas (p. 83), Baked Chimichangas (p. 86) or family-pleasing Pork Soft-Shell Tacos (p. 174).

The tomato, corn and bean mixture can also be refrigerated and eaten as a relish without the rice.

Garlic Mashed Red Potatoes

Prep/Total Time: 30 min.

☑ Uses less fat, sugar or salt. Includes Nutrition Facts and Diabetic Exchanges.

 8 **medium red potatoes, quartered**
 3 **garlic cloves, peeled**
 2 **tablespoons butter**
1/2 **cup fat-free milk, warmed**
1/2 **teaspoon salt**
1/4 **cup grated Parmesan cheese**

Place potatoes and garlic in a large saucepan; cover with water. Bring to a boil. Reduce heat; cover and simmer for 20-25 minutes or until the potatoes are very tender. Drain well. Add the butter, milk and salt; mash. Stir in Parmesan cheese.

Yield: 6 servings.

Nutrition Facts: 1 cup equals 190 calories, 5 g fat (3 g saturated fat), 14 mg cholesterol, 275 mg sodium, 36 g carbohydrate, 4 g fiber, 8 g protein. **Diabetic Exchanges:** 2 starch, 1/2 fat.

Peel Garlic the Easy Way

These creamy garlic-flavored mashed potatoes are so good, you can serve them plain—no butter or gravy is needed. With just six ingredients, you can have this super spud side dish on the table fast.

Smashing garlic with a knife may be fun to watch on food television shows, and it may work if you're going to slice, dice or squash the garlic, but there's an easier way. Soak the cloves in cold water for a few minutes. You'll find the peel slips off easily, leaving the whole clove intact.

Chili Corn Bread Wedges

Prep/Total Time: 30 min.

- 1 package (8-1/2 ounces) corn bread/muffin mix
- 1 egg
- 1/3 cup milk
- 1 can (4 ounces) chopped green chilies
- 2 tablespoons sugar
- 3/4 cup frozen corn, thawed

Place corn bread mix in a large bowl. Combine the egg, milk, chilies and sugar; stir into mix just until moistened. Fold in corn.

Pour into a greased 9-in. round baking pan. Bake at 400° for 20-25 minutes or until a toothpick inserted near the center comes out clean. Cool on a wire rack for 5 minutes. Cut into wedges; serve warm.

Yield: 6-8 servings.

Testing Bread For Doneness

With a little help from a packaged mix and a can of chopped green chilies, you'll have no trouble baking a pan of this moist corn bread. Serve these thick wedges alongside bowls of your family's favorite soup or chili, or with any Mexican-style entree.

Check for doneness 10 minutes before the end of the recommended baking time. The bread is done if a toothpick inserted near the center comes out clean. If it is not done, test again in a few more minutes.

Cool-as-a-Cucumber Salad

Prep/Total Time: 5 min.

- 1/2 cup mayonnaise
- 1/4 cup half-and-half cream
- 1/4 cup sugar
- 1/2 teaspoon celery seed
- 1/2 teaspoon dill weed
- 3 medium cucumbers, sliced

In a large bowl, combine the first five ingredients. Add cucumbers; toss to coat. Refrigerate until serving.

Yield: 4-6 servings.

The Most Common Cucumber

The fast, five-ingredient dressing for Cool-as-a-Cucumber Salad adds a slightly sweet touch to fresh sliced cukes.

The most popular cucumber is just classified as the common cucumber. It was bred to have a thicker skin than other cukes to protect it during shipping. It generally has a waxed coating on the skin to increase its freshness life.

Store unwashed cucumbers in the refrigerator crisper drawer for up to 1 week. Wash before using. Peel waxed cucumbers and seed if desired.

Tangy Cabbage Slaw

Prep/Total Time: 10 min.

　　1　package (3 ounces) chicken ramen noodles
3-3/4　cups coleslaw mix
　1/3　cup slivered almonds
　　3　tablespoons sliced green onions
　1/2　cup vegetable oil
　1/3　cup white wine vinegar
　　3　tablespoons sugar

In a large bowl, break noodles into small pieces; set seasoning packet aside. Add the coleslaw mix, almonds and onions to noodles. In a small bowl, combine the oil, vinegar, sugar and contents of seasoning packet. Pour over coleslaw mixture; toss to coat. Serve with a slotted spoon. Refrigerate leftovers.

Yield: 4-6 servings.

Slaw in Seconds

Your family will like the crunchy texture and sweet-and-sour flavor of Tangy Cabbage Slaw, which can easily be made ahead of time and stored in the re-frigerator. The recipe starts with a package of coleslaw mix, consisting of pre-mixed shredded green cab-bage, red cabbage and car-rots. The mixure is washed and ready to eat.

　To give the cabbage sal-ad a different twist, use beef ramen noodles, and toss in some sesame seeds or sunflower kernels.

Confetti Long Grain and Wild Rice

Prep/Total Time: 25 min.

2 packages (6 ounces *each*) long grain and wild rice
1 small yellow summer squash, finely diced
1 small zucchini, finely diced
1 small sweet red pepper, finely diced
1 medium carrot, diced
2 green onions, thinly sliced
1/4 to 1/2 teaspoon salt
2 teaspoons olive oil

Cook rice according to package directions. Meanwhile, in a skillet, saute the yellow squash, zucchini, red pepper, carrot, onions and salt in oil for 4-5 minutes or until vegetables are tender. Transfer rice to a serving bowl; add the vegetable mixture and toss gently.

Yield: 8 servings.

Storing and Cooking Rice

Summer squash, zucchini, sweet red pepper and carrot peek out from the tender grains of rice in this colorful side dish.

You can store white and wild rice in an airtight container indefinitely. Always rinse wild rice before cooking to remove any debris. Wild rice may become tender without absorbing all of the cooking liquid. If necessary, drain before serving or combining with other recipe ingredients.

Mock Caesar Salad

Prep/Total Time: 10 min.

    3 tablespoons mayonnaise
    2 teaspoons grated
       Parmesan cheese
1-1/2 teaspoons red wine
       vinegar
  1/2 teaspoon garlic powder
  1/2 teaspoon lemon juice
    4 cups torn romaine lettuce
  1/4 cup Caesar salad croutons
    2 tablespoons shredded
       Parmesan cheese

In a jar with a tight-fitting lid, combine the first five ingredients; shake well. In a large bowl, add lettuce; drizzle with dressing and toss to coat. Sprinkle with croutons and shredded cheese.

Yield: 4 servings.

The Creation of Caesar Salad

This 10-minute salad has the flavor of an authentic Caesar salad but without the fuss. If you like, top off the salad with chopped hard-cooked eggs and anchovies. You can also keep the dressing on hand to quickly and deliciously top a variety of other greens and vegetables, too.

Caesar salad is said to have been created in 1924 by Italian chef Caesar Cardini, who owned a popular restaurant in Tijuano, Mexico.

Blueberry-Orange Onion Salad

Prep/Total Time: 15 min.

3 cups torn salad greens

2 medium navel oranges, peeled and sliced

4 slices sweet onion, separated into rings

2 cups fresh blueberries

BLUEBERRY SOUR CREAM DRESSING:

1/2 cup sour cream

1 tablespoon white wine vinegar

1 tablespoon crushed blueberries

1-1/2 teaspoons sugar

1-1/2 teaspoons lemon juice

1/4 teaspoon salt

Arrange greens on four salad plates. Top with the orange slices and onion rings. Sprinkle with blueberries. In a small bowl, combine dressing ingredients; stir until blended. Drizzle over salads. Serve immediately.

Yield: 4 servings.

Blueberry Basics

Fresh blueberries combine nicely with navel orange slices, sweet onion rings and a tangy sour cream dressing to make this green salad really special.

Choose berries that are firm, uniform in size and indigo blue with a silvery sheen; avoid those that are shriveled or moldy.

Refrigerate unwashed blueberries in their container for up to 1 week. Wash just before using.

Veggie Potato Salad

Prep/Total Time: 15 min.

✓ Uses less fat, sugar or salt. Includes
   Nutrition Facts and Diabetic Exchanges.

1	pound small red potatoes, cooked and cubed
1-1/2	cups chopped fresh broccoli
1/2	cup sliced celery
1/4	cup chopped red onion
1/4	cup sliced radishes
2	tablespoons chopped green pepper
1/3	cup fat-free Italian salad dressing
1/2	teaspoon salt-free seasoning blend
1/4	teaspoon dill weed

In a large salad bowl, toss the potatoes and vegetables. In a small bowl, blend the salad dressing and seasonings; add to potato mixture and toss to coat. Cover and refrigerate for 1 hour or until serving.

Yield: 5 servings.

Nutrition Facts: 3/4 cup equals 79 calories, trace fat (trace saturated fat), 0 cholesterol, 177 mg sodium, 16 g carbohydrate, 3 g fiber, 3 g protein. **Diabetic Exchange:** 1 starch.

Cooking Red Potatoes

The addition of fresh broccoli, celery, red onion, radishes and green pepper makes this a nice change of pace from the traditional potato salad.

Scrub the potatoes with a brush and remove any eyes. Place in a Dutch oven or large kettle. Cover with cold water; add 1/2 to 1 teaspoon salt for each quart of water. Bring to a boil; cover and cook just until fork-tender yet firm. Don't overcook, or the potatoes might fall apart in the salad and result in a mushy texture. Cube when cool enough to handle.

Beans with Cherry Tomatoes

Prep/Total Time: 25 min.

    4   bacon strips, diced
1-1/2   pounds fresh green beans, cut into 2-inch pieces
    4   garlic cloves, thinly sliced
1-1/2   cups halved cherry tomatoes
  1/2   teaspoon salt
  1/4   cup slivered almonds, toasted

In a large skillet, cook bacon over medium heat until crisp. Remove to paper towels to drain. In the drippings, saute beans for 12-14 minutes or until crisp-tender. Add garlic; cook 2-3 minutes longer. Stir in tomatoes and salt; heat through. Sprinkle with bacon and almonds. Serve immediately.

Yield: 8 servings.

Fresh Beans Fast

You'll love this dressed-up version of garden green beans that's perfect with any meat. Store unwashed green beans in a resealable plastic bag and refrigerate for up to 3 days. Before using, wash and snap off the beans' ends.

Nothing beats the flavor of cool and crisp garden-fresh green beans. As a snack, eat them raw with French onion dip or ranch salad dressing.

Fiesta Mixed Greens

Prep/Total Time: 15 min.

4 cups torn mixed salad greens

1 large tomato, chopped

1 medium sweet yellow pepper, chopped

3/4 cup pimiento-stuffed olives

1 celery rib, chopped

1 green onion, chopped

1/4 cup olive oil

2 tablespoons plus 1-1/2 teaspoons white wine vinegar

1 tablespoon salsa

1/8 teaspoon garlic salt

1/8 teaspoon dried oregano

1/8 teaspoon dried cilantro flakes

1/8 teaspoon ground cumin

1/8 teaspoon pepper

In a salad bowl, combine the greens, tomato, yellow pepper, olives, celery and onion. In a jar with a tight-fitting lid, combine the remaining ingredients; shake well. Just before serving, drizzle over salad and toss to coat.

Yield: 4 servings.

Do Prep Work the Night Before

Chopping the vegetables the night before and refrigerating them will take the effort out of tossing Fiesta Mixed Greens, a colorful and refreshing side dish, the next day. If you like, add leftover cubed turkey, chicken or ham for a cool main course.

Don't overdress salads. Too much dressing will weigh down the ingredients and mask the flavor. The dressing should highlight, not overpower, the other items in the salad.

Tomato Rosemary Focaccia

Prep/Total Time: 25 min.

1 tube (13.8 ounces) refrigerated pizza crust
2 tablespoons olive oil
2 garlic cloves, minced
1/4 teaspoon salt
1 tablespoon minced fresh rosemary *or* 1 teaspoon dried rosemary, crushed, *divided*
2 to 3 plum tomatoes, thinly sliced
1 small red onion, thinly sliced

Unroll pizza crust onto a greased baking sheet. Combine the oil, garlic, salt and half of the rosemary; spread over crust. Top with tomatoes and onion; sprinkle with remaining rosemary. Bake at 425° for 12-15 minutes or until golden. Cut into rectangles.

Yield: 6 servings.

Tips for Cutting Tomatoes

This quick Italian flat bread is a delicious, savory snack and is also good served with soup or a salad. The recipe calls for plum tomatoes, which are meaty tomatoes with small seeds. These short, elongated tomatoes are usually red, but yellow ones are also available.

Pierce the skin of the tomato with the tip of a knife, then cut into the pierced point. Tomato slices will hold their shape better and exude less juice if you slice them vertically, from the stem end to the blossom end.

Orange-Glazed Asparagus

Prep/Total Time: 20 min.

✓ Uses less fat, sugar or salt. Includes
Nutrition Facts and Diabetic Exchang

> 3 **pounds fresh asparagus, trimmed**
> 1/2 **cup orange juice**
> 2 **tablespoons olive oil**
> 1/2 **teaspoon salt**
> 1 **teaspoon grated orange peel**

In a large saucepan, bring 1/2 in. of water to a boil. Add asparagus; cover and boil for 3 minutes. Drain and immediately place asparagus in ice water. Drain and pat dry. Transfer to a serving dish.

Add the remaining ingredients to the pan; bring to a boil. Cook, uncovered, over medium-high heat until juices are slightly thickened. Drizzle over asparagus.

Yield: 8 servings.

Nutrition Facts: 1 serving equals 59 calories, 4 g fat (1 g saturated fat), 0 cholesterol, 155 mg sodium, 5 g carbohydrate, 1 g fiber, 2 g protein. **Diabetic Exchanges:** 1 vegetable, 1/2 fat.

Preparing Asparagus

It's so simple to perk up fresh asparagus with a tangy orange glaze. This side dish is great for weeknight meals but would also be an effortless one for entertaining.

Select small, straight stalks with tightly closed, compact tips; spears should be smooth and round. Rinse asparagus stalks well in cold water to clean. Snap off the stalk ends as far down as they will easily break when gently bent, or cut off the tough white portion.

If stalks are large, use a vegetable peeler to gently peel the tough area of the stalk from the end to just below the tip. If tips are large, scrape off scales with a knife.

Even families on the go can indulge in dessert with this chapter's speedy sweets!

Peach Shortcake Towers (p. 302)

In-a-Dash **Desserts**

In-a-Dash
Desserts

Tangy Lemonade Pie (p. 317)

Blueberry Graham Dessert

Prep/Total Time: 15 min.

3/4 **cup graham cracker crumbs (about 12 squares)**

1/4 **cup chopped walnuts**

2 **tablespoons sugar**

1/4 **teaspoon ground cinnamon**

2 **tablespoons butter, melted**

1 **package (3 ounces) cream cheese, softened**

1/3 **cup confectioners' sugar**

1/2 **cup ricotta cheese**

2 **teaspoons lemon juice**

4 **cups fresh blueberries**

Whipped cream, optional

In a large bowl, combine the cracker crumbs, walnuts, sugar and cinnamon. Stir in butter; set aside. In a mixing bowl, beat cream cheese and confectioners' sugar until smooth. Beat in ricotta cheese and lemon juice.

Place 1/2 cup blueberries each in four dessert dishes. Top with cream cheese mixture, crumbs and remaining blueberries. Garnish with whipped cream if desired. Refrigerate until serving.

Yield: 4 servings.

Full of Cheesecake Flavor

When you're short on time but long for cheesecake, try this fruity dessert. Ricotta and cream cheeses give every bite the flavor of cheesecake but without all the fuss.

Instead of making individual servings, you could layer the ingredients in a glass serving bowl. Cherries can be used in place of the blueberries.

Frozen Sandwich Cookies

Prep/Total Time: 30 min.

 1/2 **cup spreadable strawberry cream cheese**
 1/4 **cup strawberry yogurt**
 16 **chocolate wafers**

In a small mixing bowl, beat cream cheese and yogurt until smooth. Spread on the bottom of half of the chocolate wafers; top with remaining wafers. Place on a baking sheet. Cover and freeze for 25 minutes. Serve or wrap in plastic wrap and store in the freezer.

Yield: 8 cookies.

Frozen Treats Can't Be Beat

These cool, creamy treats are a snap to make! Calling for just three ingredients, tasty Frozen Sandwich Cookies will be a hit with both young and old alike.

Sandwich any cookies, brownies or graham crackers with your favorite flavor of ice cream for a fast dessert. Try vanilla ice cream with oatmeal or chocolate chip cookies... fudge ripple or mint with brownies...strawberry with graham crackers...the possibilities are endless!

Hard-Shell Ice Cream Sauce

Prep/Total Time: 15 min.

   1 **cup (6 ounces) semisweet chocolate chips**
1/4 **cup butter, cubed**
   3 **tablespoons evaporated milk**
Vanilla ice cream
1/2 **cup sliced almonds**

In a heavy saucepan, combine chocolate chips, butter and milk. Cook and stir over low heat until chips are melted and mixture is smooth. Serve warm over ice cream (sauce will harden). Sprinkle with almonds. Refrigerate any leftovers. Sauce can be reheated in the microwave.

Yield: about 1 cup.

Ice Cream Shop Fun at Home

Keep the ingredients for this sauce on hand so you can make it any time you need an easy dessert. It's very rich and delicious, and forms a crunchy shell over ice cream, much like the popular treats from ice cream parlors.

Make the sauce ahead, and once it has cooled a bit, transfer it to a microwave-safe container and set it in the refrigerator. Then, when it's time for dessert, just warm the sauce up in the microwave.

Strudel Pudding Dessert

Prep/Total Time: 30 min.

4 **frozen strawberry-filled
   strudel pastries**
2 **cups cold milk**
1 **package (5.9 ounces)
   instant chocolate pudding
   mix**
1 **carton (8 ounces) frozen
   whipped topping,
   thawed, *divided***

Toast pastries according to package directions; let cool for 5 minutes. Meanwhile, in a large bowl, whisk milk and pudding mix for 2 minutes. Let stand for 2 minutes or until soft-set; fold in 2 cups whipped topping.

Place pastries in an ungreased 8-in. square dish. Spread with pudding. Cover; refrigerate for at least 20 minutes. Cut into squares. Top with remaining whipped topping.

Yield: 9 servings.

Toaster Strudels Aren't Just for Breakfast

Frozen toaster pastries make for a delightful crust in this quick, four-ingredient creation. Instant chocolate pudding mix is easily transformed into a mousse-like layer of creamy goodness that is guaranteed to get rave reviews.

You'll get equally good results if you use raspberry-filled strudel pastries in place of the strawberry.

Rocky Road Pizza

Prep/Total Time: 20 min.

Pastry for single-crust pie (9 inches)
- 3/4 cup semisweet chocolate chips
- 1/2 cup miniature marshmallows
- 1/4 cup salted peanuts

On a lightly floured surface, roll pastry into a 9-in. circle; place on a lightly greased baking sheet. Prick with a fork. Bake at 450° for 8-10 minutes or until lightly browned. Sprinkle with chocolate chips. Bake 1-2 minutes longer or until chocolate is softened.

Spread chocolate over crust to within 1/2 in. of edges. Sprinkle with marshmallows. Bake for 1-2 minutes or until marshmallows puff slightly and are golden brown. Sprinkle with peanuts. Remove to wire rack to cool.

Yield: 6-8 servings.

Dessert Pizza Is Sure to Please

Looking for a new, interesting dessert to offer your hungry clan? Chocolate lovers will relish this palate-pleasing pizza that cleverly captures the flavor of rocky road ice cream. They'll have a hard time eating just one slice!

For other flavor variations, try white chocolate chips with pistachios, or milk chocolate chips with chopped dried cherries.

Cantaloupe a la Mode

Prep/Total Time: 15 min.

- 1/2 **cup water**
- 1/2 **cup sugar**
- 2 **tablespoons lemon juice**
- 1 **tablespoon cornstarch**
- 1 **teaspoon grated lemon peel**
- 1 **cup fresh *or* frozen blueberries**
- 2 **small cantaloupes, halved and seeded**
- 4 **scoops vanilla ice cream**

Fresh mint, optional

In a small saucepan, combine the first five ingredients; bring to a boil over medium heat. Boil and stir for 2 minutes or until thickened. Add blueberries; cook until heated through. Fill cantaloupe with ice cream; top with sauce. Garnish with mint if desired.

Yield: 4 servings (1 cup sauce).

Picking Out the Perfect Cantaloupe

This special dessert is a refreshing finale to a warm-weather meal. Your family will enjoy it so much, though, you'll get requests for it year-round!

A cantaloupe has a heavy netting over its cream-colored rind; its orange flesh is very juicy and sweet. Select melons that are heavy for their size and have no cracks or dents in the skin. Avoid those that are bruised or have a strong aroma, which indicates they are overripe.

Chocolate Cheesecake Pie

Prep/Total Time: 30 min.

> 1 package (8 ounces) cream cheese, softened
> 1/4 cup butter, softened
> 1/3 cup sugar
> 1-1/2 teaspoons vanilla extract
> 1-1/2 cups milk chocolate chips, melted and cooled
> 1 carton (8 ounces) frozen whipped topping, thawed
> 1 graham cracker crust (9 inches)

Chocolate leaf dessert decorations, optional

In a large mixing bowl, beat the cream cheese, butter, sugar and vanilla until smooth. Beat in melted chocolate. Fold in whipped topping. Spoon into crust. Cover and chill until serving. Garnish with chocolate leaves if desired.

Yield: 6-8 servings.

Melting Chocolate in The Microwave

This pie's smooth, rich chocolate filling simply melts in your mouth. Slices are especially good topped with raspberry or cherry pie filling.

To melt chocolate in the microwave, place it in a microwave-safe bowl. Melt semisweet chocolate at 50% power, and milk chocolate and vanilla or white chocolate at 30% power. Stir frequently until the chocolate is melted; do not overheat.

Cherry S'mores

Prep/Total Time: 10 min.

    4 **whole graham crackers**
    1 **plain milk chocolate candy bar (7 ounces)**
    8 **large marshmallows**
    1 **cup cherry pie filling**

Break or cut graham crackers in half. Divide chocolate into eight pieces; place a piece on each graham cracker half. Top with a marshmallow.

Place two crackers at a time on a microwave-safe plate. Microwave on high for 15-25 seconds or until chocolate is melted and marshmallow is puffed. Top each with 1 tablespoon pie filling.

Yield: 8 servings.

Editor's Note: This recipe was tested with an 850-watt microwave.

Can't Get Enough Of S'mores?

If you like s'mores, you're sure to enjoy this dressed-up variation that you make in the microwave. Each open-faced treat gets a boost of sweetness from cherry pie filling.

    The name s'mores comes from the notion that they're so good, you always wants "some more." While the origin of this popular campfire dessert is unclear, the first recorded version of the recipe can be found in the Girl Scout Handbook of 1927.

Peach Shortcake Towers

Prep/Total Time: 30 min.

3 cups all-purpose flour

1/4 cup finely chopped walnuts

2 tablespoons baking powder

1 teaspoon salt

1 cup plus 1 tablespoon heavy whipping cream, *divided*

1 egg

7 to 9 tablespoons sugar, *divided*

1 teaspoon vanilla extract

1 to 2 tablespoons cold water

4 cups sliced fresh peaches

Whipped topping

In a large bowl, combine the flour, nuts, baking powder and salt. In a large mixing bowl, beat 1 cup cream, egg, 2 tablespoons sugar and vanilla until slightly thickened. Stir into dry ingredients until mixture forms a ball, adding cold water if necessary.

Turn dough onto a floured surface; knead 8-10 times. Roll out to 1/2-in. thickness. Cut into three 3-1/2-in. circles, three 2-3/4-in. circles and six 1-1/4-in. circles. Place on ungreased baking sheets. Brush the tops with remaining cream. Bake at 425° for 8-12 minutes or until golden brown.

In a large bowl, combine the peaches and 5-7 tablespoons of sugar. Split the large and medium biscuits in half horizontally. Spoon a few peach slices on large biscuit halves; dollop with whipped topping. Top each with a medium biscuit half, remaining peaches and whipped topping and a small biscuit.

Yield: 6 servings.

Picking Out Fresh Peaches

These tender biscuits make wonderful peach or strawberry shortcakes that will be greeted with oohs and aahs.

Pick out plump peaches; avoid those with bruises, soft spots or cuts. Also avoid peaches with a green tone as these will not ripen or be sweet. Ripe peaches will give slightly when gently pressed and have a sweet aroma. Store ripe peaches in the refrigerator for 3 to 5 days.

Gumdrop Cereal Bars

Prep/Total Time: 30 min.

5   **cups Corn Pops cereal**

1   **cup gumdrops**

4   **cups miniature marshmallows**

1/4   **cup butter, cubed**

1   **teaspoon vanilla extract**

Place cereal and gumdrops in a large bowl; set aside. In a microwave-safe bowl, add marshmallows and butter. Microwave, uncovered, for 1-2 minutes or until melted; stir until smooth. Stir in the vanilla.

Pour over cereal mixture; toss to coat. Spread into a greased 9-in. square pan. Cool on a wire rack. Cut with a buttered knife.

Yield: 16 bars.

Basics of Cutting Bars

These bars are a fun twist to the traditional marshmallow rice cereal treats …the recipe calls for Corn Pops instead! Gumdrops make a colorful and sweet addition.

Generally, most bars and brownies should cool completely on a wire rack before being cut. Be sure to cut Gumdrop Cereal Bars using a buttered knife; this will prevent the knife from sticking to the bars.

Mini Caramel Cheesecakes

Prep/Total Time: 20 min.

  1 **package (8 ounces) cream cheese, softened**
  2 **tablespoons apple juice concentrate**
  2 **tablespoons sugar**
1/4 **cup caramel ice cream topping**
1/2 **cup whipped topping**
  1 **package (6 count) individual graham cracker tart shells**
Additional caramel ice cream topping, optional
Chopped almonds *or* honey roasted almonds, optional

In a large mixing bowl, beat the cream cheese, apple juice concentrate, sugar and ice cream topping until smooth. Fold in whipped topping. Spoon into tart shells. Drizzle with additional ice cream topping and sprinkle with the almonds if desired. Refrigerate until serving.

Yield: 6 servings.

Softening Cream Cheese

Using individual graham cracker shells makes it easy to prepare these cute treats. They taste just like cheesecake without all the hassle.

Store cream cheese in its original wrapping in the coldest part of your refrigerator. To speed-soften cream cheese, remove from foil wrapping and place on a microwave-safe plate. For 8 ounces, cook at 50% power for about 1 minute, 3 ounces for 30 seconds. Let stand 1 minute.

Applescotch Sundaes

Prep/Total Time: 20 min.

   1 **cup packed brown sugar**
1/4 **cup all-purpose flour**
1/4 **cup water**
   1 **tablespoon lemon juice**
1/2 **teaspoon salt**
   5 **cups thinly sliced peeled
     tart apples**
   3 **tablespoons butter**
   1 **teaspoon vanilla extract**
Vanilla ice cream

In a large saucepan, combine the brown sugar, flour, water, lemon juice and salt; stir until smooth. Bring to a boil; cook and stir for 2 minutes or until thickened. Add apples; return to a boil. Reduce heat; cover and simmer for 10-12 minutes or until the apples are tender.

Remove from the heat; add butter and vanilla. Stir until butter is melted. Serve warm or at room temperature over ice cream.

Yield: 4-6 servings.

Ap-peel-ing Way To Eat Apples

Looking for a new and scrumptious way to get your gang to eat apples? This sweet sauce featuring tender chunks of apple is heavenly scooped over vanilla ice cream. Try it over gingerbread and pound cake, too.

Apples discolor quickly, so don't peel and slice them until just before stirring them into the brown sugar mixture cooking on the stovetop.

Coconut Chocolate Chip Cookies

Prep/Total Time: 25 min.

1/2 cup butter, softened
3/4 cup sugar
  1 egg
1/2 teaspoon coconut extract
  1 cup plus 2 tablespoons
     all-purpose flour
1/2 teaspoon baking soda
1/2 teaspoon salt
  1 cup (6 ounces) semisweet
     chocolate chips
1/2 cup flaked coconut

In a large mixing bowl, cream butter and sugar. Beat in egg and coconut extract. Combine the flour, baking soda and salt; add to the creamed mixture. Stir in chocolate chips and coconut.

Drop by rounded tablespoonfuls 2 in. apart onto ungreased baking sheets. Bake at 375° for 11-13 minutes or until golden brown. Remove to wire racks to cool.

Yield: about 1-1/4 dozen.

Making Drop Cookies

Here is a delicious twist on traditional chocolate chip cookies. They're great for coconut lovers, textured by coconut flakes and flavored by the coconut extract—a compatible combination that results in a crispy, chewy cookie.

For even baking, it's important that you make cookies the same size. Use a tablespoon from your flatware set. Fill it with dough; use another spoon or spatula to push the mound of dough off the spoon onto a baking sheet.

Rich Chocolate Pudding

Prep/Total Time: 25 min.

- 2 cups (12 ounces) semisweet chocolate chips
- 1/3 cup confectioners' sugar
- 1 cup milk
- 1/4 cup butter, cubed

Whipped topping and miniature semisweet chocolate chips, optional

Place chocolate chips and confectioners' sugar in a blender; cover and process until the chips are coarsely chopped.

In a small saucepan, add milk and butter. Bring to boil over medium heat. Add to blender; cover and process until chips are melted and mixture is smooth. Pour into six individual serving dishes. Chill until set. Garnish with whipped topping and miniature chips if desired.

Yield: 6 servings.

Indulge in This Chocolate Dessert

Creamy, smooth and fudgy, this after-dinner treat is a true chocolate indulgence. With just four ingredients, it might be the easiest from-scratch pudding you'll ever make. But it's so delicious and elegant-looking, your family will think you fussed stirring it up.

Top individual servings with whipped topping and miniature semisweet chocolate chips if you'd like. Or spoon the pudding into a crust and serve it as a soft-set pie.

Mousse-Topped Pound Cake

Prep/Total Time: 10 min.

- **1 cup heavy whipping cream**
- **1/4 cup confectioners' sugar**
- **2 teaspoons baking cocoa**
- **1/2 teaspoon vanilla extract**
- **1 frozen pound cake (10-3/4 ounces), thawed**
- **1 medium kiwifruit, peeled, halved and sliced, optional**

In a chilled small mixing bowl, beat cream until it begins to thicken. Add the confectioners' sugar, cocoa and vanilla; beat until stiff peaks form.

Split cake into three horizontal layers. Spread about 1/2 cup mousse on bottom layer; repeat layers twice. Garnish with kiwi if desired. Refrigerate leftovers.

Yield: 6-8 servings.

Whipping Cream

For a speedy dessert, serve Mousse-Topped Pound Cake. A smooth, creamy filling with a mild cocoa flavor is spread on layers of pound cake, then topped with sliced kiwifruit for a pretty presentation.

The bowl in which you beat cream should be deep enough so the cream can double in volume. Cream will whip faster if you chill the bowl and beaters in the freezer for 15 minutes. The cream should be as cold as possible.

Doughnut Parfaits

Prep/Total Time: 20 min.

2 cups cold milk
1 package (3.4 ounces)
  instant vanilla pudding mix
16 powdered sugar
  doughnut holes, halved
1 to 2 medium firm
  bananas, cut into 1/4-inch
  slices
2 cups whipped topping
Chopped nuts and maraschino
  cherries

In a large bowl, whisk the milk and pudding mix for 2 minutes. Let stand for 2 minutes or until soft-set. Place four doughnut hole halves in each of four parfait glasses. Top with half of the pudding, bananas and whipped topping. Repeat layers. Garnish with nuts and cherries.

Yield: 4 servings.

Dress Up Doughnuts For Dessert

Here's another delicious use for doughnuts.

In a small mixing bowl, beat 4 ounces softened cream cheese, 2 tablespoons lemon curd and 3 teaspoons sugar until smooth. Cut 4 plain cake doughnuts in half horizontally. Spread bottom halves with cream cheese mixture; replace tops. Drizzle each with 1 tablespoon blueberry preserves.

Rhubarb Cobbler

Prep/Total Time: 30 min.

4 cups sliced fresh *or* frozen rhubarb (1-inch pieces)
1 large sweet apple, peeled and sliced
1/2 cup packed brown sugar
1/2 teaspoon ground cinnamon, *divided*
1 tablespoon cornstarch
2 tablespoons cold water
8 macaroons, crumbled
1 tablespoon butter, melted
2 tablespoons sugar
Vanilla ice cream, optional

In a large skillet, combine the rhubarb, apple, brown sugar and 1/4 teaspoon cinnamon; bring to a boil. Reduce heat; cover and simmer for 10-13 minutes or until rhubarb is very tender. Combine cornstarch and water smooth; gradually add to the fruit mixture. Bring to a boil; cook and stir for 2 minutes or until thickened. Transfer to an ungreased 1-qt. baking dish.

In a small bowl, combine the crumbled cookies, butter, sugar and remaining cinnamon. Sprinkle over fruit mixture. Broil 4 in. from the heat for 3-5 minutes or until lightly browned. Serve warm with ice cream if desired.

Yield: 4 servings.

Editor's Note: If using frozen rhubarb, measure rhubarb while still frozen, then thaw completely. Drain in a colander, but do not press liquid out.

Readying Rhubarb For Cooking

Crumbled macaroons are a unique addition to this cobbler's topping. Serve hearty helpings alone or with vanilla ice cream.

Select rhubarb that is firm and crisp. Always trim and discard any leaves, which contain oxalic acid and are toxic. Thick stalks can be peeled with a vegetable peeler to remove the fibrous strings.

No-Bake Bars

Prep/Total Time: 20 min.

> 4 cups Cheerios
> 2 cups crisp rice cereal
> 2 cups dry roasted peanuts
> 2 cups M&M's
> 1 cup light corn syrup
> 1 cup sugar
> 1-1/2 cups creamy peanut butter
> 1 teaspoon vanilla extract

In a large bowl, combine the first four ingredients; set aside. In a large saucepan, bring corn syrup and sugar to a boil. Cook and stir just until sugar is dissolved.

Remove from the heat; stir in peanut butter and vanilla. Pour over cereal mixture and toss to coat evenly. Spread into a greased 15-in. x 10-in. x 1-in. baking pan. Cool. Cut into 3-in. squares.

Yield: 15 bars.

Bars Good in Any Season

Made with Cheerios, crisp rice cereal, dry roasted peanuts, M&M's and peanut butter, No-Bake Bars are big on taste but need only a little effort. They are handy to make when the weather is hot, since you never have to turn on the oven.

Change up the color of the M&M's to suit the season. Use red for Christmas or Valentine's Day, pastel colors for Easter, orange for Halloween, etc.

Ice Cream Tortilla Cups

Prep/Total Time: 25 min.

  1/4   cup butter, melted
    6   flour tortillas (6 inches), warmed
    6   tablespoons sugar
  1/2   teaspoon ground cinnamon
Strawberry ice cream *or* flavor of your choice

Brush butter on one side of each tortilla. Combine the sugar and cinnamon; sprinkle evenly over tortillas. Press each tortilla, sugar side up, into a greased muffin cup.

Bake at 400° for 6-8 minutes or until lightly browned. Cool for 5 minutes. Gently separate edges. Place a scoop of ice cream in each tortilla.

Yield: 6 servings.

Bowl Over Your Family with Tortilla Cups

Top off any supper with refreshing Ice Cream Tortilla Cups. The tasty treats look impressive, but call for just a few ingredients.

The cinnamon-sugar cups set up easily in muffin tins and bake to a crispy perfection. You can serve any flavor of ice cream you like in them. Try vanilla or caramel ice cream with honey drizzled over the top to finish off a Mexican meal.

Paradise Parfaits

Prep/Total Time: 15 min.

✓ Uses less fat, sugar or salt.
Includes Nutrition Facts.

2 cups cold fat-free milk
1 package (3.4 ounces) instant
    French vanilla pudding mix
1/4 teaspoon coconut extract
16 reduced-fat vanilla wafers,
    divided
1 medium firm banana, sliced
4 tablespoons chopped
    walnuts, toasted
1 cup sliced fresh strawberries
3/4 cup halved green grapes
2 tablespoons flaked coconut,
    toasted

In a large bowl, whisk milk and pudding mix for 2 minutes. Whisk in extract. Let stand for 2 minutes or until soft-set. Refrigerate for 5 minutes.

Meanwhile, coarsely crush 12 wafers; set aside. In parfait glasses, layer banana slices, half of the cookie crumbs, half of the walnuts and pudding and all of the strawberries. Top with the remaining cookie crumbs and pudding, all of the grapes and remaining nuts. Garnish with toasted coconut and a whole vanilla wafer.

Yield: 4 servings.

Nutrition Facts: 1 parfait equals 313 calories, 7 g fat (2 g saturated fat), 3 mg cholesterol, 484 mg sodium, 57 g carbohydrate, 2 g fiber, 7 g protein.

How to Toast Coconut

When it comes to a fuss-free dessert, you can depend on pudding and chopped fruit. Here, Paradise Parfaits give strawberries, banana, green grapes, vanilla pudding and crunchy nuts a fun twist with cookie crumbs and toasted coconut.

Spread coconut in a single layer on a baking sheet with shallow sides. Bake at 325°, tossing occasionally, for about 10 minutes or until golden brown.

Strawberry Broil

Prep/Total Time: 15 min.

  2 **cups halved fresh strawberries**
1/4 **cup sour cream**
1/4 **teaspoon ground cinnamon**
1/4 **cup packed brown sugar**
Vanilla ice cream, optional

Place the strawberries in an ungreased shallow 1-1/2-qt. baking dish. Combine sour cream and cinnamon; spoon over berries. Sprinkle with brown sugar.

Broil 4-6 in. from the heat for 3-4 minutes or until bubbly. Serve over ice cream if desired.

Yield: 4 servings.

You'll Be Sweet on This Simple Dessert

Dessert for a busy weeknight doesn't get much simpler than Strawberry Broil. A light sour cream sauce deliciously complements fresh strawberries. Or if you like, make the sauce with plain sour cream instead.

This sweet treat is satisfying on its own, but would also be scrumptious as a topping for ice cream, angel food cake or waffles.

Banana Split Pudding

Prep/Total Time: 10 min.

    3 cups cold milk
    1 package (5.1 ounces) instant vanilla pudding mix
    1 medium firm banana, sliced
    1 cup sliced fresh strawberries
    1 can (8 ounces) crushed pineapple, drained
    1 carton (8 ounces) frozen whipped topping,
       thawed
  1/4 cup chocolate syrup
  1/4 cup chopped pecans
Additional sliced strawberries and bananas, optional

In a large bowl, whisk milk and pudding mix for 2 minutes. Add banana, strawberries and pineapple; transfer to a large serving bowl. Dollop with whipped topping. Drizzle with chocolate syrup; sprinkle with pecans. Top with additional strawberries and bananas if desired.

Yield: 6-8 servings.

Split with Tradition—Serve This Pudding

This pleasing dessert is a snap to fix using packaged instant pudding. Banana and strawberry slices, and crushed pineapple stirred in, plus whipped topping, chocolate syrup and nuts on top, give it the flavor of traditional banana splits.

Store bananas at room temperature until they're ripe, then refrigerate or freeze. The skin will turn black in the refrigerator, but the flesh will remain unchanged. You can brush cut bananas with lemon, lime, orange or pineapple juice to prevent browning.

Peanut Clusters

Prep/Total Time: 15 min.

    4 **ounces milk chocolate candy coating**
    4 **ounces white candy coating**
    1 **can (16 ounces) salted peanuts (about 2-1/2 cups)**

In a microwave, melt candy coatings, stirring often until blended. Stir in the peanuts until coated. Drop by tablespoonfuls onto a waxed paper-lined baking sheet. Refrigerate until serving.

Yield: about 3 dozen.

All About Candy Coating

Have your kids help with Peanut Clusters, a sweet, three-ingredient candy that's fun to make and eat.

Candy coating is available in dark, milk or white chocolate varieties. It is sold in bulk in large blocks, in bags of flat discs and in packages of individual 1-ounce squares. Candy coating is used as a coating for candies, cookies, fruits and nuts.

In-a-Dash **Desserts**

Tangy Lemonade Pie

Prep/Total Time: 15 min. + chilling

✓ Uses less fat, sugar or salt. Includes Nutrition Facts and Diabetic Exchanges.

- **1 package (.3 ounces) sugar-free lemon gelatin**
- **1 package (8 ounces) reduced-fat cream cheese, cubed**
- **1-3/4 teaspoons sugar-free lemonade drink mix**
- **1 reduced-fat graham cracker crust (8 inches)**
- **6 tablespoons reduced-fat whipped topping**

Prepare gelatin according to package directions. Chill until almost set. Transfer to a blender or food processor. Add cream cheese and lemonade mix; cover and process until smooth. Pour into crust. Refrigerate overnight. Serve with whipped topping.

Yield: 6 servings.

Nutrition Facts: 1 piece with 1 tablespoon whipped topping equals 243 calories, 11 g fat (6 g saturated fat), 21 mg cholesterol, 273 mg sodium, 26 g carbohydrate, 0 fiber, 6 g protein. **Diabetic Exchanges:** 2 fat, 1 fruit, 1 fat-free milk.

Guilt-Free Dessert

Even those who have to watch their sugar intake can partake in this dessert! Sugar-free lemon gelatin and lemonade mix make this pretty pie light and absolutely delicious.

The pie needs to refrigerate overnight, so plan ahead. To crisp up the crust, bake at 375° for 8 to 10 minutes or until the crust is lightly browned. Cool on a wire rack before filling.

Fruit Cocktail Delight

Prep/Total Time: 5 min.

☑ Uses less fat, sugar or salt. Includes
Nutrition Facts and Diabetic Exchanges.

- **1 can (15 ounces) fruit cocktail, undrained**
- **1 package (3.4 ounces) instant vanilla pudding mix**
- **1/2 cup miniature marshmallows**

Chopped nuts, optional

In a large bowl, combine fruit cocktail and dry pudding mix; stir for 2 minutes. Let sit for 2 minutes or until soft-set. Chill until serving. Fold in marshmallows just before serving. Garnish with nuts if desired. Refrigerate leftovers.

Yield: 6 servings.

Nutrition Facts: 1/2 cup (prepared with reduced-sugar fruit cocktail and sugar-free pudding mix and without nuts) equals 95 calories, trace fat (0 saturated fat), 0 cholesterol, 667 mg sodium, 24 g carbohydrate, 0 fiber, trace protein. **Diabetic Exchange:** 1-1/2 fruit.

Shopping for Canned Fruit

Use convenient canned fruit and instant pudding to prepare Fruit Cocktail Delight. It makes a refreshing and pretty finale to any meal when served in glass dishes. Garnish each serving with whipped cream and a cherry if you'd like.

Canned fruit cocktail contains five kinds of fruit: peaches, pears, pineapple, green grapes and maraschino cherries. Small dents in a can won't harm the fruit; badly dented cans, however, should always be avoided.

Banana Berry Tarts

Prep/Total Time: 10 min.

- 4 ounces cream cheese, softened
- 2 tablespoons honey
- 1 package (10 ounces) frozen sweetened raspberries, thawed and undrained
- 1 cup miniature marshmallows
- 1 medium firm banana, chopped
- 1 cup whipped topping
- 1 package (6 count) individual graham cracker tart shells

In a small mixing bowl, beat cream cheese and honey until smooth; beat in raspberries until blended. Stir in marshmallows and banana. Fold in whipped topping. Spoon into tart shells. Chill until serving.

Yield: 6 servings.

No-Fuss Tart Fillings

If you need a no-fuss dessert that will satisfy your family's sweet tooth, try Banana Berry Tarts. Marshmallows, banana and raspberries are stirred into the creamy treats for a fun dinner finale.

Another simple filling for graham cracker shells is your favorite canned pie filling—cherry, peach, lemon, blueberry or apple. Then just top with a dollop of whipped topping.

Raspberry Pear Shortcake

Prep/Total Time: 20 min.

    2 cups fresh *or* frozen raspberries, thawed
    1 tablespoon sugar
  1/4 teaspoon ground cinnamon
    1 can (15-1/4 ounces) pear halves, drained
    4 individual round sponge cakes
Whipped topping

Place the raspberries in a large bowl. Combine sugar and cinnamon; sprinkle over raspberries and mash lightly. Let stand for 10 minutes. Place a pear half on each sponge cake. Top with the raspberries and whipped topping.

Yield: 4 servings.

Storing Fresh Raspberries

Because this recipe calls for canned pears and either fresh or frozen raspberries, you can make it year-round.

Raspberries come in red, black and golden colors. You can refrigerate a single layer of fresh berries on a paper towel-lined baking sheet covered with a paper towel for up to 3 days. You can also freeze raspberries this way. Once frozen, transfer them to a freezer container or bag and freeze up to 1 year.

Granola Banana Sticks

Prep/Total Time: 20 min.

- 1/4 cup peanut butter
- 2 tablespoons plus 1-1/2 teaspoons honey
- 4-1/2 teaspoons brown sugar
- 2 teaspoons milk
- 3 medium firm bananas
- 6 Popsicle sticks
- 2 crunchy oat and honey granola bars, crushed

In a small saucepan, combine the peanut butter, honey, brown sugar and milk; cook until heated through, stirring occasionally.

Peel bananas and cut in half widthwise; insert a Popsicle stick into one end of each banana half. Spoon peanut butter mixture over bananas to coat completely. Sprinkle with granola. Serve immediately or place on a waxed paper-lined baking sheet and freeze.

Yield: 6 servings.

Dessert on a Stick

Assemble the ingredients ahead for Granola Banana Sticks so your kids can whip them up when they get home from school. The bananas make a tasty handheld snack or dessert.

Firm but ripe bananas are best for this recipe. If you prefer, substitute crisp rice cereal as a crunchy alternative to the crushed oat and honey granola bars.

Peach Pudding

Prep/Total Time: 10 min.

1/4 cup peach *or* apricot gelatin
1/2 cup hot milk
1-1/2 cups cold milk
1 package (3.4 ounces) instant vanilla pudding mix
Sliced fresh peaches and whipped topping, optional

In a large bowl, dissolve gelatin powder in hot milk; set aside. Meanwhile, in a large mixing bowl, beat cold milk and dry pudding mix on low speed for 2 minutes. Beat in gelatin mixture. Let stand for 5 minutes. Spoon into individual dishes. Garnish with peaches and whipped topping if desired.

Yield: 4 servings.

Pitting Peaches

This light peach dessert is so fresh it tastes just like summertime! Peaches and nectarines can be used interchangeably in recipes. Nectarines have a smooth, thin skin; peaches have a fuzzy skin.

Cut the peach in half, cutting around the pit and using the indentation as a guide. Twist halves in opposite directions to separate. Using a sharp knife, loosen and remove the pit.

In-a-Dash **Desserts**

Nut-Coated Ice Cream

Prep/Total Time: 15 min.

> 7 cream-filled chocolate sandwich cookies
> 1/2 cup ground walnuts
> 1 tablespoon brown sugar
> 2 cups coffee ice cream, softened

Break four cookies in half; set aside. Crush the remaining cookies and place in a small bowl; add the walnuts and brown sugar. Drop ice cream by 1/2 cupfuls into walnut mixture; roll into four balls. Place in serving bowls; garnish with halved cookies.

Yield: 4 servings.

Crushing Sandwich Cookies

Instead of serving your family ordinary ice cream for dessert, dish out these nutty bowlfuls instead. They're an especially good way to finish off a Mexican meal. If you have time, make them in advance and freeze until ready to serve.

To crush the chocolate sandwich cookies with little mess, put them in a resealable plastic bag before crushing. Then simply crush them with your hands or roll over them with a rolling pin.

Pumpkin Pie Dip

Prep/Total Time: 10 min.

1 package (8 ounces) cream cheese, softened
2 cups confectioners' sugar
1 cup canned pumpkin
1/2 cup sour cream
1 teaspoon ground cinnamon
1 teaspoon pumpkin pie spice
1/2 teaspoon ground ginger
Gingersnap cookies

In a large mixing bowl, beat cream cheese and confectioners' sugar until smooth. Beat in the pumpkin, sour cream, cinnamon, pumpkin pie spice and ginger until blended. Serve with gingersnaps. Refrigerate leftovers.

Yield: 4 cups.

Dip into This Dessert

Make this rich, creamy dip when you have canned pumpkin left in the fridge after holiday baking, or any other time of the year.

We suggest serving Pumpkin Pie Dip with gingersnap cookies, but it would also be great served with sliced pears and apples, or as a spread on zucchini bread or nut-topped muffins.

Apricot Crisp

Prep/Total Time: 25 min.

3 cans (15-1/4 ounces *each*)
  apricot halves, drained
2 tablespoons brown sugar
1/2 teaspoon ground ginger
TOPPING:
1/4 cup all-purpose flour
3 tablespoons brown sugar
3 tablespoons quick-cooking
  oats
2 tablespoons flaked coconut
1/4 cup butter, cubed

In a large bowl, combine the apricots, brown sugar and ginger. Divide among four greased 8-oz. baking dishes. In a small bowl, combine the flour, brown sugar, oats and coconut.

Cut in butter until mixture resembles coarse crumbs. Sprinkle over apricots. Bake at 400° for 15 minutes or until filling is bubbly and top is golden brown.

Yield: 4 servings.

Quick Crisp Cut Out For Weeknights

During the week, home-made fruit crisp is a treat you likely don't have time to prepare. But these individual crisps call for canned fruit and bake for a mere 15 minutes.

Don't own 8-ounce baking dishes? Bake the crisp in an 8-inch square baking dish for 23 to 25 minutes instead. You can substitute canned peach or pear halves for the apricots.

Frosty Caterpillar Dessert

Prep/Total Time: 15 min.

8 chocolate cream-filled chocolate sandwich cookies, crushed

4 scoops raspberry orange sherbet *or* sherbet of your choice (about 1-1/3 cups)

2 semisweet chocolate chips

2 pieces red shoestring licorice (about 2 inches long)

2 miniature marshmallows

1 red-hot candy

8 assorted colored Dots

3 gummy worms

Sprinkle cookie crumbs onto a serving platter. Arrange sherbet scoops in a zigzag pattern over crumbs, forming a caterpillar. For eyes, press chocolate chips into the first scoop.

Using a toothpick, make two small holes above eyes. For antennae, insert the end of a licorice piece into each marshmallow; insert the other end of licorice piece into the holes. Add red-hot for nose. Press Dots onto the back of the caterpillar. Garnish with gummy worms. Serve immediately.

Yield: 4 servings.

Frosty Caterpillar Is Fast and Fun

Need a treat that will appeal to kids of all ages? This colorful critter will do the trick! However you shape him, this bug is sure to summon smiles from all who see him. You'll be grinning, too, because the dessert is so easy!

You can substitute any flavor of ice cream or sherbet you like to make your own garden creature. Graham cracker crumbs can even replace the cookies to create "sand."

Icy Blue Parfaits

Prep/Total Time: 20 min.

> 1 package (3 ounces) cream cheese, softened
> 1 carton (8 ounces) frozen whipped topping, thawed
> 1 package (14 ounces) blue gelatin snack cups or 1-1/3 cups cubed blue gelatin
> 1 cup fresh *or* frozen blueberries

In a large mixing bowl, beat cream cheese until smooth; beat in whipped topping. Unmold gelatin from snack cups; cut into 1/2-in. cubes.

In four parfait glasses or dessert bowls, layer half of the cream cheese mixture, gelatin and blueberries. Repeat layers. Chill until serving.

Yield: 4 servings.

Add Some Color To Supper

Your family will get a kick out of this refreshing gelatin dessert. It adds a fun, colorful touch to the dinner table.

Other kinds of gelatin and fruits can be used, too. For example, try red gelatin with raspberries or strawberries. Just leave out the cream cheese, and layer the fruit, whipped topping and jello cubes.

General Recipe Index

This handy index lists every recipe by food category, major ingredient and/or cooking method, so you can easily locate recipes to suit your needs.

✓ Recipe includes Nutrition Facts and Diabetic Exchanges.

✓ Recipe includes Nutrition Facts and Diabetic Exchanges.

✓ Recipe includes Nutrition Facts and Diabetic Exchanges.

✓ Recipe includes Nutrition Facts and Diabetic Exchanges.

✓ Recipe includes Nutrition Facts and Diabetic Exchanges.

✓ Recipe includes Nutrition Facts and Diabetic Exchanges.

✓ Recipe includes Nutrition Facts and Diabetic Exchanges.

Alphabetical
Index

Refer to this index for a complete alphabetical listing of all the recipes in this book.

✓ Recipe includes Nutrition Facts and Diabetic Exchanges.

✓ Recipe includes Nutrition Facts and Diabetic Exchanges.